THE CHURCH
IN EARLY
IRISH SOCIETY

THE CHURCH
IN EARLY
IRISH SOCIETY

Kathleen Hughes

METHUEN & CO LTD

11 New Fetter Lane, London EC4

First published in 1966 by
Methuen & Co Ltd
11 New Fetter Lane, London EC4
© 1966 Kathleen Hughes
Printed in Great Britain by
Richard Clay (The Chaucer Press) Ltd.,
Bungay, Suffolk

CONTENTS

V. TRANSMUTATION

INTRODUCTION

In this book I have been particularly interested in how the early Irish church was organized: comparatively little has been written about this, and a great deal remains to be done. I have tried to pursue a chronological development, and to base my impression of each period on the contemporary sources. Although I have occasionally referred to later texts, as a general rule the sources I have used were first recorded within a century or so of the events they describe. Ireland had no single historian of the stature of Bede, but nevertheless she has a wealth of early source material. S. Patrick's writings show us the early missionary church. For the sixth and seventh centuries there are penitentials and canons, culminating in the great collection assembled *c.* 725, while a number of the secular law tracts which throw light on ecclesiastical institutions took their present form in the eighth century. The writings of Columbanus and the Life of him written by his disciple Jonas, the letters concerning the Easter controversy, Cogitosus' Life of Brigit, Adamnán's Life of Columcille, and much of the Patrician material contained in the *Book of Armagh* are all seventh-century documents which vividly illustrate ecclesiastical organization. The ascetic revival of the late eighth and early ninth centuries inspired a number of monastic rules and related texts, and was followed by new developments in lyric poetry. From the eighth century onwards the annals provide a detailed and contemporary comment on ecclesiastical affairs, while a number of saints' Lives which go back to material put together in the Viking Age reveal some of the problems of that period. Comment and criticism of the tenth- and eleventh-century church are contained in the literature of Vision and Prophecy, while church legislation and the correspondence of popes and Anglo-Norman prelates give details of later-eleventh- and twelfth-century changes. This is to mention only the major sources.

Some conclusions, not usually sufficiently emphasized, have been forcibly brought home to me. One is the diversity existing

within the church in pre-Viking Ireland, diversity of both constitution and discipline. The 'Celtic Church' was united in its
doctrine, but it had no uniform method of government, liturgical
practice, or standard of asceticism. Practices varied from church
to church (even more than they varied in England or on the
Continent), and there was recognition and tolerance of diversity.
It is possible that the highly individual character of the early Irish
church may have encouraged practical experiment, for though her
clerics produced little speculative theology, she seems to have
been distinguished by certain innovations in church discipline.
The word used for the commutation of penance (Ir. *arre*, Lat.
arreum) is Irish in origin and 'proves beyond doubt that the practice itself is of Irish origin'. And although Irish clerics may not
have originated private penance, they made it a regular practice,
and, with the Britons and then the Anglo-Saxons, popularized the
new discipline.

Consideration of the ecclesiastical and secular legislation
suggests that certain changes in the government of the early Irish
church have often been misunderstood and oversimplified. The
transition from a church governed by bishops, each with recognizable diocesan boundaries (which seem to be the limits of
the *plebs* or tribe), to a church organized in non-territorial
monastic *paruchiae* under the control of abbots who were not
necessarily bishops, did not happen so rapidly or so uniformly as
the rigid interpretation of the *Catalogus Sanctorum* would have us
believe. Père Grosjean has shown this document to be late and
unreliable, but its clear and simple outlines of Irish constitutional
development are still the 'received' view. It seems to me likely
that differences between the 'Roman' and 'Irish' ecclesiastics in
the seventh and early eighth centuries were not confined to the
Easter question, but also concerned problems of church government. Armagh attempted to use the legal concepts of both parties
in establishing her position and, in addition, profited from the
political support of the Uí Néill overlords.

The eighth century is a period of particular interest. The
documents show that many of the practices which are normally
regarded as abuses and ascribed to the troubles of the Viking era
were already current before the 830s, and even before 800. Seen

in the context of their own age, and not judged by the standards of a post-Gregorian Catholicism, the damaging effects of these practices appear to have been exaggerated. During this period the church, which had by now gained an established position, was contributing to the peace and stability of society by legal measures of her own. Though the Vikings in the ninth century disturbed her legal and artistic development, her moral and spiritual life seems on the whole to have triumphed over physical disasters. It was in the comparatively settled conditions of the tenth century rather than in the terrors of the ninth that the damaging effects of the Viking occupation were most profoundly felt. For the Vikings indirectly widened the gap between the richer and poorer monastic houses, forced the churches into closer dependence on the secular lords, and emphasized the need of each church for its own wealth and power. As the churches re-emerged from the worst of their material tribulations (with Armagh now clearly in the ascendant) criticisms of monastic discipline become frequent. During the eleventh and twelfth centuries, as the Irish church came more closely into contact with Benedictine monasticism in Germany, with the Anglo-Normans in England, and with the Hildebrandine papacy the peculiarities of her own government became more apparent. The first movements towards improvement in the existing system were in line with earlier church policy, but before long church government was revolutionized. The transmutation of the church became inevitable.

In writing this short book I am indebted to many friends. I owe most to those who have so generously given time to read and criticize: to Professor Idris Foster, who read my manuscript in an early stage and made a number of helpful comments, to Professor D. A. Binchy, who gave me the benefit of his unrivalled knowledge of early Irish institutions, saved me from mistakes and made me rethink various problems, to Dr F. J. E. Raby who twice in his kindness went through my translation of the *Liber Angeli* with me, to Professor Kenneth Jackson, who made valuable corrections in the proofs. Any remaining errors are my own, and my critics are not, of course, responsible for views which I have expressed. The late Père Paul Grosjean, S.J. Bollandiste, has not commented on this book, but my debt to him is of many years standing. He was a master who poured out enthusiastic encouragement, savage criticism, witty asides, and ingenious ideas; a man erudite and many-sided, imaginatively at home in the world of the seventh- and eighth-century church. I am also indebted to the Rev. Dr J. G. Sheehy for allowing me to read his most interesting doctoral thesis, and to Mr R. H. M. Dolley for sending me the proofs of his important book on *The Hiberno-Norse Coins in the British Museum*. Undergraduates and former students have asked awkward questions and initiated discussion: here I am especially grateful to Dr John Bannerman and Miss Mary Anne O'Donovan. I should like to thank the University of Cambridge for its sabbatical leave, Mr Michael Behrens, whose grant gave me a year free from college duties, and my College for releasing me from them. To Professor Dorothy Whitelock I owe constant help and encouragement. Acknowledgements to institutions which have given permission to reproduce their treasures and to friends whose photographs I have used are recorded on pp. 293ff. in the notes on the plates. I am especially grateful to Dr Françoise Henry, Mr William O'Sullivan, and Mr Etienne Rynne for help and advice with the illustrations.

I. BIRTH

CHAPTER I

The heathen Celts

In various parts of Ireland the traveller may observe what remains of the homesteads of former inhabitants. Most are single-family dwellings or small groups of huts, for the population was scattered, not gathered into villages; many are fortified by a wall of earth or stone, a few (presumably the houses of the aristocracy) by a triple fortification of bank and ditch or stone cashel. Nearly all those which have been excavated, sites which were once thought to be of pre-Christian date, have proved themselves to be early Christian in period, though very occasionally a pre-historic community has been revealed.[1] The buildings were of stone, timber, clay and turf, or wattle and daub, sometimes with thatched roofs, their variety and extent depending on the social position of the holder, and the materials conditioned by the locality.

The aristocracy measured their wealth mainly in clients and stock, of which cattle was the most important element. Even as late as the sixteenth century, the diet of the Irish was reported to be whey, milk, beef broth, and meat without bread.[2] Grain was grown, but its cultivation was subsidiary to the main business of stock raising; and since Ireland has a mild climate and rich natural pasture, it may be that on the whole the rich were better fed and the poor less worn down by toil than in many other contemporary societies. Giraldus Cambrensis, a critic of Ireland during the twelfth century, remarked on the handsome physique and the natural indolence of the inhabitants, who, 'given only to leisure and devoted only to laziness, think that the greatest pleasure is not to work, and the greatest wealth is to enjoy liberty'.[3]

The people of pre-historic Ireland were self-supporting. They made sporadic raids on the Empire, and there may have been occasional trade, but they needed no coinage for large-scale

[1] O. Davies, *J.R.S.A.I.*, lxxii (1942), 98–105.
[2] Campion, *Historie of Ireland*, Chapter 6.
[3] *Topographia*, ed. O'Meara, *P.R.I.A.*, lii (1949), C 163.

exchange. The Roman legions never came to Ireland and never brought their stimulus to trade and agriculture, nor did Rome much influence the social and artistic life of Ireland, for, with a few exceptions, Irishmen never saw the roads and camps and cities, public buildings and private residences of the Empire. Irish smiths and sculptors never adopted imperial Roman tastes, and never copied the realistic naturalism of Roman art. Although some continental techniques, such as that of millefiori, reached Irish craftsmen, their patrons were a military aristocracy who appreciated little or nothing of Roman civilization.

The aristocracy recognized kings as their leaders, yet royal power, as it is revealed in the archaic law tracts or the early epic tales, was severely limited. The king could take special executive action in certain crises, he acted for his people in their relations with external kingdoms,[1] but otherwise his powers were determined by his status at the head of the noble grades. By reason of this he occupied a larger house, kept a bigger retinue, received higher compensation for offences against himself, and afforded greater legal protection than the other secular nobles. Government was aristocratic rather than monarchic, the scales weighted in favour of the nobility, with their special privileges. But one must not imagine the nobility as a consolidated class, exercising political influence as a group, like the barons in thirteenth-century England. The most important force contributing to the maintenance of order was the individual aristocrat and his kin, rather than the aristocracy, since each one maintained his own rights and looked after his dependants and was little concerned with the rights of his class. It was an intensely individualist society, with very little executive authority vested in the king.

How, then, was order maintained? Law was based on custom, and was declared through a special class of legal specialists, but, with one or two exceptions where the king had authority to execute it in special cases, it was privately enforced. There were no crimes against the state, only injuries to private persons, which must be met by compensation adjudged according to the injury received and the status of the injured party. Irish law had a well-developed surety system. Guarantors were taken to ensure the

[1] *C.G.*, lines 495–524.

performance of customary obligations: each kin-group had, for example, its representative who guaranteed the duties to which his kinsmen were bound,[1] and the king kept a 'man of pledge for base clients' permanently in his household.[2] When a man made an extraordinary contract he gave some treasure in pledge for its fulfilment, and if it was of major importance he also took guarantors who pledged themselves to see that the contract was maintained.[3] If anyone failed to fulfil his contract his guarantors were liable, and failure meant loss of status with its rights to compensation and other privileges. The man who did not keep faith was degraded and lost his honour-price.

The surety system had certain obvious disadvantages. It would only work while public morale was high and while it was supported by aristocratic prestige. It was far more complex and intimate than a system in which the same public authority is responsible for enforcing all the duties of the citizen, and the opportunities for varying reliability were as great as the considerable number of individual persons involved. Yet this system is a rational attempt to maintain the rule of law in a society where the king's powers were very limited and bureaucratic institutions unknown, it reveals a high degree of disinterest in its sense of justice transcending the bounds of kin, it shows a highly developed morality in the value which it sets upon the support of consistent friendship.

Early Irish society appears extraordinarily humane in its attitude towards certain social obligations. It seems that a wounded man had once been able to claim sick maintenance as well as the fine for his injury, according to his status. The man who had committed the injury had to provide nursing and medical attention, with half-maintenance for wife or son if they had received injury,[4] and, in certain cases, he had to provide another person to do the wounded man's work during the period of his incapacity. This law was not aimed to benefit the most powerful; indeed, some of the wealthiest persons in society were specifically

[1] C.G., lines 280-2.   [2] C.G., lines 585-6.
[3] C.G., pp. 74, 100, 102; Thurneysen, 'Die Bürgschaft', pp. 35-74.
[4] Bretha Crólige, ed. D. A. Binchy, Ériu, xii (1934), 1-77. Later the liability was commuted to a single payment, ibid., 128.

B

exempted from claiming benefit, since their maintenance would have been an impossible burden on a man of any other grade. An attempt was made in it to safeguard society as a whole, for no one could claim sick benefit unless he had already met all his own legal obligations. The old, as well as the sick, were protected by law, for their children or foster-children were required to care for them. Noble and freeborn boys and girls were sent away from home to be fostered in another household during childhood and adolescence, and special laws regulated the expenses and obligations of fosterage, defining how a boy or girl from different classes should be equipped and maintained, what he should be taught, who was liable for his misdeeds, and how the contract might be ended if it proved unsatisfactory.[1] Provision of hospitality was as important in law as regulation of education. Each man of free or noble grade, according to his status, had the right to demand hospitality under certain conditions from his equals and superiors for himself and his retinue, each man had similar obligations to provide it. One class of wealthy free men gained an honour-price equal to that of the king by undertaking to provide universal hospitality.[2] Thus, though there was no public authority in Celtic society to provide social services, things were so arranged that each individual according to his status had certain well-defined responsibilities. The more important and the wealthier he was, the greater the demands made upon him; the greater the demands he met, the more prestige he commanded.

Systematic intellectual training was provided for a special class of learned men, within which were varying degrees determined by competence, each grade with its own honour-price, the most highly skilled with a legal value equal to that of the petty king.[3] Ireland had its schools of law, and its literary schools where students learned the stories, poems, and genealogies of their people. Both types of learning were of value to the community, for one preserved its legal heritage, the other kept its historical traditions and, by their frequent recitation, maintained public morale. A king needed both a brehon and a *fili* attached to his court, the brehon to elucidate the law, the *fili* to entertain his

---

[1] *A.L.I.*, ii., 146–93.   [2] *C.G.*, p. 79.
[3] *A.L.I.*, v, 56. 'An ollam is equal in *dire* to a king of one *tuath*'.

household during feasting and inspire them before battle with the recollections of their heroic past. Our oldest surviving Welsh poem, the *Gododdin*, composed probably about 600, is a panegyric in honour of a picked force of three hundred Men of the North, defeated and killed by the advancing tide of Anglo-Saxons at Catraeth (probably Catterick in Yorkshire). The court poet describes them, gold-collared, drinking wine and mead from gold cups, happy with the bard's entertainment. But of the three hundred who rose shouting into battle, only one returned (according to one statement), and that was the bard himself: as he says, 'I from my bleeding for my song's sake'. His duty was to record the heroic deeds of the fallen and the sadness of their loss, and many a British warrior, coming after him, hearing his song, must have hoped for a similar immortality. 'Short their lives, but long the longing for them in the hearts of their kinsmen' is an enviable epitaph. The men of learning were an essential part of Celtic society, without whom the poems and tales would never have been composed and the laws never formulated.

It was they who, in the pre-Christian period, guarded the religious lore of the Celts. We can know very little with certainty about their religious ideas, for the archaeological evidence is difficult to interpret, and the mythological cycles, written down in the eighth century and much later, provide no systematic exposition of beliefs. Sacred groves and human sacrifices, the cult of the severed head are melodramatic enough, but poor substitute for a *New Testament* or even a *Meditations*. We know that the continental Celts at least were a religious people, with a great many different deities, and among the insular Celts there seem to have been mother-goddesses who controlled fertility and chieftain-gods to protect the community. After Christianity arrived the pagan divinities retreated underground into the *síd*, but the magic taboos and prescriptions which had determined the actions of the pagan heroes were handed on to Christian kings. Inauguration rites, at which the new king was 'married' to his land, seem to have continued at the age-old sites,[1] and the fertility of cattle and

---

[1] Giraldus Cambrensis in the twelfth century describes such a ceremony as taking place in Tír Conaill: *Topographia*, *P.R.I.A.*, xlii (1949), C 168. Cf. Ann. Connacht s.a. 1310, when Feidlimid was inaugurated: 'this was the most

crops was regarded as a sign of beneficent rule.[1] The mythological hero gained immortality in a happy Other-World, and the Christian literature embodied the theme in the Land of Promise, the Tír ma mBéo, the place of the *semper viventes*.

The oldest Irish epics, first recorded in the seventh or eighth century, but composed in the pre-Christian period, reveal the social ethic of the military aristocracy. Physical prowess and personal courage were, of course, essential: to be wounded in the back while fleeing from an enemy lost the king his status in ancient Irish law. A man's reputation influenced so many aspects of his life that he was prompt to defend it from any slur: the epic hero would respond to an attack on his honour by combat, and in the historic period a slander had to be met with legal action. A quick wit and a ready tongue were admired and cultivated, and the well-phrased taunt was the preliminary to many a battle. The popular literature of later hagiography turned the Irish saints into devastating cursers, so that Giraldus had some justice in his comment that Irish saints 'are more vindictive than the saints of any other region'. Boasting was also a part of the social convention, and both the epic heroes and the later saints of fiction boast of their prowess. Such a convention tends to encourage facility at the expense of literal truth, for the boaster does not need to be accurate, only stronger than his adversary. Many of the qualities of the early Irish were observed much later by the Elizabethan, Edmund Campion, who writes:

> The people are thus inclined: religious, franke, amorous, irefull, sufferable, of paines infinite, very glorious, many sorcerers, excellent horsemen, delighted with warres, great almes-givers, passing in hospitalitie . . . They are sharpe-witted, lovers of learning, capable

---

splendid kingship marriage ever celebrated in Connacht . . .' For Professor Dillon's ed. and transl. of the description see *Mediaeval Studies Presented to Aubrey Gwynn, S.J.*, pp. 186–202. In the fifteenth century the kings of Cenél Eógain were being crowned at Tulach Óg, on the 'flagstone of the kings' there. *A.U.* s.a. 1432, 1455.

[1] M. Dillon, 'Taboos of the Kings of Ireland', *P.R.I.A.*, liv (1951), C 1–36. 'It is certain of the kings of Ireland, if they avoided their *gessa* and obtained their prescriptions, that they would suffer neither misfortune nor disturbance, and neither plague nor pestilence would come in their reign, and they would not fail with age before ninety years.'

of any studie whereunto they bend themselves, constant in travaile, adventerous, intractable, kinde-hearted, secret in displeasure.[1]

How would such people receive Christianity? They were spiritually receptive, but they had a highly developed native oral culture and a firmly established learned class. Would the poets and lawyers be friendly to a different kind of learning and a new priesthood? They were a people who expressed themselves readily and immoderately in words and actions: how would they respond to Christian ideas of self-discipline? They loved fighting, much of their art and literature was devoted to its glorification: could their passion for fighting be curbed and its brutalities be mitigated? Their society was familiar, they had no urban centres and they knew nothing of centralized governmental institutions: could a church shaped by imperial administration be planted on such uncongenial soil? These are some of the questions which we shall have to consider.

[1] *Historie of Ireland*, Chapter 5.

East Mediterranean Christianity

The intellectual and sociological background of early Christianity was utterly different from that of the Celts. While a heroic society was established in the still unconquered Celtic countries of the north-western fringe of Europe, the eastern Mediterranean was following a very different pattern of life. Here were the most highly civilized, prosperous, and populous provinces of the Roman Empire, provinces which had a long history of material wealth, centralized government, and intellectual vitality.

In spite of the economic decline of the third century, Egypt and Syria still boasted splendid cities, fine palaces and luxurious villas, gymnasia and baths, all in sharp contrast to the hill cities and small enclosures of the Celtic peoples. Imperial trade was repressively controlled by the reforms of Diocletian, but industries were still carried on (though now the factories often executed orders for the state), and trade routes remained open. It would hardly be possible to imagine a sharper contrast to the insular society of the Celtic world than that afforded by the cosmopolitan centres of the east Mediterranean, by Antioch, for instance, that home of merchant shipping, or Damascus, receiving the silks and spices of India and China, or Alexandria, with its wharves and factories, bazaars and schools. The eastern Mediterranean in the fourth century still enjoyed many of the graces and refinements of a partly commercial civilization, and though Christianity set small value in theory on the material amenities of its surroundings, yet these were the commonplaces of its environment. By the time of the late Empire the normal meeting-place for Christians was not the dim austerity of the catacombs, but the civilized comfort of a Roman villa. How would Christianity transplant to the crannogs, forts, and ranches of the insular Celts?

A society under highly centralized government brought Christianity to maturity, determining the structure which framed its belief. The emperor represented public authority, and became the source of law and the symbol of divinity. He controlled the vast machine of the bureaucratic state, manned as it was by an army of officials carrying out routine administration. Ecclesiastical organization was modelled on the system used by the state, though in a modified form. In both church and state the centre of local government was the town, from which the surrounding countryside was administered. Church and state were both divided into provinces, though the boundaries were not identical. The curia of the bishops of Rome, with its system of accounting for the administration of papal estates, its courts of law, and its chancery, was the nearest approach to bureaucratic government which the barbarian west ever met during most of the early Middle Ages. However weak in fact were individual popes, the machinery of government lay to their hands, to be used and developed by an intelligent will.

Just as behind the administration of the secular church there lay a long tradition of centralized authority, so behind Christian theology lay a long history of abstract thinking. For philosophy was the very heart of a liberal education in the Hellenistic world, where educated men were expected to interest themselves in intellectual concepts. Many of the philosophical systems of the Empire were first worked out in Greek, a language whose subtleties made it a flexible vehicle for conceptual argument, where accurate expression is the essential prerequisite for clear definition. Latin speech was much less well equipped for such discussion, as the Christian theologians of the Middle Ages found, and the Celtic peoples, with their literature of poetry and lively dialogue and rhetorical description, and the highly technical language of their law tracts, had no tradition of philosophical debate comparable to that of the Greeks. In fact, their only major philosopher was the ninth-century genius John Scottus, and he had learned Greek before he conceived his system. But systems of classical philosophy did not determine the ideas of all inhabitants of the Empire. Many were conscious of the inadequacy of their own powers, and needed some sustaining power outside themselves to take transforming possession of them. Such people were aware of sin, not merely of ignorance; they wanted a superhuman experience, they longed to be united to a god, to be made partakers of divinity. The mystery religions, coming into the Empire from the East, answered this longing.

Christianity combined features of an intellectual philosophy with qualities of a mystery religion. As a religious philosophy it was probably most nearly akin to Neoplatonism, of which Philo, an Alexandrian Jew and contemporary of S. Paul, was a precursor, Plotinus, teaching at Rome in the fourth century, the chief systematizer, and Proclus the exponent in the Academy at Athens. Both Neoplatonism and Christianity provided intellectually satisfying dogmas together with opportunity for religious aspirations. Both provided philosophical system, moral discipline, and ecstatic revelation. But the Neoplatonist's revelation, though it transcended intellect, pre-supposed it, while for the Christian love was the only essential pre-requisite. Christianity, beginning with the claims that God had become man, that, by the ordeal of His passion and the miracle of His resurrection, He had brought salvation to the world (a claim which must to the casual observer have classed it with the mysteries), later had its doctrine formed in the intellectual tradition by men like Clement, Origen, Athanasius, and Augustine. Even the simple pious, who formed the main body of its adherents, were used to hearing discussion of ideas, doctrines, and philosophies. The audience which could attend with interest to the Pauline epistles was very different in its intellectual attitude from the audience which listened to the Irish tales of cattle raids and similar adventures.

Theologians of the eastern Mediterranean played a major part in the formation of Christian doctrine. Egypt and Syria also gave birth to that monasticism which was to reappear later with such marked similarities in the remote Celtic west; understandably to reappear, since the desert sloughed off much of the paraphernalia which Christianity had acquired by its development in a world of urban civilization, material wealth, and bureaucratic government. The men who sought solitude in the desert turned their backs on town and village, they abandoned property with the cares of its administration, they even left corporate worship for private communion. Monasticism meant a fresh start. Popular Christianity necessitated complex organization if the church were to be saved from degeneracy, but organization inevitably left little room for individual enthusiasm. In the burning sun and icy vigil of the desert, organization withered away, each man pursued his soul's need.

Desert theology, as expressed by the Greek Evagrius, demanded a long period of ascetic discipline which culminated in contemplative experience. Each monk chose his own solitude, natural cave, or stone hut, and applied to himself what discipline he saw fit, or voluntarily sought it from a more experienced brother. The food was meagre, the hours of prayer long, and practical work was undertaken only because it was a cure for 'accidie', 'the destruction that wasteth at noonday', that neurosis of frustration which was the occupational disease of contemplatives. Difficult as this life was, many contemporaries found its objects worth striving for. The men who attempted it believed that its attainable goal was a state of indescribable blessedness. The readers of the *Life* of the early hermit, S. Antony, saw in him not a gloomy fanaticism, but a realization of the felicity for which they longed.[1]

The solitude and fasting of the desert brought with it some of the marvellous phenomena common to many ascetic religions. It was probably inevitable that, with many simple people fleeing to the desert, some should mistake the means for the end, and behave as if the phenomena were the prime object of monasticism; but the theologians leave no doubt that ascetic discipline was for the emptying of the self, for the cultivation of a state of passivity, so that God might take possession. 'Moses, fasting, talked with God,' writes Athanasius, 'Elijah, fasting, saw visions and was finally taken up by a chariot into heaven.' The contemplative ideal was the object of the desert, solitude and ascetism were its necessary conditions.

The solitary had no obligations to work, no social responsibilities, no outside authority to exercise discipline. Sitting alone among the rocks of the desert, he either pursued his spiritual warfare with intense activity or the terrifying monotony of the desert became intolerable. Desert solitude was not in fact always total or perpetual. The beginner usually lived for a time alongside

[1] Athanasius, *Life of St Antony*, transl. R. T. Meyer, London, 1950, cc. 14, 44, 50, 56, 73 etc.

some experienced hermit. In some areas, such as Nitria in northern Egypt, many hermits lived in the same neighbourhood, with common bakeries and common church, a guest house and some minimum standard of common discipline.[1] It was possible to spend months or years in the desert and then return to the world, for each man, though he might ask advice, was entirely free to follow his own judgement. 'Be to them an example, not a lawgiver', was the typical maxim of one desert father. Indeed, the individualism of the desert was far too difficult a responsibility for ordinary men, who needed the pressure of public opinion to sustain them when their love was cold and their wills weak.

It was the Egyptian Pachomius who revolutionized monasticism by introducing three entirely new elements – corporate life, obedience, and work. He organized fully resident communities under the direction of a superior, where a considerable part of every day was spent in materially productive work for the benefit of the monks and of the world outside. The Pachomian prior had disciplinary powers, while the superior of the whole confederation of all Pachomian houses had extensive economic resources as well as moral authority, rather as a great Celtic abbot was later to have. But even within the authoritarian régime of Pachomius there were still opportunities for individual judgement, for the standard of asceticism set within the community was a minimum standard, which any monk might better if he willed. The harshness of the desert was still not far from Pachomius' demands.

His younger contemporary Basil the Cappadocian crystallized that union of the contemplative ideal of monasticism with the conception of social obligation towards which Pachomius had worked. 'If a man love God,' said Basil, 'then he must love his brother also': so even while he encouraged his monks in contemplative prayer, he built an almshouse and a hospital, and attached a school to his monastery. His sister Macrina, acting in the same spirit, turned the family residence into a convent for women, but in times of famine went out to gather up the babies

---

[1] 'On the mountain live some five thousand men with different modes of life, each living in accordance with his own powers and wishes, so that it is allowed to live alone, or with another, or with a number of others.' Palladius, *Lausiac History*, transl. W. K. L. Clarke, S.P.C.K., 1918, pp. 57–9.

who had been abandoned at the roadside.[1] His younger brother set out intending to lead the hermit's life, but came across some helpless old people, so stayed near them, fishing and providing for them all.[2] The ruthlessness of the desert is absent from Basil's monasticism. 'He reconciled . . . and united the solitary and the community life,' writes his friend Gregory Nazianzen, 'so that the contemplative life might not be cut off from society, nor the active life be uninfluenced by contemplation.'[3] The combination of the two was to prove a truly creative element in western monasticism.

Within a few decades of its beginning, monasticism had already developed along varied lines. Antony is the type of the complete solitary, but before long parts of the desert were a honeycomb of hermits' cells, the more accessible being visited by serious inquirers and even pestered by tourists, so that one hermit built himself an underground passage into which he could crawl away when sightseers arrived. Pachomius, the Egyptian and ex-soldier, was the desert's first great organizer, who built houses, installed priors, drew up rules, and set his monks to hard practical work, separating them into residences according to their trade, so that his monasteries had some elements of a factory. Basil, the educated Greek, from a family familiar with social service, encouraged his small household of monks to set before their imaginations the service of those in want, a service not incompatible with the heavenly vision.

The period of pre-Benedictine monasticism was a great adventure, when the potentialities of monastic life for good or ill were still only half-realized. Monasticism was then varied, fluctuating, dependent on the views of a founder, subject for its fulfilment to the will of the individual monk. Born in a flight from the world, it was not nearly so conditioned, as was the secular church, by the structure of contemporary society. Towns and bureaucratic government were not essential to its origin or development.

---

[1] Gregory of Nyssa, *Life of Macrina*, transl. W. K. L. Clarke, S.P.C.K., 1916, p. 60.

[2] Ibid., pp. 30–1.

[3] Panegyric on St Basil, §62, transl. C. G. Browne and J. E. Swallow, *Nicene and Post-Nicene Fathers*, 2nd ser., vii, Oxford, 1894, pp. 415–6.

Monasticism was therefore a form of Christian life which could be easily transplanted to a completely alien society. Nevertheless, a journey of nearly three thousand miles separates the eastern Mediterranean from the lands of the Celtic west, a country on the outer edge of the world of which Syria and Egypt lie at the heart. How did monasticism transfer itself from the eastern deserts to the plains and forests, the coasts and highlands of the Celtic west?

CHAPTER 3

The western provinces

Christianity reached the western provinces of the Empire not by formal missions but by casual contacts, establishing itself first in the towns, where it was organized on the same lines as in the eastern Mediterranean. By the end of the fourth century it had become a socially respectable religion, professed by many of the well-to-do and well-born; its leaders the bishops were responsible administrators, performing a number of social services, respected by the population.

S. Martin was one of the first to practise the monastic life in Gaul. The well-bred Gallo-Roman bishops did not all welcome his consecration as bishop of Tours about 372, for he was a social outsider who inherited no traditions of command, an ex-soldier of insignificant appearance, ill-dressed and unkempt and excitable.[1] The monasticism he established was of a semi-eremitic kind, following a strictly ascetic régime. About two miles outside Tours, where the Loire bends gently, on the level land between the cliff face and the river, Martin lived with eighty or so monks, who spent their time almost entirely in private prayer, not maintaining themselves by their own labour.[2] His disciple Sulpicius Severus had already written a popular Life of the saint before

[1] 'They said . . . that Martin was a despicable individual and quite unfit to be a bishop, what with his insignificant appearance, his sordid garments and his disgraceful hair.' Sulpicius Severus, *Life of Martin*, c. 9, transl. Hoare, *The Western Fathers*, pp. 22–3.

[2] Ibid., p. 24. 'His own cell was built of wood, as were those of many of the brethren; but most of them had hollowed out shelters for themselves in the rock of the overhanging mountain. . . . No one possessed anything of his own; everything was put in the common stock. The buying and selling which is customary with most hermits (*monachi*) was forbidden them. No craft was practised there except that of the copyist, and that was assigned to the younger men. The older ones were left free for prayer. It was seldom that anyone left his cell except when they assembled at the place of worship. All received their food together after the fast was ended. No one touched wine unless ill-health forced him to do so. Most of them wore clothes of camel's hair; softer clothing was looked on as an offence there.'

Martin's death in 397, and he followed it with Letters and Dialogues, that with Postumianus containing anecdotes of the life and teaching of monks in the African and Syrian deserts, on whose practices Martin seems to have modelled his own.

It is hard to discover a theory of the monastic life either in the career of Martin or in the writings of Sulpicius. The solitary life was apparently valued highly, the attitude to work was negative, there was no conception of social service by the monks as a body, though Martin himself went out on preaching and healing tours. In spite of Sulpicius's humour and the fluency of his literary style, the intellectual content of his work is meagre: extreme asceticism and miracles which are the phenomena of early monasticism take the place of any reasoned exposition of the nature and purpose of monastic life.

It was the eastern monk Cassian who made the theory of Egyptian and Syrian monasticism widely known in the west, translating some of the technical terms of Greek ascetic theology into Latin speech and thought. Cassian was no legislator, although, as it happens, we are familiar with his ideas because he wrote them down to provide regulations and teaching for bishop Castor's new foundation at Apt, forty miles north of his own settlement at Marseilles. He was interested primarily in contemplative prayer, that state of blessedness in which the individual soul is possessed by God. He believed in the superiority of the solitary over the community life, and he shared the desert Fathers' negative attitude to work. Love of one's neighbour was desirable only as a means to perfection, it was not the fruit of a good life: on the contrary, it was a state of mind inconsistent with that tranquillity which is essential to contemplation. 'Who can, with tranquil mind, . . . gaze upon the glorious majesty of God while engaged in works of charity?' asks Cassian. 'Who can contemplate the immeasurable blessedness of heaven at that very moment when he is ministering alms to the poor, when he is welcoming visitors with gracious hospitality, when he is concerned with caring for the needs of his brethren?'[1] There is little conception

---

[1] *Collationes*, xxiii, 5, transl. E. C. S. Gibson, *Nicene and Post-Nicene Fathers*, 2nd ser., xi, Oxford, 1894, p. 522. For Cassian's thought see O. Chadwick, *John Cassian*, pp. 120–33, 137–67.

here of social obligation, little consciousness of the needs of the world outside the monastery, troubled and devastated as it was by invasions and disasters. Yet Cassian performed an immense service to Latin monastic thought by rationalizing for the west the asceticism of Egypt, emphasizing that an ascetic activity like fasting is a means to an end, stressing the need for absolute obedience to superior direction during the preliminary period of training in a community before the monk could proceed to the high adventure of solitude.

Honoratus, a contemporary of Cassian, founded, on one of the islands of Lérins off the coast of the French Riviera, a monastic settlement which seems to have combined a high degree of individualism with a definite conception of social obligation. Lérins had both a *coenobium* and hermitages to which the senior brethren could withdraw to pursue their own standard of perfection. Honoratus ruled his monks with strict discipline, yet, if we are to judge by the moving portrait of him drawn by his disciple Hilary of Arles, his rule cannot have been irksome. For he was clearly a man of unusual imagination and human sympathy: 'You would hardly believe what trouble he took to see that no one became depressed,' writes Hilary. 'He discerned what was troubling anyone as easily as if he carried everyone's mind in his own.'[1] One of his favourite verses from the Psalms was: 'Let the hearts of those who seek the Lord be glad.'[2] He saw the monastic life as the means by which individuals might express their love for God and join themselves to Him.[3] Yet he joined the contemplative ideal with awareness of the needs of the world. Whereas many of the Egyptian monks were not allowed to bring their property to the group which they joined,[4] Honoratus and some of his disciples brought substantial patrimonies to Lérins, which enabled them to

---

[1] Discourse on the Life of S. Honoratus, transl. F. R. Hoare, op. cit., p. 263, for the consideration he gave to each personality and the different treatment to suit each monk. Cf. p. 270. Honoratus may have inherited something of this understanding from his own pagan father, who had tried to distract him from Christianity and to 'renew his own youth in a kind of comradeship with his young son'. Ibid., p. 252.

[2] Ibid., p. 279, quoting Ps. 105[3].

[3] 'binding me with the chains of love for Thee'. Ibid., p. 268.

[4] See Chadwick, *Cassian*, p. 53.

offer practical relief to refugees from areas devastated by the barbarians.[1] Honoratus himself accepted the invitation to Arles as bishop, at a time when Gallic bishops were having to take over some of the administrative functions of the older Roman magistracy. His disciple and biographer Hilary succeeded him at Arles, and, indeed, Lérins provided so many candidates for episcopal sees that it became known as a 'nursery of bishops'.

Even more important, several of the monasteries of southern Gaul were noted for their intellectual enlightenment. Martin had been simple and unlearned, Honoratus was from a cultivated family. Whereas Sulpicius, writing of S. Martin, is the true *vulgarisateur*, stylistically facile and intellectually thin, Cassian of Marseilles is writing for a more intelligent public. For Cassian virtue, not miracle, is the sign of perfection.

The schools of Marseilles and Lérins joined with vigour in the great theological dispute on the relative place of grace and free-will which shook the church in the early fifth century. They formed an influential section of the anti-Augustinian party, refusing to accept that God had predestined some to salvation and others to damnation, a doctrine which they recognized as perversive of all moral effort. Cassian saw the human will as sick rather than dead to all good, needing divine help, but sometimes able to make the first faint turnings, *naturaliter*, in the direction of God. Throughout his teaching he emphasized the necessity for constant effort by the individual in the spiritual life.[2]

The anti-Augustinians of Marseilles and Lérins have sometimes been described as semi-Pelagians, but the insular Celt Pelagius[3] had gone much farther than they were prepared to go in his insistence on the power of man's will, independent of grace. It is possible that 'grace' had a sinister meaning for Pelagius, for in the

---

[1] Hoare, op. cit., p. 265. 'His material resources matched his bountiful spirit . . . those who had dedicated possessions to works of mercy were eager to take them to him to be dispensed. . . . This was the cause of the continual stream that came to him from so many devastated regions.'

[2] For a full discussion of Cassian's position see Owen Chadwick, *Cassian*, pp. 109–38.

[3] He is called an Irishman by Jerome in a vituperative passage, of which the phrase 'Scotorum pultibus praegravatus' is a sample. But see Grosjean, *A.B.*, lxxv (1957), 206–11, who argues for a British origin.

contemporary Theodosian Code it often signifies 'favouritism'. Thus, a God who was *gratiosus* might have seemed to some a corrupt God, the *potentia* he wielded might imply oppression, while *gratia* must be sought by the defenceless to escape from tyranny.[1] Pelagius had been trained in Rome in legal studies. He believed both in the goodness of God and the dignity of man, and maintained that God had given man free will, which enabled him to choose between good and evil. Man was capable of perfection because God had so created him, but the desire for good was the action of his own will, and man would ultimately be judged on his own achievements by an impartial God.

Pelagius' doctrine was condemned in 418, but in the distant province of Britain the 'enemies of grace' gained power. By this time Christianity had long been established in Britain. It had arrived at least as early as the second century, for Tertullian, writing about 200, suggests that it had even penetrated beyond the territory under Roman occupation.[2] The British church had organized itself along the same imperial lines as the church on the Continent: bishops from three British cities attended the Council of Arles in 314, British bishops were present at the Councils of Sardica in 347 and of Rimini in 359, where three of them had their travelling expenses paid from public funds. In the following century British Pelagianism was felt to be sufficiently menacing for two bishops, Germanus of Auxerre and Lupus of Troyes, to head a Gaulish mission in 429 intended to stamp out the heresy. This was only partially successful, and a second mission was dispatched in the 440s. Even so, some of the writings of Pelagius must have been preserved and treasured, for Irish scholars were quoting from him several centuries later.

The mission of Germanus, as reported by his fifth-century biographer Constantius, proves that Roman Britain had a population sufficiently educated to interest itself in theological discussion. The debate, presumably held in Latin, between the Pelagian disputants and the Gaulish bishops was attended by a vast crowd,

[1] J. N. L. Myres, 'Pelagius and the End of Roman Rule in Britain', *J.R.S.* L (1960), 21–36. It is, however, impossible to believe that Augustine and his supporters were using the words in this way.

[2] *Britannorum inaccessa Romanis loca Christo vero subdita.*

C

who followed the argument with enthusiasm; the Pelagians came forth 'flaunting their wealth in dazzling robes' and made speeches of 'empty words drawn out to great length', before the Gauls answered with their 'floods of eloquence'. Constantius' account also demonstrates the close links between the church in Gaul and in Britain. The Gauls clearly felt some responsibility for Christians in the neighbouring province. According to the contemporary chronicler Prosper of Aquitaine, Pope Celestine, advised by the deacon Palladius, sent Germanus of Auxerre to Britain.[1] Constantius, writing about sixty years later, reports that a deputation of Britons appealed for help directly to a Gaulish synod.[2] The British church was not to be abandoned to heresy, even though the province was finally lost to the Empire.[3]

The churches of Gaul and Britain were at this time very similar in organization. But whereas monasticism in Gaul was firmly established by the middle of the fifth century, and beginning to exercise a profound influence on the secular church through its learning and its personalities, there is no evidence of any comparable monastic movement in Britain. Monasticism was known there. Pelagius is called a monk, but his active life was spent abroad. The British bishop Fastidius wrote treatises on 'The Christian Life' and 'The Preserving of Widowhood'. Faustus, another Briton and semi-Pelagian, journeyed south to the Mediterranean to become a monk at Lérins. We see the monk Riocatus travelling back home to Britain, carrying with him books from southern Gaul.[4] Britain had monks, but, as far as we know, she had no monastic schools in any way comparable to Lérins or Marseilles, no monastic bishops like Martin or Honoratus. Monasticism in Gaul was still a comparatively recent development in the fifth century, and there was probably a time-lag before it grew to strength in the remoter parts of the Christian world.

---

[1] *Chronicon* s.a. 429; Migne, *P.L.*, li, 594–5; Mommsen, *Chronica Minora* i (1892) 473. For Palladius, see *infra*, pp. 32–3.

[2] *M. G. H. Script. Rer. Mer.*, vii (1920), 259; Hoare, *Western Fathers*, p. 295.

[3] Dr Myers argues that Pelagianism provided a rallying point for men in revolt against Rome, and that the Gaulish mission had political as well as theological motives.

[4] Sidonius Apollinaris, *Epistolae* ed. Krusch, *M.G.H.*, viii, 157.

Britons at this period were travelling even beyond Gaul, and might go on pilgrimage to the eastern Mediterranean. 'The Briton, sundered from our world,' writes Jerome in Bethlehem, 'if he has made progress in religion, leaves his western sun and seeks a place known only to him by fame and the narrative of the scriptures.'[1] The author of the semi-Pelagian letter *De vita Christiana*, who may be the British bishop Fastidius,[2] left his young daughter with a Sicilian lady before proceeding eastwards. In the late fourth century Britons were still part of the Empire, and journeys within the imperial frontiers were still possible.

A few Britons went far afield, but Gaul was their nearest neighbour, and the most immediate outside influence on the British church. The church of Gaul had, at this time, incorporated but not yet fused together a number of varied and even incompatible elements. There were the well-born and often cultivated Gallo-Roman bishops, benevolent officials performing public duties. Some men of this type would naturally find themselves in opposition to the ill-educated wonder worker, Martin, and the unsophisticated approach to Christianity which he represented. They were also suspicious of the more extreme forms of eastern asceticism which were filtering into Gaul. Gregory of Tours wrote in the sixth century of a would-be stylite who found the country folk worshipping an image of Diana, so set up a pillar beside her on which he stood through summer and icy winter preaching the new faith. So successful a rival to Diana did he become that the village people helped him to drag down and smash the image. But in spite of this, the bishops disapproved his manner of life: 'A base-born man like you,' they told him, 'cannot be compared with Simon of Antioch, who lived on a column.' So, arguing the unsuitable climate and the needs of his brethren, the bishops persuaded him to come down, and one day, having summoned him to a village some way off, they had his pillar destroyed.[3] Such forms of austerity were not to be encouraged.

---

[1] *Ep.* xlvi. 10, ed. and transl. J. Labourt, *Saint Jérôme, Lettres*, ii, Paris, 1951, p. 110.
[2] Ed. C. P. Caspari, *Briefe, Abhandlungen und Predigten, Ep.* I; see R. S. T. Haslehurst, *The Works of Fastidius*, London, 1927, pp. 2 ff.
[3] *History of the Franks*, viii, 15.

The intellectual monasteries of southern Gaul followed a more rational asceticism, using it as a way towards contemplative experience, and combining it in some cases with a high degree of social obligation. To all these varieties of Christian thought and organization the Celtic west lay open.

CHAPTER 4

The first missionaries

It seems likely that the leaders of the Romano-British church were the gentry; men like the wealthy villa-owner at Lullingstone, who set aside for Christian worship rooms decorated with painted wall-plasters depicting praying figures, or at Frampton, where the chi-rho emblem was incorporated into a mosaic.[1] Near, even alongside, the Christian motifs might be purely pagan scenes, for the tastes of these men had been formed by Roman traditions. It was the church of the lowland zone which sent Christianity out to the highlands, so it is not surprising that the new converts became conscious, as Christians, of their part in Roman civilization.

The Roman roads drove a clear highway far beyond the towns and villas of the lowlands to regions where the evidences of Rome were walls and camps and signal stations, with Celtic fortifications on the hilltops. Wales, northern England, and the Scottish low-lands were a crisscross of roads, which penetrated even beyond the Forth–Clyde line. Here in the highland zones the natives and the army had fraternized: the Celts sold their produce in the townships which grew up round the Roman camps, and took home such things as iron tools and glass-ware. At Traprain in Gododdin, twenty miles east of the rock of Edinburgh, some of the inhabitants wanted to read and write simple Latin: they scratched their alphabets and left them here on the hill-top bet-ween the Lammermuirs and the sea.[2] Such people welcomed Roman civilization. As early as the fourth century certain princes of Strathclyde and Gododdin (the peoples who occupied territory at the west and east ends respectively of the Antonine Wall) had been adopting Roman names: Clemens and Quintilius appear,

[1] J. M. C. Toynbee, 'Christianity in Roman Britain', *Jrnl. of the Br. Arch. Assoc.*, 3rd ser., xvi (1953), 1–24.

[2] J. Curle, *Proc. Scot. Ant. Soc.*, lxvi (1931–2), 359 f. 42–3. I. Richmond, *Roman and Native in North Britain*, p. 119: they represent 'the need to read inscriptions and perhaps even documents, the kind of accomplishment most necessary among merchants or chiefs'.

under their Celtic forms, in the genealogies of Strathclyde, Tacitus, Paternus, and Aeternus in a genealogy of Gododdin. Paternus even has an epithet, *Pesrut*,[1] a title which reminds us of the scarlet tunic worn by the Roman military officer. Strathclyde and Gododdin, so strategically located on the frontiers of Roman Britain, may have been deliberately cultivated by Rome as buffer states, or as *foederati*. The late-fifth- and sixth-century inscriptions of Wales show that the Irish settlers there adopted Roman names, sometimes writing them in ogam on their memorial stones, sometimes inscribing their stones in Latin. Latin, with a provincial pronunciation, was a spoken language in the Celtic west of Britain.[2] Even in Ireland a few Latinized names appear on the ogam stones, mainly in areas accessible from the sea. The highland zone in the fifth century must have been in a mood receptive to ideas from the Romanized world.

Ninian is the first Christian of the Celts beyond the frontier about whom we have any historical information, and that scanty, for our earliest records of him date from the eighth century, more than three hundred years after his own time. Bede briefly relates the information which he had been able to collect,[3] possibly (though he does not say so)[4] from his friend Pecthelm, who was the first to occupy the newly founded English see of Whithorn. Later in the century a cleric of Whithorn familiar with Bede's works composed verses on S. Ninian,[5] and Ailred of Rievaulx, writing of Ninian in the twelfth century, used 'a book on his life and miracles written in barbarous style' (*barbarice scriptus*) which

---

[1] From the Latin *pexa* 'woolly [tunic]' + *rut* (Mod. W. *rhudd*) 'red'.

[2] Jackson, *L.H.E.B.*, pp. 172 ff. The late-fifth- or early-sixth-century stone from Lewannick in Cornwall gives the Latin inscription *Ingenvi Memoria*, with the ogam transliteration *Ingenavi Memor*, where the engraver tries to give the sound of the British Latin. Cf. p. 366.

[3] *H.E.* III. 4, Plummer's edn. ii, 128 ff. for notes.

[4] Merely 'ut perhibent'. He refers explicitly elsewhere to Pecthelm as a source of information, *H.E. V.* 13, 18. His information might possibly have come from Pictland, for relations between Northumbria and Pictland were friendly during Bede's time. (*H.E. V.* 21).

[5] W. Levison, 'An Eighth Century Poem on S. Ninian', *Antiquity*, xiv (1940), 280–91. The poems edited by C. Strecker, *M.G.H.*, iv (1923), 943–62, are almost certainly to be identified with those sent to Alcuin from York.

may date from the eighth century or perhaps earlier. It appears that Ninian was arousing interest in the eighth century.

Bede tells us that he was a Briton and a bishop, 'who had been regularly instructed in the mysteries of the Christian faith at Rome', that he built a stone church at Candida Casa (now usually identified as Whithorn in the west of Galloway), where he was buried, and that he evangelized the southern Picts. When Bede wrote, Candida Casa was dedicated to S. Martin, and the see, English by this time, was famous for its fine church; the southern Picts were occupying the territory from the Tay as far north as the Mounth, so this was presumably the country which Bede understood Ninian to have evangelized.[1]

How far can we trust our information on S. Ninian? The group of eighth-century works strongly suggests that there was a revival of interest in him then, almost certainly encouraged by the new English foundation at Whithorn, and probably also by the friendly relations established recently between Northumbrians and Picts, which must have facilitated the exchange of information. It has been suggested that political relations were just then so favourable to the establishment of Ninian's cult at Whithorn that the eighth century probably marks the beginning of his connexion with that church;[2] but it is far more likely that the English revived a cult and fostered traditions which were already established.

The material remains provide unequivocal evidence that Christians were settled in western Galloway at least as early as the fifth century. A stone found at Whithorn bears the earliest of a group of inscriptions, which commemorates Latinus, aged thirty-five, and his daughter, aged four.[3] Barrovadus, grandson of Latinus, set up the stone, probably soon after 500, so Latinus was presumably alive in the fifth century. On the neck of the next peninsula to the west, at Kirkmadrine, is a sixth century stone

[1] The poem says that Ninian evangelized the Picts *quae naturae dicuntur*. Levison suggests emending to *Niuduera*, as in the Anon. Life of S. Cuthbert (ed. B. Colgrave, p. 82; cf. p. 192).

[2] N. K. Chadwick, *Trans. of the Dumfriesshire and Galloway Natural History and Antiquarian Society*, 3rd ser., xxvii (1950), 9–53. Cf. E. A. Thompson, 'Origin of Christianity in Scotland', *S.H.R.* xxxvii (1958), 17–22.

[3] R. Radford and G. Donaldson, *Whithorn and Kirkmadrine*, H.M.S.O., 1927, p. 38. I am following Professor Kenneth Jackson's dating for these stones.

incised with the Christian monogram, the alpha and omega signs, and the inscription: *Hic iacent sancti at praecipvi sacerdotes, id est Viventius et Mavorius*.[1] This would suggest a church of some local importance. The monogram appears on another stone, of the late fifth century, which bears a Latin name (Florentius) in a defaced inscription, and a third Christian inscription occurs in the seventh century. There can be no doubt that a church under Roman influence flourished in Galloway in the fifth and sixth centuries.

This does not, of course, prove the full reliability of the tradition reported to Bede. The late Père Grosjean protested that a fourth-century dedication to S. Martin at Whithorn was an impossibility, for the consecration of an altar or church to a confessor outside the place where his body rested would have been an enormous anachronism in the fourth or early fifth century.[2] S. Martin died in 397: Bede certainly believed that the ancient church of S. Martin at Canterbury had been built and dedicated during the Roman occupation. But whether or not Whithorn was from the beginning dedicated to S. Martin, with Ninian as its first bishop, there were Christians here in the fifth century, and the southern Picts had been converted before Patrick addressed his letter to Coroticus referring to the 'apostate', that is the iniquitous, immoral, Picts.[3] The late-fifth- and early-sixth-century inscriptions of the Scottish lowlands bear Christian formulae.[4] One, at Overkirkhope in Selkirkshire, shows a figure with hands raised in the classical attitude of prayer, in the same position as the praying figures at Lullingstone, though in this northern stone the execution is crude.[5] Christianity must have filtered gradually from the province into the north British highlands, and all the evidence which we have suggests that the church

[1] R. Radford illustrates the stone (opp. p. 40) and reads *Ides, Viventius et Mavorius*. The reading I have given is that of Macalister, *Corpus* i. 494, and was accepted by the late Père Grosjean, S. J.

[2] *A.B.*, lxxvi (1958), 357; see also W. Levison, 'Medieval Church dedications in England', *Trans. of the Architectural and Archaeological Soc. of Durham and Northumberland*, x (1946), 60–75.

[3] Grosjean, *A.B.*, lxxvi, 374; L. Bieler, *Libri Epistolarum*, ii, 194–5.

[4] Jackson, *Angles and Britons*, pp. 63–5; Macalister, *Corpus* i. nos. 498, 510, 514–20.

[5] Report of the Royal Cmsn. on Anc. and Hist. Monuments of Scotland, *Selkirkshire* (Edinburgh, 1957), pp. 69 f.

there followed the same pattern of organization as the Romano-British church.

We have no early narrative account of the Christian church in Wales. Later Welsh tradition associated S. Germanus with Powys, the kingdom in central–east Wales. According to the reading made by Edward Llwyd in 1696 (but now largely indecipherable), the Pillar of Elised was set up by Elised's great-grandson Concenn in the first half of the ninth century. Concenn took the opportunity to record the splendours of his ancestors, and one of the traditions he thought deserved honour concerned Britu, son of Vortigern and Severa (daughter of Maximus), who had been blessed by Germanus.[1] Nennius, writing in the early ninth century, believed that Germanus had prophesied the prosperity of the royal dynasty of Powys. But such stories belong to legend rather than history.[2] It is, however, significant that Dubricius, whom the early Life of S. Samson and many of the later Lives of Welsh saints regard as spiritual father and senior, was active, as his dedications show, in Archenfeld, the highly romanized area of south-east Wales, an area penetrated by a network of Roman roads and villas.[3] It looks as if the father (*papa*) of the Welsh saints may have gained his inspiration from Roman Britain.

Patrick, the apostle of the Irish, author of the Confession, was a Briton from a partially Romanized area in the west.[4] When he was sixteen, as he himself tells the story in his Confession, he was captured by a raiding party and carried off from his father's estate to Ireland, where he became a slave. Looking back over a lifetime of successes and defeats, the writer of the Confession recognized himself as spiritually unawakened to meet this first crisis of his adolescence: 'I did not know the Lord.' In the anguish of his isolation he came to know God: 'I was like a stone lying in the

[1] Nash-Williams, *E.C.M.W.*, pp. 123–5. On the authenticity of this evidence see Bu'lock, *Antiquity*, xxxiv (1960), 50–3.

[2] A saint named Garmon was once active in Powys, as the dedications prove.

[3] Bowen, *Settlements*, pp. 33–9.

[4] The text of Patrick's Epistle and Letter is edited by L. Bieler (1952) and translated by him (1953). On the problems arising from these and other Patrician texts, see D. Binchy, 'Patrick', pp. 7–173.

deep mire; and He that is mighty came, and in His mercy lifted me up.' That communion maintained him in a state of serenity and joy throughout the physical hardships of his tasks: 'I felt no harm, and there was no sloth in me – as I now see, because the spirit within me was then fervent.'

He spent six years in slavery, apparently without thought of escape, until one night in a dream there came to his ears the voice which then and later was to change the pattern of his life. First came the promise: 'Soon you will go to your own country,' then after a short time the words: 'See, your ship is ready.' Upon that sign he fled from his master, travelling about two hundred miles over country previously unknown to him to where a merchant ship waited. Here, after some difficulty, he was taken aboard by the pagan crew, and after a three days' voyage, landed with them in a deserted countryside, we do not know where. Ultimately he reached home, to be re-united with his family.

But in spite of their kindly welcome, he did not settle down at home, and again a dream redirected him. A messenger arrived from Ireland with many letters, one of which he handed to Patrick, who read the opening words. Instead of the personal name of the sender with which a fifth-century letter normally opened, Patrick saw written on the page before him *The Voice of the Irish,* and as he read, in his dream, it was as if he heard their voice, calling to him in unison, beseeching him to return and be with them again. He was so much moved that he could read no further, and awoke. Confusing dreams followed: 'Another night . . . they called me most unmistakably with words which I heard but could not understand, except that at the end of the prayer He spoke thus: 'He that has laid down his life for thee, it is He that speaketh to thee.' In the end, his bewilderment and resistance were overcome, and Patrick returned to Ireland.

His work in Ireland, covering a whole generation according to the Irish records, seems to have taken place in the fifth century.[1] He endured many hardships at the hands of the Irish – twelve times, he tells us, he was in mortal danger, once he was fettered – but his mission was crowned with success: 'Many were reborn in

[1] For the controversy on the date and identity of Patrick, see Binchy, 'Patrick'.

God through me and afterwards confirmed, and clerics were
ordained for them everywhere, for a people just coming to the
faith, whom the Lord took from the uttermost parts of the earth.'

Patrick writes as though the people to whom he preached were
entirely heathen, though we know that in 431 Pope Celestine, who
had interested himself in the Pelagian controversy, sent Palladius
as the first bishop to 'the Irish believing in Christ'. It seems likely,
on grounds of general probability (there is no direct evidence),
that communities already Christian were resident in the south, in
the areas which we know had sent out settlements to Britain and
where Roman imports have been found, and that Patrick's mission
spread over a wide area in north-east, central, and western Ireland,[1] among people hitherto untouched by Christianity.

What was the character of this church which had been introduced into the Celtic north and west of the British Isles by the
late fourth or early fifth century? The Patrician mission seems to
have been rather unconventional, and needs separate consideration. For north and west Britain the fifth-century inscriptions,
though few in number, provide decisive evidence on the contacts
maintained by the British church, as well as a few clear hints on its
organization. Dubricius' work on the western border of Roman
Britain and Ninian's on the northern border may have received
impetus from the church already established in the province, but
the inscriptions of Celtic Britain borrow their styles not from
Roman Britain, but from the Christian inscriptions of Gaul. A
generation ago it used to be said on the best authority that the
Anglo-Saxon invasions isolated the Celtic west from the Continent, and divorced her from contemporary developments there,
as her conservative attitude on the Easter question well illustrated.[2]
More recent epigraphical studies have shown this view to be
completely false.[3] The formulae prove that the British church of
the north and west was in touch with Gaul in the fifth and sixth
centuries. The fashions in inscriptions which started in Italy in the

[1] The areas, in fact, where Tírechán, writing in the later seventh century,
claims that his foundations were located.

[2] Kenney, *Sources*, pp. 171, 183, 212.

[3] Nash-Williams, *E.C.M.W.*; Jackson, *L.H.E.B.*, pp. 149–93; Foster,
Prehistoric and Early Wales, pp. 213–35; Alcock, *ibid.*, pp. 177–212; see also
Bowen, *Settlements*, pp. 15–17.

fourth century spread to Gaul and were thence transmitted to Britain: there is a specially close connexion between the epigraphy of Wales (where the evidence is more plentiful than elsewhere) and that of the Lyon–Vienne region of Gaul. Gallic influence seems to have come in by the sea routes, routes which are proved to have remained open by the discovery of Mediterranean pottery on Cornish, Welsh, Scottish, and Irish sites.[1] From the coasts travellers from Gaul followed the roads inland, bringing Christian Gaulish fashions into Celtic Britain.

The inscriptions show that the leaders of the north and west British church in the fifth century were bishops and priests, as we know them to have been in Roman Britain and in Gaul; for the stones speak of *sacerdotes*[2] and *presbiteri*. Occasionally there is evidence of a Christian cemetery, as at Capel Anelog near Aberdaron, where two priests are commemorated in the first half of the sixth century: one *Senacus presbyter* lay here *cum multitudinem fratrum*, and his stone was re-used about a century later.[3] In such Christian communities the memory of Roman civilization lived on, as we can see in the Roman names, and in the reference to a 'citizen' (*civis*), or magistrate[4] or doctor (*medicus*).[5] But whereas, during the period of Roman rule, the cultural life of the province, and even of the highland zone, had been mainly directed to the south-east, in the fifth and sixth centuries the 'romanity' of western Britain seems to have survived partly at least through her contemporary contacts with Gaul via the western sea routes.

Ireland's connexions with the continental church are more controversial. Pope Celestine sent Palladius in 431 as first bishop to the Irish believing in Christ (as we know from the continental chronicler Prosper of Aquitaine). It seems likely that this missionary is to be identified with the deacon Palladius, who two years earlier had urged the Pope to send bishop Germanus to fight the

---

[1] Radford, *Dark Age Britain*, pp. 59–70; Thomas, *Mediaeval Archaeology*, iii (1959), 89–111.

[2] At this time (the fifth and sixth centuries) the word *sacerdos* normally means bishop, but is occasionally applied to a priest. See P.M. Gy, *The Sacrament of Holy Orders*, pp. 105–15.

[3] R. Radford, *Caernarvonshire Hist. Soc. Trans.*, xvi (1955), 6–7; *E.C.M.W.* No. 78.

[4] *E.C.M.W.* No. 103.   [5] *E.C.M.W.* No. 92.

Pelagian heresy in Britain. If so, Palladius almost certainly knew something of Auxerre, where Germanus had his seat, and it has been suggested that he may even have been a deacon of that church. In the late seventh century there was a well-established tradition that Patrick the Briton had spent some time in Gaul, and there are continental elements in Patrick's own use of Latin.[1] Tírechán says he spent seven years in Gaul, Italy, and the islands of the Tyrrhene Sea; Muirchú gives him a long stay, some thirty or forty years, at Auxerre; and Cellanus abbot of Péronne, who died in 706, knew that 'Gaul educated him'. Patrick himself says nothing of this, and historians have found it difficult to reconcile the seventh-century claims for a long residence at Lérins or Auxerre with Patrick's halting and unskilled Latin, his rather limited and poor vocabulary on ecclesiastical matters, and his difficulties when dealing with non-ecclesiastical affairs.[2] Dr Mohrmann has recently shown that S. Patrick's Latin is in any case not the Latin of southern Gaul.[3] But what of Auxerre? Muirchú's account may contain, in a very corrupt form, two place-names from the region of Auxerre, and his bishop 'Amathorex', who consecrated Patrick, may be Amator, predecessor of Germanus. If this is so, some early connexion between Ireland and Auxerre would be most probable. The suggestion that Palladius, first bishop to the Irish, may originally have been a deacon at Auxerre, may have known something of conditions in the British Isles and for this reason been sent by Pope Celestine to Ireland, provides the most likely solution to the difficulty, for traditions of his ministry may subsequently have been confused with the mission of Patrick the Briton.

The early Irish church owed much both to Gaul and to Britain, and naturally took its ecclesiastical organization from familiar models: it was led by bishops and priests,[4] it included persons who had taken monastic vows.[5] Yet from the first there may have been unusual features. The activities of Palladius were soon forgotten: it was Patrick whom seventh-century tradition chose to

---

[1] C. Mohrmann. *The Latin of St Patrick*, pp. 50 ff.
[2] Mohrmann, *Latin*, pp. 22 ff; Binchy, 'Patrick', pp. 80 ff.
[3] Mohrmann, *Latin*, pp. 19, 50.
[4] *Conf.* cc. 38, 40.   [5] *Conf.* cc. 41, 42.

remember, and Patrick's mission was distinctly unconventional. It is doubtful whether his mission was even officially recognized. He was bitterly criticized by contemporaries on two grounds, both of which he admits to be true. During his boyhood he had committed some 'sin' (unspecified) which some of his ecclesiastical seniors considered incapacitated him. Exactly what it incapacitated him from being or doing is not clear, for Patrick's audience knew the circumstances to which he only needed to allude. The most probable interpretation of this obscure passage in the Confession seems to be that his opponents thought him unfit to hold orders, an interpretation which receives support from his own insistence that his episcopacy was conferred on him by God: 'I, Patrick, a sinner, unlearned, resident in Ireland,' he begins his letter to Coroticus, 'declare myself to be a bishop. Most assuredly I believe that what I am I have received from God.' The second ground for their objection was his lack of learning. At this period the most influential members of the church in Britain could boast considerable intellectual attainments, while in Gaul Martin had met opposition because of his lack of sophistication. Patrick admits his rusticity, but gives as an excuse his early enslavement and the necessity to learn the language of his captors.

These two faults he admits, but he defends himself with spirit against the injustice of another allegation. His enemies had been asserting that he had made profits from his ministry in Ireland. Never has he taken the smallest payment from one of the thousands whom he baptized, he has accepted no gifts from those he ordained, and he has returned to his woman converts even the personal ornaments which they laid on the altar.[1] 'See,' he writes in his conclusion, 'again and again would I set forth the words of my confession . . . that I never had any reason except the Gospel and its promises, why I should ever return to the people from whom once before I barely escaped.' His central defence against his detractors is a positive one, the success of his mission: not his own success, for Patrick is no Pelagian,[2] but, as he concludes his apologia, 'it was the gift of God'. Yet though his defence is

[1] *Conf.* cc. 48, 49, 50.
[2] *Conf.* cc. 36, 38, 62. The care which he takes to set himself alongside the 'sons of grace' shows that he was very much aware of the controversy.

moving and convincing, the Confession makes it evident that the conversion of much of Ireland was conducted by a bishop of whom influential sections of the church disapproved.

The situation which he had to face was different from that of Gaul or even of Britain. Roman towns were non-existent in Ireland. Armagh was founded two miles from the royal fort of Emain Macha, from which may be seen the hill on which the church stood. Yet Patrick himself never mentions his seat, as a continental bishop might have done had he been writing a Confession: 'resident in Ireland,' he says of himself. The idea of an ecclesiastical city seems to have been only gradually grafted on to Irish thinking. Patrick himself was constantly on the move, and he travelled with a retinue of the sons of princes, rather as any important Irishman might have travelled with a retinue suited to his rank. Generosity was essential to prestige in a heroic society, so Patrick made gifts not only to his own retinue but to rulers and brehons: 'I think I distributed not less than the price of fifteen men.' It may have been such munificence which gave rise to slanders at home. An ill-educated, itinerant bishop, travelling with a paid retinue of young nobles, distributing largesse to petty kings, may well have been regarded with misgivings by unimaginative churchmen in Gaul and Britain. Patrick's mission demonstrates that from the beginning the peculiar conditions of an extra-imperial, heroic society compelled unconventional measures of evangelization.

Yet though the Patrician mission had its critics, we may conclude that the church established in Ireland was similar in its main features to the church of the western provinces of the empire. Epigraphy shows that Britain and Gaul, neighbouring parts of the same empire, were in close and intimate touch, though there is no comparable evidence for Irish reliance on the fashions of Gaul in the fifth and sixth centuries. Yet the church fostered by the papal-sponsored Palladius and the maligned Briton Patrick was the church already established elsewhere. It was not until later that its peculiarities hardened into a markedly different organization.

II. GROWTH

CHAPTER 5

The problems of the sixth-century church

The problems of the sixth-century church in Britain[1] and Ireland were by no means identical. The British church was an old-established institution, while the Irish church was still struggling towards maturity. In both countries the church represented Latin civilization, but while this had been naturalized in Britain, it was completely foreign to Ireland: thus, the church in Ireland found none of the administrative structure which was its normal foundation elsewhere in Europe. Moreover, although Irish political life was superficially troubled by frequent minor battles, her society was fundamentally secure and intensely conservative: Britain, on the other hand, had recently been almost overturned by a hostile invasion, for in the second half of the fifth century heathen Germanic barbarians had settled in the eastern half of the island, where they had massacred, expelled, or enslaved the civilian population. Under Aurelianus a British army had fought its way to victory, and at Badon Hill (led by Arthur, according to a tradition recorded by Nennius) it held the Saxon advance, so that after fifty years of fighting for survival the Britons experienced the relief of a respite. For the first two generations of the sixth century Britons and Saxons each occupied their own parts of the country. The majority of Britons alive in 550 had experienced only such conditions, and Gildas, the contemporary writer, implies that, lulled into a false security, they had given themselves up to relaxation. Yet there must have been many others, like himself, who understood how imminent was the danger.

Gildas is our chief authority for the state of the British church in this period of comparative peace before the barbarians closed in. The inaccuracy of his account of Britain's early history is notorious,

[1] By 'Britain' I here mean the area now known as Wales, plus the western part of England not yet overrun by the Anglo-Saxons. I am not attempting to discuss Northern Britain or Scotland, because, apart from the inscriptions and burials already mentioned, we have no contemporary evidence.

and his philosophy of events does not permit a balanced survey. He saw the disasters of the preceding century as a judgement, and writes as a prophet calling men to repentance from the sins and sloth of his own day. Nevertheless, his indictment of princes and priesthood gives us, incidentally, some reliable sidelights on the British church. Further contemporary illustration comes from the inscribed stones, evidence of much in little. We are thus fairly well informed about the sixth-century British church.

The British princes of this period were Christian. One, Maelgwn of Gwynnedd, had entered a monastery, which he later abandoned, and had been taught by a distinguished Christian master.[1] They were professedly pious, making their oaths on Christian altars, though prepared to break them without scruple:[2] they were almsgivers, like Maelgwn, though *largior in dando, profusior in peccato*.[3] They exercised some control over ecclesiastical appointments, for Gildas complains bitterly that unsuitable persons bought episcopal office from the *tyranni*,[4] and that princes were prepared to use their influence in the church to further political intrigues.[5] The bishops were well-to-do men who commanded prestige. Episcopal office was worth buying; indeed, there was so much competition that would-be purchasers were sometimes disappointed.[6] Bishops were not withdrawn, but were active in the world, and did not expect to pursue the ascetic life. Gildas' strictures on the hollowness of their profession serves to emphasize the fact that they were a socially acceptable class.

The position of the fifth-century church in Gaul provides conditions in many ways parallel with those of sixth-century Britain. The Gallo-Roman bishops were often aristocrats with private means, representing a Latin culture, trying to maintain order in a disturbed society. Sees were rich, and men of the world

[1] Gildas, ed. Williams, pp. 78–82 (cc. 33–5).

[2] Ibid., p. 66 (c. 27).

[3] Ibid., p. 76 (c. 33)

[4] Ibid., p. 168 (c. 67). This practice sometimes continued in the same family for more than one generation.

[5] Constantine, '*sub sancti abbatis amphibalo*, cruelly tore the tender sides of two royal children', ibid., p. 68 (c. 28).

[6] Gildas, pp. 164–72 (cc. 66–7), 246 (c. 108).

were needed to administer them.[1] The bishops were not only responsible for all the clergy in their dioceses; they had to hold courts for the laity,[2] negotiate with the invaders,[3] buy back captives.[4] Detractors complained that they were proud and worldly, taken up with the state they kept;[5] the procedure for the election of bishops in fifth-century Gaul was ambiguous, and was sometimes abused by intrigue and the purchase of ecclesiastical office.[6] These criticisms of the fifth-century church during the first generations of the barbarian invasions are similar to those which Gildas makes of the British church in his day, but the clergy he describes do not compare in debauchery and dishonesty with the Merovingian clergy a few decades later, after Gaul had suffered a century of barbarization.[7]

Gildas and the contemporary inscriptions provide evidence on the practice of celibacy among British clergy, but their evidence is controversial. Up to the fourth century the church had accepted that married men who took orders should continue to live with their wives. Celibacy began as a voluntary practice of asceticism and, though it came to be much admired, it was not regarded as obligatory. From the fourth century onwards a movement within the church attempted to make celibacy binding on the higher grades of clergy. The provincial Council of Elvira in Spain, held *c*. 300, required bishops, priests, and deacons *abstinere se a conjugibus suis et non generare filios*. Similar prohibitions, passed at a Roman Council held in 386, were conveyed to the bishops of Spain and Africa, and Leo the Great (440–61) extended the practice to subdeacons. During the fifth century Gaulish custom was diverse. But as early as the fourth century Gaulish bishops had begun to separate from their wives on consecration. By the sixth century a custom was established by which the wife of a married man gave her consent to his consecration as a bishop, and after this, though

[1] *Letters of Sidonius*, translated O. M. Dalton, Oxford, 1915, ii. 117.
[2] C. E. Stevens, *Sidonius Apollinaris and his Age*, Oxford, 1933, pp. 118–20.
[3] E.g. *Letters*, ii. 120.
[4] Stevens, p. 116 note 6 for references.
[5] Sulpicius Severus, *Dialogue* I.21, transl. F. R. Hoare, p. 93.
[6] E.g. *Letters*, ii, 104–5.
[7] O. M. Dalton, (ed.) *The History of the Franks by Gregory of Tours*, Oxford, 1927, i, 282–7.

she continued to be recognized as his wife, she lived apart from him.[1] She might take part in charitable works within the diocese, and was sometimes known as *episcopa*. All the same, complete continence was required from both husband and wife, though lapses are not infrequently recorded. Priests and deacons, and according to some legislation subdeacons, were also expected to live in continence, but these grades were allowed to keep their wives in their houses. Suspicion often attached to such relationships, and the Council of Lyons in 583 found it necessary to forbid domestic contacts between all the higher clergy and their wives.[2]

British evidence shows clearly that the higher clergy were married and their wives recognized. One inscription at Llantrisant in Anglesey records the burial place of a lady 'who was the very loving wife of Bivatig(irnus), servant of God, *sacerdos* and disciple of Paulinus'. It goes on to name the people to whom the husband belonged, possibly the Gaulish Andecavi, whose territory was on the Loire, and to say that he was 'an example to all his fellow citizens and relatives both in character (and) in rule of life'.[3] If we bear in mind the practice required by canon law in contemporary Gaul the British inscription would suggest (though not conclusively) that Bivatigirnus and his wife lived in continence. Yet the implication to be drawn from Gildas may be that a bishop and his wife were part of the same household. Gildas repeats the Pauline injunction that the bishop must be the husband of one wife and that he must rule his own house well, having his children in subjection with all chastity.[4] This seems to suggest a joint household, but it would be dangerous to attach too literal a meaning to Gildas' comments. He also points out that the Britons too often behave as if they had heard Paul require them to be 'the husband of wives', though some, he admits, are continent.[5] Others, perhaps under the guise of piety, 'drive out of the house a religious mother maybe, or sisters, and unbecomingly make light of strange women'.[6] We may conclude that in Britain a number of the higher

---

[1] Article by H. Leclercq *Célibat* in *Dict. d'arch chrét.*, ii, 2, cols. 2802 ff.; Beck, 'Pastoral Care', pp. 24–9; for general bibliography on celibacy, p. 26, note 97.

[2] Beck, 'Pastoral Care', pp. 88–9.   [3] *E.C.M.W.*, No. 33.

[4] Gildas, pp. 246–8 (cc. 108–9).   [5] Ibid., p. 250 (c. 110).

[6] Ibid., p. 164 (c. 66).

clergy were married, and that at least monogamy was demanded. The crucial question is whether they formed a joint household with their wives, and though the evidence seems to suggest that they did, it is not conclusive. As long as the clergy were allowed to continue in residence with their wives, it is difficult to see how the practice of celibacy could be enforced.

Gildas shows that by his own day monasticism was firmly established in Britain. The monks are excluded from his indictment; indeed, Gildas expressly commends their godly manner of life.[1] It is possible that he is referring to monks when he describes the few true sons of the church, who are 'counted at so small a number that our revered mother . . . does not observe them as they rest in her bosom'.[2] It seems unlikely that Gildas was himself a monk,[3] and the church he describes is certainly not administered by monastic priests and bishops. Nevertheless, the monastic order was able to exercise considerable influence on a minority, and their discipline formed a marked contrast to the easy-going habits of the secular clergy.

The sixth-century British church had identified itself with Latin civilization. Gildas himself wrote a fluent, pedantic, and ornate Latin style, lacking in taste perhaps, but not in erudition. Heathen barbarism threatened not only the political security but the cultural heritage of the Britons. Gildas speaks of the Picts and Scots in tones of disgust, as men who would rather cover their villainous faces with hair than their naked bodies with decent clothing, who pour out in their currachs like swarms of worms.[4] Of all the invaders, however, the Saxons are the most deeply accursed, 'hated by God and men'.[5] Church legislators of the sixth or seventh century[6] passed decrees against Britons who betrayed their fellow-countrymen to the invaders. The ecclesiastics at the Synod of the Grove of Victory demand light penances in comparison with those required by their Irish colleagues (three

[1] p. 78 (c. 34). [2] p. 64 (c. 26).
[3] See O. Chadwick, *J.T.S.*, v (1954), 78–80.
[4] Gildas, p. 44 (c. 19).
[5] Ibid., p. 54, (c. 23).
[6] I cannot date these canons satisfactorily. They are usually said to be sixth century (see L. Bieler, *Penitentials*, p. 3), but I think they are probably later han Gildas' day. Monasticism is here well developed.

years, for instance, for adultery or for killing in anger), but by
far the heaviest penance they impose is for the crime of treason.

> They who afford guidance to the barbarians, thirteen years, provided
> there be no slaughter of Christians or effusion of blood or dire
> captivity. If, however, such things do take place the offenders shall
> perform penance, laying down their arms for the rest of life. But if
> one planned to conduct the barbarians to the Christians, and did so
> according to his will, he shall do penance for the remainder of his
> life.[1]

The scale of penances laid down by this Synod suggests that
national defence was a Christian duty, and that national betrayal
was a sin beside which other sins assumed minor proportions.

For the sixth-century church in Ireland we must turn to the
Penitential of Vinnian (*Vi.*), a work ascribed to either the founder
of Clonard (died *A.U.* 549) or to the founder of Moville (died
A.U. 579). But it seems to me likely that the canons attributed to
Patrick, Auxilius, and Iserninus (*Pa. I*) contain even earlier legislation, so it is necessary first to consider their date. Bury's argument in favour of the substantial authenticity of the canons[2] has
been generally accepted during the present century until recently,
and Professor Bieler still upholds the attribution to Patrick and
his fellow-workers, even venturing on a date, 457, for the synod
where they were promulgated.[3] Professor Binchy, on the other
hand, believes that the canons were promulgated in Ireland
between the late sixth and mid-seventh century by the party of
Roman sympathizers in the contemporary Irish church.[4]

After considerable hesitation I find myself differing from both
these views. It is very difficult to believe that the church depicted
in these canons is the first-generation missionary church. Its
organization is well developed, with *paruchiae* each under the
control of their own bishops and having well-defined boundaries,
for no one must invade the *paruchia* of another. All seven clerical
grades are established, and lectors sing the office in each church.
Clerics must come, when summoned, to sing the offices of matins

---

[1] Bieler, *Penitentials*, p. 68.   [2] *Life of St Patrick*, pp. 233–45.
[3] *Mélanges offerts a Mlle. Christine Mohrmann*, Utrecht/Anvers, 1963, pp.
96–102.
[4] 'Patrick', pp. 45—9.

and vespers (much as they were ordered to come by the Justinian Code)[1] on pain of exclusion from the clergy. The last canon in the collection implies a form of monasticism no longer at its most primitive, for the monks live a community life under the rule of an abbot, and may not take journeys without his permission. It seems that the church would need some little time to reach this level of organizational development.

Yet the Christians depicted in the canons are not yet identical with Irish society. The church is not merely legislating against pagan survivals (as it was to do for centuries to come), it is still struggling against a pagan environment. The canonists require Christians to avoid the secular courts and bring their disputes to the church for settlement,[2] a hint that the secular lawyers still clung to the old ways. By the seventh century, Irish church legislators seem to have been anxious rather to define the church's position within the native system of government than to separate her from it.[3] The legal technicalities into which they enter in the seventh-century rulings suggest that, by this time, the secular law schools were not any longer the declared enemies of the church. Moreover, the later canonists accept the support of secular penalties in enforcing their decrees, and such penalties must have been sanctioned by a Christian society.[4] It is significant that the canons attributed to Patrick, Auxilius, and Iserninus mention no penalties other than penance and excommunication, though the thief is required to return stolen goods, 'if possible'.[5] The early canons require that alms offered to the church by pagans are to be refused, whereas later the church legislates for the payment of tithes and other church dues. All the evidence suggests that the Christians of the canons were living in a predominantly pagan society, whereas seventh-century church legislators show us a society which is predominantly Christian. Ireland was almost certainly not converted with the rapid universality which seventh-century Patrician apologists imply, yet the ascetic example of the later-sixth-century

---

[1] *ut omnes clerici per singulas ecclesias constituti per se ipsos et nocturnas et matutinas et vespertinas preces cantent.* Cod. Just. 1. I tit. III. lex. 41. Cf. Council of Agde, 506 canon 30: *hymni matutini vel vespertini diebus omnibus decantentur.* Cf. *Pa. I.* 7.

[2] *Pa. I.* 21.   [3] See *infra*, pp. 127–32.

[4] See *infra*, pp. 131–2.   [5] *Pa. I.*, 15.

church and the growth of monastic *paruchiae* had their effect. Pagan survivals certainly remained long after the seventh century, but by that time, as the legislation shows, the church had been generally accepted.

If we set the canons attributed to Patrick, Auxilius, and Iserninus alongside secular law and seventh-century ecclesiastical legislation we may note some significant contrasts which suggest that our canons belong to an earlier stage of development. Secular law recognizes that the ecclesiastic may act as a *naidm*, that is, as the surety who stakes his honour on the principal's performance of his obligations, who compels the principal to pay, if necessary using physical force even to the extent of wounding or slaying him (for the shedding of blood by a *naidm* when enforcing his suretyship is one of 'the immune bloodsheds' in Irish law). Canon 8 of the collection attributed to Patrick, Auxilius, and Iserninus seems to allow the cleric to act as a *ráth*, the surety who answers for the principal's default by discharging the debt from his own property, while forbidding him to act as the *naidm* or enforcing surety.[1] The canon reads:

> If a cleric has given surety for a pagan (*si pro gentili homine fideiusor fuerit*) in whatsoever amount, and it so happens – as well it might – that the pagan by some ruse defaults upon the cleric, the cleric must pay the debt from his own means; should he contend with him in arms (*nam si armis compugnauerit*) let him be reckoned to be outside the church, as he deserves.

This canon is repeated in the later *Collectio Canonum Hibernensis*, but the canons on surety passed by the *Synodus Hibernensis* and contained in the *Collectio* appear to belong to a later stage of development than canon 8 of the synod attributed to Patrick, Auxilius, and Iserninus. These canons of the Irish Synod are much more detailed and elaborate, with a clear differentiation of terms, for they discuss the part played by witnesses (*testes*), by the enforcing surety or *naidm* (*stipulator*), and by the paying surety or *ráth*.[2] Whereas *Pa.I.* 8 uses the genuine Latin legal term *fideiussor*,

---

[1] I am indebted to Professor Binchy for this interpretation.
[2] *Coll.* XXXLV. On this collection see *infra*, pp. 123. ff., and discussion by Thurneysen, *Z.C.P.*, xviii, 364–72.

'surety', the *Synodus Hibernensis* also employs the word *rata*. Thurneysen pointed out that the Irish canonists arrived at this word via a misinterpretation of the Latin *ratum* contained in Jerome's Commentary, gave it a long *ā* and made a feminine noun, to provide the 'Latin' for their own legal term *ráth*.[1] Such a development cannot be very early, whereas the use of the word *fideiussor* in *Pa.I.* 8, though it does not in itself prove an early date, is perfectly consistent with one.

The enforcing surety or *naidm* must, according to Irish law, be a member of the noble grades. So, if the canons attributed to Patrick and his helpers forbid the cleric to act as a *naidm*, such a cleric must have been of the noble classes. We know that by the time the church had been fully integrated into the tribal order the clergy had been assimilated, as a class, to the noble grades of society. But this state of affairs, which is a commonplace of the law tracts, had not yet been achieved when canon 7 of our collection was issued. This canon speaks of the cleric held 'under the yoke of slavery'.[2] Our canons seem, in fact, to reveal a society in which a cleric might be either a noble or a slave, that is to say, a society in which taking orders did not affect a man's status as it later came to do. Such conditions belong to a period before the church was fully adjusted to Irish society in the way revealed in seventh- and eighth-century legislation.

It has been argued that canon 6 was drawn up during the period of the Easter controversy and issued by the Romanizing party. This canon reads:

> Whichever cleric, from *ostiarius* to *sacerdos*, shall be seen without a tunic, and does not cover the nakedness and unsightliness (or 'shame', *turpitudinem*) of his belly (*ventris*), and if his hair is not shorn in the Roman custom (*more Romano*), and if his wife (*uxor*) goes about with her head unveiled, such are to be despised by the laity (*laicis*) and separated from the church.

It is true that the phrase *more Romano* is frequently employed in the seventh century, but it should be noted that Patrick uses the term *Romani* two centuries earlier in his Letter to Coroticus. The Britons who have enslaved his converts have, he argues, the habits of barbarians: he will not address them as 'my fellow-citizens, or

[1] Z.C.P., xviii, 367–8.   [2] *nisi forte iugo seruitutis sit detentus.*

fellow-citizens of the holy Romans',[1] for Romans are civilized Christians, distinct from barbarians such as the Picts and Scots. In our canon clerics are told that they must conform in three ways to civilized Roman conditions: by wearing a tunic, shaving their heads, and seeing that their wives go veiled. It seems to me that the tenor of the canon, dividing civilized Roman practices from barbarous customs, fits at least as well with the earlier usage as it does with seventh-century injunctions, where tonsure in the Roman manner has a special significance. A comparable ruling of a Welsh synod requires that no catholic (*catholicus*) should let his hair grow *more barbarorum*.[2] Such rulings need not necessarily belong exclusively to the period of the Easter controversy.

There are other elements in the canon which seem to fit a sixth-century more readily than a seventh-century context. The clerical grades range from *ostiarius* at the bottom to *sacerdos*, presumably at the top. In the sixth century both *episcopus* and *sacerdos* are being used for the bishop, but in later legislation the more usual word is *episcopus*. The ruling in the eighth-century *Collectio*[3] or in MS. C.C.C.C. 279 (p. 156) which describes the duties of the various grades starts with the *episcopus* and moves down through the *sacerdos* (priest) and the rest to the *ostiarius*. Our canon also recognizes the wife of the cleric of every grade, and calls her *uxor*, not *clentella*, the word used by Vinnian and Columbanus.[4] None of these usages are conclusive proof of an early date, but they give no support whatever to a seventh-century date.

If this group of canons had been first formulated in Ireland in the seventh century I think we should not expect to see so deliberate an attempt to separate the Christian church from the surrounding population of pagans: by this time the canonists' usual grouping is of clergy and laity, not of Christians and pagans. We might, on the other hand, in a seventh-century collection observe some awareness of lay support for the church's penitential discipline: in this group of canons the very opposite is the

---

[1] c.2. *non dico ciuibus meis neque ciuibus sanctorum Romanorum.*

[2] *Wa.* A. 61.

[3] *Coll.* VIII. 2. On the *Collectio*, see *infra*, pp. 123 ff.

[4] See *infra*, p. 51. In referring to the 'laity' here, the canon clearly means the Christian layfolk, as distinct from pagans.

case, for the canonists are trying to avoid being indebted to the pagans among whom they live. And in the seventh century we might also expect some more definite allusion to the Easter controversy. The arguments based on canon 33 seem to me quite unconvincing. This canon reads:

> A cleric who comes from the Britons without letters, even though he is resident in the tribe (*in plebe*) is not allowed to minister.

It has been assumed that this canon was drawn up by Irish *Romani*, who were hostile to the conservative Britons. But the implication is that Britons coming with letters of introduction *will* be allowed to minister, and its sense is fully in harmony with other canons in the same collection, which seek to prevent unauthorized clergy from setting up in Irish dioceses without episcopal sanction. There must have been considerable coming and going between the British and Irish church in the sixth century, and it would be most reasonable for Irish bishops to protect themselves against unsuitable British clergy.[1] This canon, with its rational and moderate tone, should be compared with the seventh- or early-eighth-century ruling in the *Collectio*, which explicitly warns against the Britons, 'who are contrary in all things and cut themselves off from Roman custom and from the unity of the church'.[2] Seventh-century clerics with an axe to grind, fortunately for later historians, usually grind it quite openly.[3]

It seems to me that the canons attributed to Patrick, Auxilius, and Iserninus probably contain our earliest Irish ecclesiastical legislation, legislation which dates from the sixth century. But the possibility of interpolation need not be discarded. Our earliest MS. of these canons (C.C.C.C. 279) dates from the ninth or tenth century, and seems not even to have been written in Ireland. Thus, there may be a number of intermediaries between the original promulgation and the present text. It seems to me possible, and

---

[1] Some of the place-seekers described by Gildas would not have been very desirable colleagues in a half-converted society. All the same, this canon does not suggest the shortage of clergy you would expect in a first-generation church.

[2] *Coll.* XX. 6.

[3] The other canons, 25, 30, and 34, which Bury, with his fifth-century date, rejected as later interpolations, provide no difficulty in a sixth-century context.

even likely, that an early group of canons was preserved, that, known to be ancient, it later came to be associated with S. Patrick, and that it was re-issued during the seventh century, when the case for a diocesan clergy as against a monastic church must have been debated. Under such circumstances slight alterations could be made, and an extra canon or two could be slipped in; indeed, it is perfectly clear from the sense that canon 4 once followed canon 1, whereas now two canons stand between. Nevertheless, I think we are justified in regarding this collection as evidence for the government of the sixth-century Irish church. Even if the reader remains unconvinced, and prefers to regard this as seventh- (or fifth-) century legislation, it none the less describes an ecclesiastical system modelled on that of the church elsewhere, of the kind which must have been originally introduced into Ireland, and quite unlike the monastic church which had subsequently grown up. Thus, it would still be permissible to use the canons as evidence for sixth-century church government.

The canons quite unambiguously show a church under the rule of bishops. Each bishop held authority within his own *paruchia*, and could not exercise his functions in the *paruchia* of another bishop without his brother's permission.[1] No priest might say mass in a church he had built until the bishop of his *paruchia* had consecrated it;[2] no stranger might minister in the *paruchia* without the bishop's authority.[3] The *paruchia* seems to have been co-terminous with the *plebs*;[4] it was the land inhabited by a particular group of people, possibly the *sept* or even the *tuath*,[5] for the bishop had a number of churches in his diocese in which he was expected to officiate on occasions.[6] He was supported by clergy of all grades, who were obliged to attend the services of matins and vespers in the church,[7] and to adopt Roman conven-

---

[1] *Pa*. I. 30.   [2] *Pa*. I. 23.
[3] *Pa*. I. 24.   [4] *Vi*. 48; *Pa* I. 27.
[5] The *tuath* is the Irish petty kingdom, the *sept* one of the groups within it.
[6] *Pa*. I., 25. I should like to translate the word *plebs* as tribe, using the word loosely as some modern anthropologists use it. This would suit all the occasions when it is mentioned in the documents edited by Professor Bieler. He normally translates 'community'; occasionally 'people' (*Hi*. II. 4, *Pa*. II. 16) or 'parish' (*Vi*. 48).
[7] *Pa*. I. 7.

tions of personal appearance by shaving their heads and wearing a tunic, so distinguishing themselves from the non-Christian population.[1] Some had entered the clerical order as adults, others had been educated as clerics from boyhood,[2] some were nobles, some slaves.[3]

The clergy were allowed to live at home with their wives. This is the rational inference from canon 6, which, when ordering the clerics' own appearance, requires them to see that their wives are veiled when they go out. A similar ambiguity of interpretation attaches to this, as to the British evidence. Were the early Irish clergy living in compulsory continence, or were they allowed now, as later, to live in monogamy?

In the later sixth century complete continence is definitely required by some writers. Whereas Gildas, the British inscription, and the early Canons all use the word *uxor* for wife, Vinnian rejects it in favour of *clentella* to mean the cleric's former wife, and the ascetic Columbanus follows him in this usage.[4] Vinnian recognizes that the cleric may continue to live with his family after ordination, but both Vinnian and Columbanus say that if a cleric cohabits with his former wife he commits a sin as great as by cohabiting with a casual stranger.[5] Columbanus calls it adultery, 'which among our teachers is reckoned to be no less guilt'.[6] Here he is quoting Vinnian. But is there any justification for assuming that this had been the practice of the Irish church from the beginning?

In the sixth-century group of canons there is no ruling enjoining continence on the clergy and their wives. The Irish practice of divorce and remarriage is forbidden;[7] so, by implication, is the practice of concubinage.[8] A canon on the marital relations of the clergy would not be out of place here, but we must not place much reliance on any argument *ex silentio*, for some such canon may have been lost. It must, however, have been difficult enough to persuade Irish converts, used to the practice of concubinage, to

---

[1] *Pa.* I. 6.   [2] *Vi.* 27.
[3] *Pa.* I. 7 and 8.
[4] See note 12 by Bieler, *Penitentials*, pp. 243–4.
[5] *Vi.* 27, *Co.* B. 8.   [6] Walker, *Opera*, pp. 8–9.
[7] *Pa.* I. 22.   [8] *Pa* I. 19.

confine themselves to one wife. It is hardly credible that the
early Irish clergy, not just one or two, but all of them, practised
continence while continuing to live with their wives at very close
quarters in small huts, not in large Roman villas where physical
privacy was possible. The later legislators Vinnian and Columbanus find it necessary to condemn explicitly the cleric who
continues to have sexual relations with his wife. The early Irish
church certainly required monogamy from all its clergy, but it
may have made no serious attempt to impose complete continence.
This was the work of the ascetics of the later sixth century. The
evidence for monogamy or celibacy in the early Irish church is
not conclusive, but, bearing in mind contemporary practice in
Gaul and social conditions in Ireland, we should not assume that
the early bishops thought on this matter in precisely the same way
as Vinnian and Columbanus. There may have been considerably
more tolerance and more variety of opinion than is usually
supposed.[1]

Sixth-century legislation shows that monasticism was established in Ireland, but it seems as yet to be of no great importance in
ecclesiastical administration. Vinnian speaks of the cleric who
despoils monasteries, thus suggesting that foundations had been
endowed with property, but the monks have apparently no
duties in the *paruchia*, for they are forbidden to baptize or to
receive alms.[2] The final clause of the canons attributed to Patrick,

---

[1] There is a hint in a ninth- or tenth-century manuscript in Corpus Christi
College Cambridge (No. 279) that a later scribe may have felt that married
bishops were out of place. This scribe has copied out a number of canons
which are closely paralleled by rulings from the eighth-century *Collectio*,
though in the opinion of Henry Bradshaw he was not copying from the
Collectio itself, but both compilers were using a common source. One canon
which he transcribes lays down the qualities required in a bishop. He is to
be prudent, teachable, temperate, sober, chaste in life, and so on. But the
words *vita castus* are written over an erasure. The erasure has been so well
effected that it is impossible, even under ultra-violet light, to read anything
under it, but the space was originally intended to take a rather longer entry,
and the words *vir unius uxoris* would fit neatly into it. I would suggest that,
following S. Paul's advice, the Irish bishop was originally required to be a
man of one wife, and that the passage in its original form appeared thus: the
later scribe, realizing the discrepancy between this advice and the teaching of
the church, altered the requirement to chastity.

[2] *Vi.* 30, 50.

Auxilius, and Iserninus legislates against the *monachus vagulus*.[1]
Monks and virgins from different places are prohibited from
lodging together in the same hospice, travelling in the same
carriage, or conducting long conversations together.[2] The woman
who has taken a vow of virginity and later broken it to marry is
to be excommunicated.[3]

Though Christians are required in the canons to observe habits
different from those of the surrounding pagans, and keep themselves unspotted from the world, they must observe certain
obligations to their heathen neighbours. Debts must be paid,[4] the
obligations of the *ráth* must be met.[5] Moreover, the Christian may
not act at society's expense by kidnapping a captive,[6] though
collections for the redemption of captives are a regular part of
Christian charity.[7] The church, though conscious of its moral
separateness, is in process of integration with the customs of a
pagan society.

The canons legislate for a people still coming to the faith; they
are concerned mainly with external actions, and their style is
laconic. Vinnian is legislating for Christians, and he writes 'compelled by love of you', *suis visceralibus filiis*. His tone is markedly
ascetic. The Christian laity should support the needy, receive
pilgrims, visit the sick, minister to prisoners.[8] Standards of sexual
self-discipline, as laid down by Vinnian, are extremely severe. His
conception of Christian marriage makes no concessions to a
society accustomed to divorce, remarriage, and concubinage.
Both partners in the marriage are required to be faithful, and to
maintain this principle the innocent partner may have to suffer
for the sins of the guilty. If a wife deserts her husband he is not to
remarry; if she returns to him he must receive her, and she must
serve him as though she were his slave. If an innocent woman is

---

[1] *Pa* I. 34.
[2] *Pa.* I. 9.
[3] *Pa.* I. 17.
[4] *Pa.* I. 20.
[5] *Pa.* I. 8, *supra*, p. 46.
[6] *Pa.* I. 32.
[7] *Pa.* I. 1, 4, 5. Cf. *Vi.* 30, 31, 32. In this matter the church had to protect
herself from her own members, for some clerics had abused generosity. Thus,
anyone making such a collection had to obtain the bishop's permission, must
ask only for what was needed, and must place anything left over on the
bishop's altar for the needs of the poor.
[8] *Vi.* 32, 33.

E

put away by her husband she may not take any other man.[1] If either partner is unfaithful sexual union is to be suspended for a year as part of the penance.[2] If a man has a barren wife he may not turn her away, but both are to live together in continence.[3] Concubinage is completely rejected.[4] Moreover, married people are to abstain from each other by mutual consent on Saturday and Sunday, in the period between conception and birth, and during the three forty-day periods of abstinence in each year. If they add to this, self-mortification, alms, fulfilling the commandments of God, and expelling their faults, they may expect to receive 'the thirty-fold fruit which the Saviour in the Gospel in his account has set aside for married people'.[5] With the prospect of such meagre reward, it is hardly surprising that the devout in the next generation turned to the religious life, nor that it proved impossible to impose these standards on the Irish laity. Vinnian's Pauline attitude to the flesh, elaborated soon afterwards by S. Columbanus, set the tone for subsequent teaching. The wholehearted enthusiasm with which the pagan Irish hero had entered on his feasts and combats was being applied by some Irishmen in the sixth century to the ascetic life.

The purpose of sexual continence among the lay folk is 'that they may be able to have time for prayer for the salvation of their souls'.[6] The spiritual sins are to be cured by their contrary virtues: 'Patience must arise for wrathfulness; kindliness, or the love of God and one's neighbour, for envy; for detraction, restraint of heart and tongue; for dejection, spiritual joy; for greed, liberality.' Vinnian is concerned not only with the physical sins. 'If a cleric is wrathful or envious or backbiting or gloomy or greedy, great and capital sins are these, and they slay the soul and cast it down to the depth of hell. But there is this penance for them, until they are plucked forth and eradicated from our hearts through the help of God and through our own zeal.'[7] Vinnian, like the men who framed the canons, is concerned with the conduct of Christians in

---

[1] *Vi.* 43–4.   [2] *Vi.* 51.
[3] *Vi.* 41.   [4] *Vi.* 39, 40.
[5] *Vi.* 46. Cf. Matthew 13, 3–9, where the seed yields fruit 'some a hundredfold, some sixty and some thirty'.
[6] *Vi.* 46.   [7] *Vi.* 29, following Cassian.

society; but he is also concerned much more specifically than they with the individual soul. So he assesses motive and opportunity as well as action.[1] His discipline is based on familiarity with the complexities of human nature, on a deep affection for his spiritual sons and a passionate concern for religion.[2]

Vinnian writes as a man who is spiritually responsible for clerics and laity. Those who minister to the population are priests and deacons, not monks. Yet the clergy are living under close control, not allowed to cohabit with their former wives, subject to penitential discipline. The lives of the Irish clergy, in this heroic period, followed an ascetic régime. It has recently been suggested that the fifth-century Irish missionaries may have modelled their church on the fusion of clerical and monastic life known on the Continent, by which bishops who were also monks lived together with their clergy, all following an ascetic routine, without private property.[3] Attractive as this suggestion seems, there is little to support it in our two sixth-century Irish documents. The Irish clergy there revealed lived a canonical life, meeting for prayers together,[4] but the canons speak of clergy who seem to be living with their wives and who certainly have their own private property,[5] while Vinnian, though less explicit, implies that the cleric has the means to repay his debt fourfold.[6] At the same period there were also monks, living under an abbot's jurisdiction, who must not leave the monastery without his sanction.[7] Yet the clergy of the *paruchia* may have regarded their bishop as *abbas*, father. Canon 34 says that no deacon is to go to another diocese without

---

[1] The first chapters of the Penitential deal with the man who sins in thought and immediately repents; the man who constantly contemplates sinful action, but hesitates to perform it; the man who seriously intends to do evil, but lacks the opportunity; the man who has committed an act of sin, but inadvertently.

[2] *Vi.* Conclusion.

[3] G. B. Ladner, *The Idea of Reform*, 1959, calls this fusion 'the Augustinian synthesis'. It existed at Tours under S. Martin, and probably at Arles under S. Caesarius and at Auxerre under Germanus. Cf. M. Sheehy, *Irish Theol. Quart.*, xxix (1962), 136–44.

[4] *Pa.* I. 28.

[5] *Pa.* I. 6 (wives); 8, 32 (property).

[6] *Vi.* 25.

[7] *Pa.* I. 34. Vinnian's letter to Gildas is quoted by Columbanus, *Opera*, p. 8.

consulting his own *abbas* and without a letter. The words *in-consultu suo abbate* may have intruded, by the scribe's mistake, from the final clause of the canon, where they are repeated,[1] but on the Continent the word *abbas* could be applied to the head of a community of clerics.[2] The differences between a clerical and monastic life in Ireland should certainly not be exaggerated. Once Irish legislators tried to enforce the rulings against priests cohabiting with their former wives a common life for the clergy becomes a practical convenience. Patrick had been sympathetic to the monastic ideal: the asceticism of Vinnian may have encouraged Irish churchmen further towards it.

[1] Professor Bieler suggests this, *Penitentials*, p. 240.
[2] Ladner, *Idea of Reform*, pp. 388–90.

CHAPTER 6

The foundation of monastic paruchiae

Vinnian heralded a movement of devotion. The second half of the sixth century[1] saw the foundation of the great monastic *paruchiae*. Before the century was out, Columcille had founded Derry, Durrow and Iona, Comgall had established Bangor, and Columbanus had left the schools of Bangor for the Continent, where, before his death in 615, he had set up monastic houses at Annegray, Luxeuil, and Bobbio. These are only a few among the many monasteries founded during the later sixth and early seventh centuries.[2] The first missionaries had aimed to preach the gospel to the heathen laity: the monastic founders were primarily concerned to build up the individual Christian into the perfect man.

The writings of Columbanus present the compelling ideas of one such monastic founder. In the violence and insecurity of Merovingian society Columbanus summoned each of his disciples to found his personality on the rock of Christ. The way was by the abandonment of self, for the asceticism which is Columbanus' dominating theme is of the mind and will, as well as of the body. 'Idle then is a religion decorated with prostrations of the body, equally idle is the mere mortification of the flesh':[3] to mortify the flesh alone is as though a man were to dig outside and on his boundaries, leaving his land within untilled.[4] We must die to ourselves, 'that is, to our wills', in order to live in Christ.[5] This means stripping oneself of all the desires and possessions which bind a man to the present world. *Ne parcas caducis, ne aeterna perdas; alienus tibi totus mundus est, qui nudus natus nudus sepeliris.*[6] 'Born and

---

[1] See *infra*, pp. 65 ff.

[2] See Kenney, *Sources*, pp. 309 ff. One of the most important of these early monastic founders was Ciarán of Clonmacnois, who is said to have died prematurely in the plague of 549, but his Life is considerably later and provides no contemporary evidence.

[3] Walker, *Opera*, pp. 70–1.   [4] Ibid., pp. 68–9.

[5] Ibid., pp. 102–3.   [6] Ibid., p. 78.

buried bare.' So it must be on earth, for human existence is 'a way to life, not life'.[1]

In the régime of Columbanus there is no place for compromise or moderation.[2] Apart from God, man's will is insatiable, and the Christian's life must be a constant warfare against it. Without God, human nature is rotten.[3] The *dies irae* approaches (Columbanus quotes the moving passages of the prophets), and 'not to fear these things is the part of dead and hopeless minds'.[4] Thus, there can be no half-measures: 'It requires great violence to seek by toil and to maintain by enthusiasm what a corrupted nature has not kept.'[5]

The rules and penitential of Columbanus apply the philosophy expressed in the sermons. He follows Vinnian in legislating for the common sins, but whereas, like Vinnian, he speaks of the cure of penance,[6] he also definitely regards it as a punishment[7] which is beneficial in itself. *Maxima pars regulae monachorum mortificatio est*,[8] both physical mortification[9] and the subjection of pride. Thus, the monk is not to grumble or contradict, he may do nothing without asking leave of his superior,[10] he may not excuse himself, or even explain himself.[11] Columbanus does not intend his perfect monk to enjoy either comfort of body or freedom of will:

Let him not do as he wishes, let him eat what he is bidden, keep as much as he has received, complete the tale of his work, be subject to whom he does not like. Let him come weary to his bed and sleep walking, and let him be forced to rise while his sleep is not yet finished. Let him keep silence when he has suffered wrong, let him fear the superior of his community as a lord, love him as a father, believe that whatever he commands is healthful for himself, and let him not pass judgement on the opinion of an elder.[12]

---

[1] Walker, *Opera*, pp. 84–5; cf. pp. 94–6.

[2] Ibid., p. 104: *ille enim bene diligit, qui seipsum salubriter odit, hoc est, afligit.*

[3] Ibid., pp. 90–2: 'Defiled skin, in vain are you washed that are unclean by nature', etc.

[4] Ibid., p. 100.   [5] Ibid., p. 102.

[6] Vinnian, *de penitentiae remediis*, Columbanus, *spiritales medici . . . sanare debent.* Bieler, *Penitentials*, pp. 92, 98.

[7] *damnandus est*, Walker, p. 170.

[8] Walker, p. 138.

[9] Columbanus' dislike and distrust of the body can be seen in his bathing regulations, Walker, p. 180.

[10] Walker, p. 170.   [11] Walker, p. 142.

[12] Walker, pp. 140–2.

The rules of Columbanus outline a hard and fierce régime. Alongside the ferocity of his legislation should be put his own care for his community,[1] and the mystical experience of love to which his asceticism was directed.[2] Moreover, the society which held his community was not conducive to gentleness; and the violence of Columbanus' régime, willingly undertaken, must be compared, not with the civilization of a later age, but with the violence of Merovingian Gaul, involuntarily endured.

How far were the ideas of Columbanus shared by contemporary Irish monastic founders? It is impossible to say with certainty, for there are no other contemporary accounts. Columbanus himself experienced some opposition from within his own community.[3] The Penitential of Cummean, drawn up about the middle of the seventh century, suggests that other abbots did not attempt to impose so severely autocratic or ascetic a rule upon their monks. This can best be seen by listing the comparable passages:

COLUMBANUS	CUMMEAN
He who does something by himself without asking, or who contradicts and says: 'I am not doing it', or who murmurs, if the matter is serious, let him do penance with three special fasts, if slight, with one. Simple contradiction of another's word is to be punished with fifty strokes; if out of contention, with an imposition of silence. If it is made in a quarrel, the penance should be for a week.[6]	If any work is imposed on anyone and he does it not, on account of contempt he shall go without supper.[4] He who murmurs shall be put apart and his work shall be rejected; he shall remain with the due half loaf of bread and water.[5] He who offers an excuse to the abbot or the stewards, if he is ignorant of the rule, he shall do penance for one day; if he knows the rule, he shall keep a special fast.[7]

[1] Seen most clearly in the letter written after he had been taken from them to be extradited, Walker, pp. 26–36.

[2] Walker, p. 120. 'Wound our souls with thy love. . . . Show me Him whom my soul has loved, for by love am I wounded. . . . Blessed is such a soul, which is thus wounded by love; such seeks the Fountain, such drinks, though it ever thirst in drinking. . . .'

[3] Walker, p. 28: 'Since I have felt the desires of many to differ in respect of maintaining the strictness of the rule. . . .' Cf. p. 36.

[4] Ibid., p. 126; *Cu.* ix. 5.   [5] Ibid., p. 122; *Cu.* viii. 6.

[6] Bieler, *Penitentials*, pp. 96–8; *Co.* A. 9.   [7] Ibid., p. 124; *Cu.* viii. 17.

COLUMBANUS

He who slanders . . . if it concerns the superior, let him do penance for a week.[1]

He who has despised his superior in pride, or has spoken evil of the rule, is to be cast out, unless he has said immediately: 'I am sorry for what I said'; but if he has not truly humbled himself, let him do penance for forty days, because he is infected with the disease of pride.[4]

CUMMEAN

He who for envy's sake defames another or willingly listens to a defamer . . . if the offence is against a superior, he shall do penance thus for seven days, and shall willingly serve him thereafter. But . . . to speak true things is not to defame; but, according to the Gospel, first *rebuke him between thee and him alone*, afterwards, *if he will not hear thee*, call another; and if he will not hear you (both), *tell the church*.[2]

The disobedient shall remain outside the assembly, without food, and shall humbly knock until he is received; and for as long time as he has been disobedient he shall go on bread and water.[3]

He who intentionally disdains to bow to any senior shall go without supper.[5]

Cummean protects the monastic officials from insolence and disobedience, but takes a more moderate view than does Columbanus of offences against their dignity. On the whole, he follows Columbanus in assigning penances for sexual offences, theft, anger, and gluttony, but he seems to recognize the practice of commuting penances to shorter periods, or in the case of sick persons, to almsgiving.[6] Cummean, half a century later than Columbanus, has adopted similar ascetic principles, but seems to have applied them with rather more discretion.

Our knowledge of the monastic régime at Iona is based on the Life of Columcille written by Adamnán, almost certainly between the years 688 and 692, and in any case before his death in 704.[7]

---

[1] Bieler, *Penitentials*, p. 99; *Co.* A. 10.
[2] Ibid., p. 122; *Cu.* viii. 8–10.   [3] Ibid., p. 122; *Cu.* viii. 4.
[4] Ibid., p. 98; *Co.* A. 11.   [5] Ibid., p. 124; *Cu.* viii. 18.
[6] Ibid., p. 124; *Cu.* viii. 25–7.
[7] Anderson, *Adomnan's Life of Columba*, p. 96.

Although Adamnán wrote almost a century after Columcille's death (s.a. 597), he drew on an uninterrupted oral tradition.[1] Columcille had thirty-four years on Iona in which to found a tradition,[2] his memory was proudly revered, and it is unlikely that conditions on Iona changed essentially in the hundred years following his death. It seems therefore legitimate to compare the ascetic régime at Iona which Adamnán describes with that laid down by Columbanus.

The references are incidental, not systematic. Economic necessity might at any time impose hardship. In the May of 597, a period in which he felt his death approaching, Columcille went to bless the monastery barn and noted the two heaps of grain with thankfulness, commenting to his disciple that the monks would have enough bread for the year, even though he were unable to look after them. Most of the monks worked in the fields and might be tired at the day's end,[3] but their régime was not so severe as to exclude help: a white horse carried the milk vessels between the pasture and the monastery, and in his old age Columcille was drawn in a wagon to visit the monks at work.[4] The monks had milk and fish as well as corn in their diet. The abbot's discretion was absolute, but Columcille's practice of austerity seems to have

---

[1] In some cases Adamnán, in his youth, had the stories directly from old men who had been concerned (e.g. III. 23 from 'a very aged soldier of Christ', who, as a young man, had been out fishing when he learned of Columcille's death), Cf. I. 20; in other cases there was one intermediary, e.g. two monks of S. Comgall heard a prophecy made by Columcille, and reported it to Fínán, anchorite of Durrow, who told Adamnán I. 49, Cf. I. 2, III. 23. Adamnán obtained some of his oral information from Abbot Failbe his predecessor (ob. 679), who had it from Ségéne the fifth abbot (624–52), e.g. traditions of the English king Oswald. I. 1; cf. I. 3. Adamnán may also have had written sources. Cummene, seventh abbot 657–69 (not to be confused with Cummean, i.e. Cuimíne Fota, author of the Penitential mentioned above, who was his contemporary) had written a *Liber de virtutibus sancti Columbae*, though it is doubtful whether Adamnán used it. A passage from it is inserted into the manuscript written by Dorbene early in the eighth century. Adamnán seems to suggest that Baíthéne, disciple and successor of Columcille, used to make notes of some of his utterances, III. 18.

[2] Adamnán, III. 22.

[3] Adamnán, I. 37. The presence of the saint's spirit lightens his monks' fatigue in harvest time.

[4] Adamnán, III. 23. Some later Saints' Lives prohibit cows or animal labour.

been less extreme than Columbanus'. He was saddened by knowing that the monks of Durrow, 'my monks', were being over-
worked in cold weather on the construction of a new building,
and glad when their superior ordered a meal and the cessation of
work until the rough weather had passed.[1] There is no suggestion
anywhere in Adamnán's Life of harshness deliberately imposed by
the abbot on his monks. Although the abbot's decision was final,
his senior monks might advise him,[2] and his disciples sometimes
questioned his actions.[3] The affairs of lay-folk were mentioned in
the monastery.[4] Columcille did not believe that complete chastity,
for the laity, was desirable for its own sake in all circumstances.
When a woman who had taken a physical aversion to her husband
offered to enter a nunnery the saint refused to allow it; instead he
prayed and fasted with the pair so that the woman came to love
her husband.[5] Monks came and went, though with the abbot's
consent,[6] sometimes on enterprises which demanded great initiative and courage.[7] Columcille himself travelled abroad with his
company,[8] and was accessible to monks, visitors, and laity. We
gain an impression of a government more moderate and humane
than that of Columbanus.

Although the way of life depended to a large extent on the ideas
of the founder, certain principles of government seem to be
constant. When compared with the early canons (Pa.I) and the
Penitential of Vinnian, they reveal major differences in the organization of the church. Authority is now in the hands of abbots,

[1] Adamnán, I. 29.

[2] Baíthéne suggests accepting the penitence of a man who has committed
fratricide and incest. Columcille does not believe he is prepared to fulfil the
penance and refuses him, I. 22.

[3] I. 42. 'When the poet Crónán was leaving us, why did you not according to the custom ask for a song of his own composition, sung to a
tune?'

[4] E.g. III. 10. Where Columcille speaks of the death of a lay-woman to his
baker (incidentally an Englishman) or, II. 40, where he prays for the relief of
a kinswoman in painful childbirth.

[5] II. 41. What would Columbanus have done under similar circumstances?

[6] I. 19. A brother 'intending to sail to the island of Eth' comes in the
morning to the saint for his blessing. He receives advice about the route he
should follow, deliberately disregards it, and gets into difficulties.

[7] I. 20; I. 6; II. 42.

[8] I. 1; I. 33; I. 31, 32, 33.

and the abbots of many monastic churches founded from the mid-sixth century onwards were priests, not bishops as the early church leaders had been. Bede reports that 'Iona is always ruled by an abbot in priest's orders, to whose authority, by an unusual custom, the whole province must be subject; according to the practice of that first doctor (Columcille) who was not a bishop but a priest and monk.'[1] Bishops within such monasteries fulfilled their own functions of order, but under the abbot's jurisdiction, and the abbot's authority was so far accepted that a bishop might be forced into action of which he disapproved. Adamnán has an interesting story of a priest-abbot Findchán and a young Cruithnian prince, Aed Dub, who had entered the monastery after a career of some violence. After Aed had spent some time in pilgrimage (presumably to expiate his sins) his abbot, whose judgement was deceived by his own partiality for the young man, wished to have him ordained to the priesthood. He summoned a bishop, who was reluctant to perform the ceremony unless the abbot took responsibility: 'The bishop dared not lay his hand on Aed's head until first Findchán, whose love for Aed was earthly, (*carnaliter amans*) laid his right hand on Aed's head, for confirmation.'[2] Probably all bishops were not as weak-willed as this. Certainly Columcille deplored the bishop's action, and the abbot's even more.

Both Columbanus and Columcille were heads of a *paruchia* of monasteries founded either by themselves or their disciples. Whereas the *paruchia* of the early Irish bishop of the Canons was a small territory, coterminous with the *plebs*,[3] the monastic *paruchia* consisted of scattered houses. While Columcille was abbot of Iona one of his disciples ruled as *praepositus* over each of his other houses,[4] 'my monasteries', as the saint called them.[5] Columbanus, torn away from his monks, appointed 'my true follower Attala' as his successor: should Attala decide to follow Columbanus into exile, Waldelenus was to be *praepositus*.[6] The *paruchia* or diocese of the priest-abbot was by no means the same thing as the diocese of the bishop revealed in the early canons.

---

[1] *H.E.* III. 4.
[2] Adamnán, I. 36.
[3] *Supra*, p. 50.
[4] E.g. Adamnán, I. 31, 45.
[5] Ibid., II. 39.
[6] Walker, p. 26.

The system of ecclesiastical government was thus markedly different from the episcopal system already established. We need to know when and why monastic *paruchiae* developed, what were their relations with the old episcopal dioceses, and what was the effect of their development upon the Celtic church.

CHAPTER 7

The when and why of early monastic paruchiae

Three sources inform us of when the Irish monastic *paruchiae* were founded. All give a clear and unambiguous statement, which has been generally accepted as true; but all are late witnesses. We must therefore begin by examining their credibility.

The Annals name twenty-eight Irish clerics in the period before the great plague which began in 549: of these, twenty-five are bishops, one an abbot, and two are unidentified in rank. Between 549 and 600 thirty-three men are named, of whom thirteen are bishops, seventeen abbots or priests, and three unidentified. In the period 601–64 there are more names, ninety-seven in all. The ecclesiastical rank of twenty-five of these cannot be identified; but of the remainder, twenty-four are bishops and forty-eight abbots. Thus, the annals clearly show an overwhelming preponderance of bishops before 549. The second half of the sixth century is the period of change, with almost as many bishops as there are abbots mentioned, and from the seventh century onwards the preponderance of abbots is decisive.

The extant Irish annals survive in a number of versions, but the entries prior to the early eighth century, in the form in which we now have them, are not contemporary. O'Rahilly expressed this by saying that all the early entries for the Christian period share a common source, a chronicle drawn up in Ulster about 730 × 40.[1] Professor Kelleher has more recently asserted that all the entries up to about 590 and a large number of entries between 590 and 735 'were either freshly composed or wholly revised not earlier than the later half of the ninth century'.[2] Thus, both these scholars agree that the Annals do not become contemporary

---

[1] *Early Irish History*, pp. 253–4. Cf. MacNeill, *Ériu*, vii (1914–16), p. 77, had argued along similar lines, but dated the original compilation to *c.* 712.

[2] *Studia Hibernica*, iii (1963), 122. I adopted the date 730 as the beginning of my own study of Irish *scriptoria* (published 1958), since this seemed to be the earliest date when the Annals could be accepted as reliable contemporary sources.

records until after 735. Everyone also agrees that the men who compiled the chronicle for the period before 735 drew on earlier records. What sort of records, and how reliable were they?

We are here concerned only with the obits of clerics, with their dates and the description of their ecclesiastical rank. In the seventh century the names of the dead were read out at mass. The first Irish reference to this custom of which I am aware is in the mid-seventh-century Penitential of Cummean.[1] The diptychs of the Stowe Missal, drawn up between 792 and 812,[2] provide a list of Irish saints divided into bishops and priests. Liturgical commemoration began very soon after a saint's death,[3] and there would thus be a continuous tradition of the name and rank of many saints. There is no reason in the vast majority of cases why this should have been falsified.

In the early eighth century the most important churches probably possessed lists of their early bishops and abbots. Armagh claimed to have such a list in the eleventh century stating the number of years that each man had held office.[4] Though the liturgical commemoration is almost certainly early, the lists, with their chronological data, were probably not commenced until several generations after the foundation of the church. An instructive list is appended to the Life of Monenna in Cotton Cleop. A.ii. It provides the saint's own pedigree; then, beginning with the fifth abbess, it provides the name and patronymic of each abbess, and the period of her reign up to the fifteenth successor.[5] Thus, in the ninth century a monastic scribe was able to record the succession for a period of two hundred years. The Life itself contains the names of the second, third, and fourth abbesses, though without the chronological data of the list. The hagio-

---

[1] *Cu.* XI. 11 'A deacon who forgets to bring the oblation until the linen is removed when the names of the departed are recited shall do penance . . .'

[2] See Kenney, *Sources*, p. 699 for argument.

[3] Adamnán, III. 12 'When in the course of this service (mass) the customary prayer was chanted, with melody, in which the name of St Martin is mentioned, suddenly S. Columba said to the singers, when they came to the place of that name: "Today you must sing, 'For St Colman, the bishop'"'. Colman, a bishop of the Laigin, had died the previous night.

[4] Ed. Lawlor and Best, *P.R.I.A.*, xxxv (1919), C 316–62.

[5] Ed. Esposito, 'Conchubrani Vita', pp. 244–5.

grapher must have been familiar with the names from liturgical usage, but it looks as if a formal list, with regnal years, was not kept at this monastery until the early seventh century. It seems likely that the dates of the earliest saints in ecclesiastical lists were, in most cases, added much later by scribes whose calculations were not based on reliable early written sources. The great plague of 549–50, which carried off so many clergy, may have made memories of the earlier period even more inaccurate than they would otherwise have been. I would therefore suggest that the dates of saints who died before 549 are very likely to be inaccurate, and that, in most cases, we have no means of telling whether they are not decades out; that the possibility of an accurate record increases after *c.* 550, and that by the seventh century the obits are likely to be correct on the whole.[1]

In some cases the *floruit* of a saint may be dated by external references. Gildas was writing in the period of peace in the first half of the sixth century, which followed the Battle of Badon and preceded the further Saxon advances of the later sixth century. *Vennianus auctor*, presumably the author of the Penitential, asked Gildas' advice on problems of ecclesiastical discipline, and Vinnian was himself an authority used by Columbanus.[2] This suggests that Vinnian was active some time around the middle or third quarter of the sixth century. He had been concerned about the undisciplined asceticism of some monks in their flight to the desert, and from this we may infer that monasticism at the time commanded great enthusiasm, but was as yet very unorganized. Bangor (in Ireland) was well established considerably before Columbanus left it for the Continent. The letters of Columbanus mention Frankish and Lombardic kings, church councils, and popes who can be identified from other sources, and the saint's death in 615 is safely attested. The scribal tradition at Iona seems to date from Columcille's own lifetime. Ciarán of Clonmacnois is said to have died prematurely in the great plague, a date likely to be remembered. Thus, we have safe evidence that the monastic ideal was being encouraged and that some great monastic

---

[1] See Binchy, 'Patrick', pp. 70–5, 159. This is also in accordance with Professor Kelleher's conclusions, op, cit.

[2] Walker, *Opera*, p. 8.

paruchiae were being founded between about 540 and 615. It may be knowledge of this kind which led later monastic chroniclers to synchronize the period of the great monastic founders with the second half of the sixth and early seventh centuries.

In any case, the total picture which the annals give of the sixth century, especially of the earlier period, may well be inaccurate in its emphasis, since it represents only those houses which enjoyed considerable importance in the early eighth century. Thus, the annalists tell us nothing of the history of the early episcopal sees founded by Iserninus, Auxilius, and Secundinus, whom seventh-century tradition claimed as the Gaulish helpers of S. Patrick, though they knew of these men and assigned them obits. Churches were dedicated to them: to Auxilius, Killashee near Naas, a royal fort; to Secundinus, Dunshaughlin not far from Tara; to Iserninus, Kilcullen lying just to the north of Dún Ailline. These episcopal sees, in close proximity to royal seats, must have been important in the life of the fifth- and early-sixth-century church. Yet, with the exception of Mac-Táil of Kilcullen, who died in the plague, these churches do not enter the annals until the very end of the eighth century. There must have been other churches like them, of which we are totally ignorant.

The other two documents by which the accepted authorities have tried to date the beginnings of a monastic church are of even more dubious value. The list of coarbs of Patrick found in the Book of Leinster probably took its present form in the eleventh century.[1] This list is open to the same kind of objections as the obits found in the annals, with the added danger that Armagh had stronger motives for reshaping her early history than had most other houses. The document gives a list of coarbs from Patrick onwards, with the number of years each ruled. In the Annals some of these coarbs are described as abbots, some as bishops. Professor Ryan concludes that until the second half of the eighth century (750–90) all the rulers of Armagh held the office of both bishop and abbot.[2] Between 749 and 793 the annals mention only abbots at Armagh, and in 793 abbot Airechtach and bishop Affiath died

---

[1] For Binchy's comments on its unreliability in the early period, see 'Patrick', p. 159.

[2] *Irish Monasticism*, pp. 170–2.

on the same night: from this time forward the offices were distinct.[1]

It seems almost certain that at least up to the early eighth century the *temporalia* of Armagh were administered by bishops. When the Book of the Angel was compiled in the seventh or early eighth century Armagh was controlled by a chief bishop, of whom the word *archiepiscopus* is used. The church in Ireland had not been, as far as we know, divided into provinces under metropolitical jurisdiction. We know that at the period when the Book of the Angel was written there were other bishops at Armagh,[2] but the *archiepiscopus* administered property and exercised jurisdiction. The chief bishop of Armagh exercised functions held by the abbots of monastic *paruchiae*, and he is sometimes referred to as abbot even in the early documents. When Conchad of Sletty accepts Flann Febla of Armagh as overlord Flann is described as abbot.[3] The scribe of one of the fifteenth-century manuscripts of the Annals of Ulster hesitates between 'bishop' (in the margin) and 'abbot' (in the text) when noting Flann's obit. Tómméne appears as a bishop in the papal letter of 640, but the compiler of the Martyrology of Tallaght, writing about 800, describes him as 'comarba', heir, a word usually translated as abbot, implying control over *temporalia*.[4] By 800 men thought of the rulers of Armagh as abbots, even though they might still be occasionally in bishop's orders, for by this time the character of the office had changed.

Our remaining source is the *Catalogus Sanctorum Hiberniae*. Until recently this text was thought to belong to the early or mid-eighth century, but Père Grosjean, who has re-edited it from six manuscripts, has shown it to be a ninth- or tenth-century compilation.[5] It thus belongs to the period when, according to Professor Kelleher, the annals for the period before 735 were being revised.

---

[1] At least this is what I understand pp. 171–2 to mean.
[2] *Arm.* 21 a 1.   [3] *Arm.* 18 b 1.
[4] *M.T.*, Jan. 10.
[5] *A.B.*, lxxiii (1955), 197–213, 289–322. I am afraid that, when I reviewed Père Grosjean's edition in *I.H.S.*, xi (1958), 170–2, I did not realize the implications of his redating, and accepted the *Catalogus* as substantially true. So have Dr Kenney, Dom Louis Gougaud, and Professor Ryan, writing before Père Grosjean's commentary.

F

The *Catalogus* describes a first 'ordo' of saints, *sanctissima*, made up of bishops only, under the authority of S. Patrick, and it gives chronological data which place this first order in the period 432–544. The second 'ordo', *sanctior*, is made up mainly of priests, though with some bishops, and belongs to the period 544–98. Irish monastic historians of the ninth and tenth centuries conceived a church ruled by bishops until about the middle of the sixth century, after that by priests. The author of the Catalogue used sources like those available to the men who compiled the annals. He was a successful teacher: the statement he gave was clear and dogmatic, and thus gained general acceptance.

If, then, these three explicit sources are of such doubtful value for the first century or so of Christianity in Ireland, can we draw any conclusions about the date when the monastic *paruchiae* were founded? Fairly good authority permits us to say that the nucleus of the monastic *paruchiae* founded by Columcille, Comgall of Bangor, Columbanus, and probably Ciarán of Clonmacnois had been established by the end of the sixth century. The period which the ninth-century historians accepted for the foundation of monastic *paruchiae*, i.e. the second half of the sixth century, had its foundation in fact, though other aspects of their account are, as we shall see, entirely tendentious.

The reasons why this peculiar system of ecclesiastical organization developed in Ireland are difficult to determine. Two sources of foreign influence have been suggested. Professor Ladner has asked: 'Could the monastic organization of the Irish church, still rather enigmatic as to its origins, be a peculiarly inverted adaption to Celtic rural clan society of the western Mediterranean and Gallic, originally urban, fusion of monasticism and clericate?'[1] Father Sheehy has taken this further, and has suggested that the early missionaries to Ireland brought from Gaul, and in particular from Auxerre, an ecclesiastical organization in which monks and clerics lived a very similar life.[2] But while Irish enthusiasm for the monastic life may well have been encouraged by the example of Martin or Germanus or Caesarius, the Irish version of a monastic church was so 'peculiarly inverted' as to amount to something

---

[1] *The Idea of Reform*, p. 396.
[2] *Irish Theol. Quart.*, xxix (1962), 136–44.

different. Although Ireland had no native *civitates*, she had royal forts and small kingdoms, and the bishops of the canons attributed to Patrick, Auxilius, and Iserninus appear to have been territorial bishops, while early churches seem to have often been founded near a royal fortress. Dr Mohrmann has shown that there are very few typically monastic terms in Patrick's works:[1] he was above all a bishop, and when he writes with authority to Coroticus he insists on his episcopal orders. The abbots of Iona, on the contrary, from the first were priests, and the *paruchia* of Columcille a confederation of far-flung monasteries not coterminous with any tribal kingdom. Ascetic enthusiasm developed in many different areas of Christendom, and the practice of bishops following the monastic life may have reached Ireland from Gaul as early as the fifth century; but this does not explain in itself the peculiarities of the later Irish system.

Was the development of Irish monastic institutions indebted to British influence?[2] Britain and Ireland must have been in close and frequent contact. Irish immigrants had established themselves in south-western Wales, possibly as early as the end of the third century,[3] and here they later erected ogam-inscribed stones, and stones bearing bilingual inscriptions in Latin and Goidelic (the Irish branch of the Celtic language). Though the majority of the ogam stones are in the south-west, a few survive in south-central and north-western Wales, proving the existence in the fifth and sixth centuries of a population which understood Irish,[4] and of the ease with which conventions might pass from one side to the other of the Irish Sea. Moreover, the Irish borrowed into their own language words from Latin as it was spoken in Britain, though the precise period when these borrowings occurred is a

---

[1] *The Latin of St Patrick*, p. 26.

[2] Ryan, *Irish Monasticism*, pp. 164–6, concluding: 'Gildas, therefore, not David, seems to have been chiefly responsible for the peculiar line of development on which the Irish church entered about the middle of the sixth century.' Cf. pp. 108 ff.: 'We may regard it, too, as certain that in the opening half of the sixth century the relation between the (British and Irish) churches was largely that of master and disciple. Britain, the elder sister, taught, whilst Ireland, the younger sister, gladly learnt.'

[3] Jackson, *L.H.E.B.*, pp. 155 ff.

[4] Nash-Williams, *E.C.M.W.*, p. 6: the main incidence of the ogam inscriptions probably falls before 550. Cf. Jackson, *L.H.E.B.* pp. 169 ff.

matter of dispute. Again, the great Apostle to the Irish was a Briton. But can we be confident that, in the development of monastic institutions, Britain was the teacher and Ireland the learner?

The author of the *Catalogus* believed that this was so: he states categorically that the second order of Irish saints, in the period 544–98, obtained a mass from David, Gildas, and Doccus the Britons.[1] But this is much later testimony, representing a tradition which may or may not be reliable. Another, less-well-known, tract, by a man who seems to be from a Columban house on the Continent, possibly Luxeuil, provides a different account of the origins of the Irish liturgy.[2] According to his version it was first chanted by S. Mark, passed to eastern ascetics, and then to southern Gaul, and was brought by Germanus and Lupus to Britain. They taught it to Patrick, who brought it to Ireland, and from Bangor it returned with Columbanus to Gaul. This author, in his opening phrase, recognizes that other untaught persons have given a different account of the origins of the liturgy, which his own is intended to supersede: he does not subscribe to the theory that the Irish obtained a peculiar mass in the later sixth century from the British saints. Both this tract and the *Catalogus* represent not what happened in the sixth century but what different churchmen later believed to have happened. If we are to believe either of those accounts they must be supported by independent evidence.

There is plenty of support for contacts between British and Irish saints in the saints' Lives, but all except one are so much later that they are of very doubtful value.[3] Only the Life of Samson, which may go back to a seventh-century source, may throw light on sixth-century conditions.[4] This tells how certain learned and distinguished Irishmen, on their way back from Rome, called on the British saint, who returned with them to Ireland.[5] Before

---

[1] Grosjean, *A.B.*, lxxiii (1955), 206–10.

[2] Haddan and Stubbs, *Councils*, I. 138–40. Kenney, *Sources*, pp. 687–8.

[3] This point needs to be stressed. The Lives of Finnián, Cadoc, David, Maedóc, Cainnech, and Teilo all use the same incidents, relating them to different saints.   [4] Kenney, *Sources*, pp. 173–5.

[5] Ed. R. Fawtier, *La vie de saint Samson*, pp. 133 ff., translated T. Taylor, *The Life of S. Samson of Dol*, c. 37 ff.

doing this, *he obtained the bishop's sanction*. Samson was at this time an abbot, but not yet a bishop, and his action implies that abbots in Britain were still subject to episcopal jurisdiction. In Ireland Samson cured a mad abbot, who 'gave his monastery and all its substance' to him. As soon as Samson had returned home, his uncle, Umbraphel, was ordained to the priesthood and dispatched to be abbot of the Irish monastery. The Life of Samson shows monastic life established in both Ireland and Britain, the monastic *paruchia* in process of development, while the abbot in Britain is still under his bishop's authority.

The British church described by Gildas is governed by bishops, and the monks are still a minority. Yet Gildas was a warm supporter of monasticism, and Vinnian consulted him about over-enthusiastic ascetics. The Preface on Penance attributed to Gildas[1] is written for monks (some of whom are in orders) and for priests. Not all the priests are under monastic vow, but they seem to be subjected to a similar discipline. By the early seventh century, if Bede's information is correct,[2] Bangor Iscoed in north-east Wales was a great monastery of well over two thousand monks, divided into seven sections, each under an abbot. Monasticism, then, seems to have developed in Wales between the writing of the *De Excidio* and the Battle of Chester, that is to say, at the same time as it developed in Ireland.

It seems impossible to say with certainty that the Welsh church shaped the monastic institutions of Ireland. The dedications of the most important saints of south-eastern Wales are concentrated in fairly confined areas: those to Dubricius mainly in Erging, those to Illtud in Glywysing, those to Cadoc mainly in Glywysing and Gwent, though with outliers.[3] The cults of David (whose main church was St David's in the extreme south-west), Teilo (of Llandeilo Fawr in Carmarthenshire), and Beuno (of Powys stock) are, by contrast, widely scattered. This may suggest that in the Romanized areas of Wales there were strong traditions of a

---

[1] Ed. Bieler, *Penitentials*, pp. 60–5. J. T. McNeill. R.C. xxxix (1922) 265 accepts Gildas' authorship.

[2] H.E. II. 2. *in quo tantus fertur fuisse numerus monachorum*, etc.

[3] Bowen, *Settlements*, pp. 36 ff., and maps. Both Cadoc and Illtud have dedications in Brittany.

territorial diocese of continental type, whereas in the non-Romanized areas the monastic-type *paruchiae* carried all before them. It is quite possible that, though Ireland received her Christianity mainly from Britain, in the later sixth century British Christianity was no longer the dominating influence.

The development of monasticism in Ireland undoubtedly owed much of its impetus to the ascetic spirit which may have been present from the beginning, but which was certainly powerful in the second half of the sixth century. Vinnian imposed standards of austerity on clerics and laity so severe that, if men really intended to keep them, it is not surprising that they sought the support of communal life under rule. Both he and Columbanus preached asceticism with passionate sincerity as a life higher, more noble, more rewarding. The ascetic life was arduous, but the Christian was sustained by his love of God; and, as everyone knows, love, even while it is all the trouble in the world, is yet no trouble.[1] Great monastic founders called men, with burning eloquence, to learn the hidden mysteries of God.

> Lord, grant me, I pray Thee in the name of Jesus Christ Thy Son, my God, that love which knows no fall, so that my lamp may feel the kindling touch and know no quenching, may burn for me and for others may give light.[2] Do Thou, Christ, deign to kindle our lamps, our Saviour most sweet to us, that they may shine continually in Thy temple, and receive perpetual light from Thee the light perpetual, so that our darkness may be enlightened, and yet the world's darkness may be driven from us. Thus do Thou enrich my lantern with Thy light, I pray Thee my Jesus, so that by its light there may be disclosed to me those holy places of the holy, which hold Thee the eternal Priest of the eternal things, entering there in the pillars of that great temple of Thine, that constantly I may see, observe, desire Thee only, and loving Thee only may behold, and before Thee my lamp may ever shine and burn.[3]

But ascetic enthusiasm in Ireland did not merely lead the bishops and their clergy to adopt the monastic life, or monks to

---

[1] *Numquid, possumus dicere, laboriosum est, durum est? Non est labor dilectio; plus suave est, plus medicale est, plus salubre est cordi dilectio.* Walker, p. 110.

[2] This image is used more effectively in the *Navigatio S. Brendani*, where the arrow of fire enters the window to light the lamps on the altar. ed. C. Selmer, pp. 36–7.

[3] Walker, p. 114.

establish themselves in religious communities within the tribe under their bishop's control. The evolution of abbatial jurisdiction and monastic *paruchiae* seems, rather, to have occurred independently of the tribal bishops. As Christianity gained popularity in the sixth century, why was the endowment of monasteries more attractive to Irishmen than the endowment of tribal bishops? The ownership of land was carefully guarded in Irish law. Property was normally held by the family,[1] and the family's inheritance must not be diminished.[2] The individual was his family's responsibility, and the property which he inherited must return to the kin. In certain cases a man might have to pay for his crimes with moveable property, and as a last resort be liable to sell himself; when that condition arose his kin decided whether to give the family land in compensation for the crime, or keep the land and let their kinsman lose his freedom. The family inheritance was not at a man's personal disposition. He could make grants outside the family, but only from property which he had acquired himself, and even then he had to leave a proportion of it to his kin. It appears that certain exceptions to these rules could be made with the common consent of the whole kin-group, but the principle remained that inherited land should normally be left in the family. This is the situation as it appears in the secular law tracts. The texts included in the Book of Armagh suggest, however, that laymen sometimes had churches built on hereditary land (presumably with the consent of the *fine*), and that the king confirmed their grants, 'freeing' the property and giving 'regnum'.[3] Thus, the king liberated the land from obligations such as tribute or billeting troops, which were due to him as ruler.

The written sources which tell us how the fifth-century church was endowed all belong to the seventh century and later. Patrick, though he declares himself a bishop, resident in Ireland, never mentions any settlement, and gives no indication of his sources of income. He accepted nothing for performing baptism or ordaining clergy, and he returned the ornaments which women converts

[1] Usually the *derbfhine*, the four-generations family group. Binchy, *Early Irish Society*, p. 58.
[2] Thurneysen, *Irisches Recht*, p. 33, § 35.
[3] *Arm.* 17a 2, 17b 1.

laid on the altar:[1] yet he was able to make diplomatic presents to kings and brehons ('for you' he says to his correspondents, 'that they' that is, the Irish, 'might receive me'), and to reward the retinue of young princes who travelled with him.[2] The proximity of many early church sites to royal settlements, however, suggests that the churches were often under royal patronage; as might be expected, for kings had more influence and greater resources than other men. Armagh was founded within two miles of Emain Macha, the ancient capital of Ulster, and Professor Binchy has argued convincingly that when the church was established there the kings of Ulster must still have been resident at Emain.[3] Auxilius' church at Killashee was near to Dún Ailline, capital of North Leinster, Secundinus' church at Dunshaughlin was about six miles from Tara and two from Lagore.[4] The church of bishop Fiacc of Sletty, according to the Book of Armagh, was founded on land provided by Crimthann (king of Leinster), who was buried at Sletty.[5]

In the sixth century, as Christianity gathered force and the ascetic movement attracted admiration, the Irish aristocracy wanted to found monasteries. Was it possible for them to reconcile this desire with their obligations to family property? The whole family might turn to the religious life, using the family lands for the endowment of monasteries. The Life of the British saint Samson describes how the saint's father and mother, his five brothers and sister, his father's brother with his wife and three sons all dedicated themselves to the monastic life. His father and mother were the first to make the decision, and, with their children's co-operation, they decided to offer their property to God. 'Let not only me and you,' says his father, 'as is fitting and proper, serve God, but let us link together all our children in the service of God, and let all that is ours become wholly God's.'[6] Part of the family property was used to found churches, conse-crated by Samson, and referred to by his mother as 'our churches'.[7]

---

[1] *Conf.* cc. 49, 50.   [2] *Conf.* cc. 51, 52, 53.   [3] 'Patrick', p. 153.
[4] Archaeological evidence for the earliest occupation of this site belongs to the seventh century. Hencken, *P.R.I.A.*, liii (1950), C 5–7.
[5] *Arm.* 18b. 1.   [6] *Life of Samson*, c. 29.
[7] Ibid., c. 31; cf. 46, 52.

The author of the Life of Samson says that he has many times heard the names of Samson's father and mother read out in church at mass 'among the names of those by whom the offering was made'; he also mentions the names of Samson's uncle and aunt.[1] Samson's own family were thus the founders of a group of monasteries, out of their own family property. Perhaps Illtud, the British master to whom Samson was sent for education, was also founder of a family monastery: his nephew in orders certainly thought that he had a right to succeed his uncle, and regarded the monastery as 'a hereditary worldly possession', 'a hereditary monastery'.[2] The property of such a church would belong, by hereditary right, to the family of the founding saint (or patron), and succeeding abbots would be heirs to the founder. The evidence provided by the Life of Samson relates primarily to the British rather than to the Irish church, but the Irish aristocracy also seem to have founded churches, while retaining to themselves certain rights. In Ireland succession to the abbacy rested with the family of the donor when the line of the patron saint failed to produce a suitable candidate.[3] Thus, the donors of the land retained a powerful interest in the property.

It seems likely that, from their foundation, some Irish monasteries at any rate may have made concessions to the familiar basis of Irish society; that families built churches on their own lands, with their own kin as abbots, or that they retained interests in the monastery. The tribal bishops, however, as we see them in the canons attributed to Patrick, Auxilius, and Iserninus, seem to have been trying to exclude the authority of the laity, making every effort to keep the clergy of the *paruchia* under their own control. If a priest in the *paruchia* builds a church[4] the bishop must consecrate it before it can be used. A newcomer to the territory may not exercise his ecclesiastical orders or build a church without the bishop's permission, and anyone who looks to laymen for permission shall be *alienus*, an outsider.[5] The tribal bishop seems to have been somewhat wary of independent lay influence within his territory.

---

[1] *Life of Samson*, c. 1. [2] Ibid., cc. 14, 16.
[3] *A.L.I.*, iii, 72–4. [4] *Pa.* I. 23. Where? On his own land?
[5] *Pa.* I. 24.

We need not, however, assume that there was at first any spirit of competition between the tribal bishops and the early monasteries. Ireland was hardly Christianized in a century, and early monastic churches may have been founded in places where the bishops had little influence. Iona was established in an Irish colony,[1] and Bangor sent out monks across the Irish sea. The career of Columcille himself may have provided a powerful stimulus to monastic development. He was a man of the very highest birth, with all the natural advantage of command which such a circumstance gave in an aristocratic society. He had the gift of second sight, combined with a power to control other men by the force of his own personality. He was a shrewd judge of character, and yet at the same time a man of warm sympathies. His monks, the laity, even the animals felt his attraction. He could terrify, he could comfort, he could delight. A recruit with such qualities must have outshone most of his contemporaries.

We must also remember that Ireland had no tradition of centralized organization which would accommodate a hierarchy of urban and provincial bishops. Desert monasticism, dependent on the individual, varied in its forms, had sloughed off much of imperial organization and could be adapted much more easily to Ireland than could the better-defined episcopal system of Gaul.

The position of the tribal bishop corresponded to the position of the petty king within his *tuath*. Once a confederation of monasteries was founded, the position of the abbot of the major church corresponded to the position of an over-king. Other houses were founded, perhaps sometimes on unappropriated land, and houses already in existence joined the confederation, recognizing the overlordship of the patron saint and his heirs. The monastic *paruchia* had great powers of expansion: however far the monks travelled, they were still part of the family. Thus, the new monasticism was able to use the desire for wandering which was still alive in a people who had been, within tribal memory, on the move.

[1] Or possibly an island which was still claimed by the Picts. Bede says that the Picts granted the site. *H.E.* III. 3.

CHAPTER 8

Bishops and monastic confederations in the seventh century

Scholars using the *Catalogus Sanctorum*, the annals, and the abbatial lists have generally assumed that by the end of the sixth century a church governed by presbyter-abbots had completely superseded a church governed by bishops. This transition is in itself unlikely: it would surely take more than half a century for the peculiar structure of Celtic society to triumph over an ecclesiastical institution universally accepted throughout the Christian west. It is, moreover, directly contradicted by early sources of far greater historical authority than the *Catalogus*.

The ecclesiastical legislation of the period proves that bishops continued to exist outside the monastic system, and that a secular clergy who were not following a monastic discipline remained active in the seventh century. In the Penitential of Cummean there are priests and deacons without monastic vow, and monks who have not taken orders, as well as men who both hold major orders and follow a monastic life.[1] The penances performed by the bishop are the most severe of all, on the principle stated at the end of the same penitential, that 'to whom much is entrusted, from him shall more be exacted'. The *Canones Hibernenses* speak of a bishop (*episcopus*) and a 'bishop of bishops', who has a higher compensation value:[2] the *episcopus episcoporum* must be a bishop holding some powers of government over the rest, since there is no ecclesiastical order above that of bishop. His position may have parallels with that of the *archiepiscopus* mentioned in other seventh-century sources. Much of the ecclesiastical legislation of

[1] *Cu.* II. 4.
[2] *Hi.* v. 7, 9. Seven *ancillae* for the bishop's rejection, eight and two-thirds *ancillae* for that of the *episcopus episcoporum*. For the *ancilla* (Ir. *cumal*) as a unit of value, see *infra*, p. 134.

the seventh century gives the bishop more prominence than the abbot,[1] though the Old Irish Penitential[2] (compiled after the Penitential of Cummean) and some of the *Canones Hibernenses* class the great abbot (*excelsis princeps*) with the bishop.[3] Whatever the *Catalogus* may say, the much better evidence of church legislation shows that in the seventh century a considerable number of bishops continued to act as ecclesiastical administrators in much the same way as they had done earlier.

Some of the secular law tracts similarly emphasize the importance of the bishop's authority and dignity, and give him an honour-price higher than that of any other ecclesiastic. *Crith Gablach*, drawn up in the early eighth century,[4] asks: 'Which is more illustrious, king or bishop?' and the answer is that the bishop has the higher dignity.[5] In Irish law the value of a man's eye-witness testimony (*fiadnaise*) depended on his rank, and that of king and bishop was of equal value.[6] The interest accruing from a bishop's pledge was worth twice that of a priest's.[7] The honour price of a chief bishop (*uasal-epscop*), like the bishop of Emly or Cork, two great churches of Munster, was equal to that of the king of Munster, the overlord of the Southern Half of Ireland.[8] It is the bishop, not the abbot, whose dignity some of the early law tracts emphasize.

But it is not only the dignity of the bishop of which the law tracts speak. According to the early eighth-century *Crith Gablach*, the bishop goes on visitation, 'for the profit of church and kingdom' with a company of twelve men.[9] Thus, he has jurisdictional authority, though another law tract of the same period,

---

[1] 'Synodus II S. Patricii' emphasizes the authority of the abbot more than either Cummean or the *Canones Hibernenses*. I am not at all convinced that this text is as early as the other two texts. The marriage law is now considerably relaxed, cc. 28–9.

[2] V. 17. Professor Binchy says 'not later than the end of the eighth century'.

[3] *Hi.* I. 29, IV. 1, V. 11.

[4] Ed. Binchy, p. xiv.   [5] Ibid., lines 604–6.

[6] Law of Distress, *A.L.I.* i. 78.

[7] *A.L.I.*, v, 388–90. The pledge (*gell*) was a valuable object given as security.

[8] Small Primer, *A.L.I.* v. 110–12.

[9] Binchy, *C.G.*, lines 599–600. Cf. *A.L.I.* iii. 408, for the bishop saying mass at the 'hill of meeting'.

which formed part of the *Senchas Már*, implies that the abbot is the chief administrator.[1] Some, if not all, of the bishops mentioned in the contemporary law tracts must have been administering their dioceses from a monastic residence, but it was their episcopal and not their abbatial office which the legislators chose to emphasize. Moreover, a secular clergy existed without monastic vows. We are forced to the conclusion that an episcopacy controlling ecclesiastical administration survived into the seventh century, where it co-existed with the monastic *paruchiae* under presbyter-abbots which had been founded in the sixth.

It was inevitable that, once established, the monastic *paruchiae* should gain a power greater than that of the territorial bishoprics. The old bishopric was limited to a narrow territorial area, almost certainly to the boundaries occupied by the population-group in which the bishop was resident: the monastic *paruchia*, on the other hand, might keep on growing, for land might be offered to the patron saint (or his heirs) anywhere in the Celtic areas, and even in England and on the Continent. The abbot was thus overlord of a number of monasteries with their tenants, buildings, and lands. The abbot of Iona visited Ireland at least four times during the last three decades of the seventh century. The *paruchia* of Comgall of Bangor made new foundations across the Irish Sea: Comgall had been a friend of Columcille, and in 673 Máel-ruba of Bangor, then a young man of thirty, founded a church at Applecross, on the Scottish mainland opposite Skye, where he died in 722. The settlement was protected from the hinterland by a ridge of mountains, and the sea must have been the monks' highway. Máel-ruba's successor was drowned in it with twenty-two men thirteen years after the founder's death, and the dedications to Máel-ruba show that he, or if not he, his disciples, travelled by sea along the coasts and islands of western Scotland and through the Great Glen to the east.[2] Applecross retained its connexion with Bangor, at least until the Viking age, for one of its monks in

---

[1] *A.L.I.* iii. 14. 22, Collotype facsimile, R. I. Best and R. Thurneysen, Dublin, 1931, p. 47 col. 1, p. 48 col. 1. Cf. Thurneysen, *Z.C.P.*, xvi (1927), 168–96.

[2] See map W. D. Simpson, *The Celtic Church in Scotland*, Aberdeen 1935, Fig. 10.

the later eighth century became abbot of Bangor.[1] Another Irishman named Fursey, this time in episcopal orders, left Ireland and founded a monastery at Cnobheresburg in East Anglia (probably within the massive late Roman fortification at Burgh Castle), proceeded to the Continent, leaving his brother Foílleán at Cnobheresburg, and himself settled at Lagny on the Marne to the east of Paris. He was buried in the monastery of Péronne, completed soon after his death. Nivelles, ruled by an abbess, was added to his *paruchia*, and his brother Foílleán, who succeeded him, founded Fosse near Namur.[2] The *paruchia Fursei* was supported by the Frankish nobility and played some part in Frankish politics. The old-type diocesan sees could not possibly have made any comparable expansion.

Yet the early bishoprics were inevitably influenced by the monastic movement. The difference in manner of life between an apostolic bishop of the Patrician period and a monastic bishop of the heroic age cannot have been great,[3] and the adoption of monastic life by diocesan bishops may from the first have been common. Professor Ryan, on the evidence mainly of lists and annals, argues that the bishop of Armagh and his *familia* had adopted the monastic way of life before the end of the fifth century.[4] The association of monastic and episcopal institutions may be seen in the régime at Lindisfarne in the seventh century. About the year 721 Bede described how bishop Aidan, ruling the Northumbrians from his seat at Lindisfarne, followed the monastic life, and left the domestic affairs of the monastery to the rule of an abbot. Bede seems to have thought this arrangement needed some explanation:

> And let no one be surprised that, though we have said above that in this island of Lindisfarne, small as it is, there is found the seat of a bishop, now we say also that it is the home of an abbot and monks;

[1] Died *A.U.* 802. Very late sources attribute other Scottish foundations to men who went out from Bangor: see Simpson, op. cit. pp. 77–81.

[2] See Grosjean, *A.B.*, lxxv (1957), 373–420, reviewed Hughes, *I.H.S.*, xii (1960), 63–4.

[3] This point, though it is not a new one, has been very clearly expressed by Rev. Maurice Sheehy in a lecture delivered to the Franco-Irish Historical Congress at Auxerre, 1961.

[4] *Irish Monasticism*, p. 101.

for it is actually so. For one and the same dwelling-place of the servants of God holds both: and indeed all are monks. Aidan, who was the first bishop of this place, was a monk and always lived according to monastic rule together with his followers. Hence all the bishops of that place up to the present time exercise their episcopal functions in such a way that the abbot, whom they themselves have chosen by the advice of the brethren, rules the monastery; and all the priests, deacons, singers and readers, and the other ecclesiastical grades, together with the bishop himself, keep the monastic rule in all things.[1]

Aidan had come from the monastery of Iona to be bishop of the Northumbrians. He was a bishop, under monastic vows, ruling a see whose boundaries were coterminous with the kingdom. He might have acted as both abbot and bishop. Instead the offices were divided, and Aidan, as bishop, appointed an abbot to conduct the domestic affairs of the monastery, leaving himself free for wider administrative duties. In Iona it had been the abbot who administered the external, as well as the internal, affairs of the *paruchia*, while the bishop, whom he appointed, officiated at the sacraments reserved to the episcopal office. This was the arrangement in other Irish monasteries, while in yet others abbot and bishop were one and the same person. Patrick had claimed to be bishop of the Irish, and at Armagh his seventh-century successors administered the see of Armagh as bishops;[2] yet it is likely that they adopted the monastic life, themselves acting as abbots. Amidst the developments of the seventh century, if they wished to retain the administrative authority which they exercised as bishops, the appointment of an abbot might have led to a dangerous division of power.

The most revolutionary change which some of the early sees underwent occurred not when the bishop adopted the monastic life but when his church tried to follow the example of the monastic confederations and build up a *paruchia* not limited by the narrow territorial boundaries of the old diocese. We can glimpse this attempt to establish a *paruchia* at Kildare in the 630s, and see it much more clearly at Armagh towards the close of the century.

[1] c. 16. Ed. B. Colgrave, *Two Lives of S. Cuthbert*, Cambridge, 1940, pp. 206–8.

[2] *Supra*, p. 114.

By this time Kildare and Armagh must both have had about two centuries of activity, but the great monastic *paruchiae* founded much later than their own churches had probably already out-stripped them in influence.

Cogitosus, writing in the 630s, describes a church at Kildare served by clerics and nuns, ruled jointly by a bishop and an abbess. The church was presumably locally endowed with land and clients, for Aed Dub, 'bishop of Kildare and all the Leinstermen' in the time of Cogitosus, was a son of the king of Leinster,[1] 'the treasures of kings' were kept there,[2] and the church was richly decorated.[3] Cogitosus calls Kildare a 'great metropolitan city',[4] by which he presumably means at the least that she was the chief church in the province of Leinster, and probably that she claimed lordship over churches of other provinces. Moreover, it is also clear from the prologue that by this time Kildare had built up, or was trying to build, a *paruchia* of monastic type, unconfined by the boundaries of any kingdom. The bishop of Kildare is the 'chief bishop (*archiepiscopus*) of the Irish bishops', and the abbess is 'the abbess whom all the abbesses of the Irish venerate'.[5] The *paruchia* of S. Brigit 'is diffused throughout all the Irish lands and extends from sea to sea'; it has 'spread throughout the whole Irish island'.[6] It is difficult to be sure what these claims amount to, for the vague-ness and ambiguity of them does not inspire confidence; but at least we may be sure that the church of Kildare with its high altar flanked by the sarcophagi of 'archbishop Conlaeth and the noble virgin Brigit', tombs decorated with gold, silver and many-coloured precious stones and surmounted by crowns of gold and silver, had received solid material support, and it is clear that Cogitosus was claiming a widespread *paruchia*.

The seventh-century church of Kildare accommodated the archbishop with his school of clerics (*regularis schola*), the abbess with her virgins and pious widows, and the laity.

---

[1] O Briain, 'Hagiography of Leinster', p. 460.

[2] *P.L.* lxxii, col. 790B

[3] Ibid., cols. 789-90. Col. 790C mentions the gifts brought by those attending the festival of S. Brigit.

[4] Ibid., col. 790.   [5] Ibid., col. 778.

[6] Ibid., col. 778.

The church, however, is not the original one; (writes Cogitosus) a new church has been erected in the place of the old one, in order to hold the increased numbers of the faithful. Its ground plan is large, and it rises to a dizzy height. It is adorned with painted tablets. The interior contains three large oratories, divided from one another by walls of timber, but all under one roof. One wall, covered with linen curtains and decorated with paintings, traverses the eastern part of the church from one side to the other. There are doors in it at either end. The one door gives access to the sanctuary and the altar, where the bishop, with his school of clerics and those who are called to the celebration of the holy mysteries, offers the divine sacrifice to the Lord. By the other door of the dividing wall, the abbess enters with her virgins and with pious widows in order to participate in the supper of Jesus Christ, which is his flesh and blood. The remainder of the building is divided lengthwise into two equal parts by another wall, which runs from the western side to the transverse wall. The church has many windows. Priests and lay persons of the male sex enter by an ornamented door to the right hand side; matrons and virgins enter by another door on the left hand side. In this way the one basilica is sufficient for a huge crowd, separated by walls according to state, grade and sex, but united in the spirit, to pray to Almighty God.[1]

The *archiepiscopus* of Kildare had a share in administering the church: the words Cogitosus uses are 'government' and 'rule'. He was not confined to functions of order exercised more or less at the discretion of a monastic superior. It seems likely that from early times Kildare was the *cathedra* of a bishop, whose *paruchia* occupied a contiguous area, and that a community of women was closely associated with the church.[2] By the 630s the *paruchia* had become, or was becoming, an overlordship analogous to the confederation of monasteries headed by Iona.

Such a transition can be much more clearly discerned at

---

[1] *P.L.* lxxii, col. 789, trs. Bieler, *Ireland*, p. 28.
[2] R.A.S. Macalister (*P.R.I.A.*, xxxiv (1919), C 340–1) has suggested that a pagan college of priestesses came over to Christianity. There can be no decisive proof for such a suggestion, but it is significant that Brigit is the name of a pagan goddess, that the saint's feast, 1 February, falls on the same day as *Imbolc*, one of the four great festivals of the pagan year, and that, according to the twelfth-century report of Giraldus Cambrensis, the nuns of Kildare maintained a perpetual fire surrounded by a circular fence which no man might pass.

G

Armagh in the late-seventh- and early-eighth-century sources.[1] The Book of the Angel defines the *terminus* of Armagh as a compact territorial area comprising Airgialla with parts of the adjacent kingdoms of Ulaid and Dál Araide.[2] This may well be the extent of the early episcopal see of Armagh. Yet the Book of the Angel also claims for Patrick and his successors judicial and financial control throughout a much wider area,[3] while Tírechán specifies the churches granted to Patrick all over the Northern Half of Ireland, with a few in the Southern Half. It is thus abundantly clear that the bishop of Armagh in the late seventh century was not only claiming to govern a compact territorial diocese but was also trying to assert overlordship over a widespread *paruchia*.[4] The Additions to Tírechán provide some illustration of the process of expansion. Aed, bishop of Sletty, accepted Ségéne bishop of Armagh as his overlord, and his successor Conchad accepted Ségéne's successor, Flann Febla. Here, at the end of the seventh century, there seems to have been a formal acknowledgement of overlordship,[5] though it is the only known instance.

It would appear that in the second half of the seventh century the church of Armagh, then the chief church within a territorial diocese and ruled by a bishop following the monastic life, deter-

---

[1] Tírechán, writing 670 × 700; Muirchú, writing 680 × 700; the Additions to Tírechán, written in the early eighth century; the Book of the Angel, which Kenney dates to the eighth century (*Sources*, p. 336), but which Binchy, O'Rahilly, and Carney regard as earlier than Tírechán ('this strange document, or at least the substance of it, was in existence before Tírechán's day', 'Patrick', p. 60). The Book of the Angel is, in fact, a collection of statements, apparently from different sources, and occasionally inconsistent. See Appendix. All these texts were copied into the Book of Armagh at the beginning of the ninth century. See Binchy, 'Patrick', for an illuminating discussion of these sources.

[2] E. MacNeill, *J.R.S.A.I.*, xviii (1928), 95–100.

[3] *Arm.* 20b 2.

[4] 'The *terminus* means the area immediately subject to the abbot of Armagh, that portion of territory over which he exercises direct rule, like the *rí tuaithe* or tribal king; the *paruchia* is a much wider area over which he exercises indirect suzerainty similar to that enjoyed by the *ruiri* or superior king.' See Binchy, 'Patrick', p. 61.

[5] According to *A.U.*, Ségéne died in 688, Aed in 700; Flann Febla in 715, Conchad in 692. *Tr. Life*, p. 347.

mined to establish a *paruchia* analogous to that of Iona. The territorial diocese introduced from the Continent was based on the Roman *civitas*; the monastic-type *paruchia* was based on Irish ideas of overlordship. Under native law the petty king was the highest grade of the nobility, directly controlling more assets in land and clients than anyone else within his kingdom; the over-king of a group of petty kingdoms exercised overlordship, a position which brought increased dignity and prosperity. Highest of all was the superior king, or the 'king over kings', such as the Uí Neill king of the Northern Half, or the king of Munster. The earliest ecclesiastical overlordship of which we have *certain* knowledge was that founded by Columcille, of the Uí Neill dynasty. The advantages of such a system must have become rapidly apparent. Other monastic confederations were similarly constituted, and before long the older diocesan sees had to adopt it or fade into insignificance.[1]

The statement of the prerogatives of Armagh contained in the Book of the Angel sets out those classes of churches which Armagh lawyers were claiming as part of the *paruchia Patricii*. They describe the churches as follows, saying that they 'ought to be in special union with S. Patrick':

> *Omnis aeclessia libera et civitas ab aepiscopali gradu videtur esse fundata in tota Scotorum insola, et omnis ubique locus qui Dominicus appellatus.*[2]

'Every free church and (its) city is seen to have been founded by episcopal authority in the whole island of the Scotti,' the passage begins. The claim is that every church now free from obligations was founded by episcopal order, and all those churches must be associated with Armagh. The *Collectio Canonum Hibernensis* distinguishes between a church *catholica et ab omni censu libera* and a church *sub censu regali*,[3] while the Additions to Tírechán describe how a king 'frees' a property which its owner had granted to Patrick, in the phrase *liberavit rex Deo et Patricio*.[4] A church thus freed from secular burdens surely belongs to the class of which

---

[1] Cf. Kenney, p. 329.

[2] *Arm.* 21 a 2. For a discussion of this passage see Binchy, 'Patrick', p. 64. For translation of the *Liber Angeli* see Appendix.

[3] *Coll.* XXIX. 6.   [4] *Tr. Life*, p. 338.

the Book of the Angel speaks. In addition, as Professor Binchy says, the group must also include those churches which are still unattached to any of the great monastic federations. The Book of the Angel also claims for Patrick 'every place which is called *domnach*', and Professor Binchy has shown that the *domnach* names belong to a very early, possibly a pre-Patrician, strata of loan-words.[1] Tírechán makes a somewhat similar claim that *omnia primitivae aeclesiae Hiberniae* belong to Patrick.[2] Thus, the Armagh lawyers were trying to build up for Patrick a widespread *paruchia* such as Columcille's, a *paruchia* quite unlike that of the early bishop of the *plebs*. They were claiming for it early foundations, churches founded by episcopal authority and free from obligations to an existing overlord.

Tírechán specifies many of the properties claimed by Armagh in the provinces of Meath, Connacht, and the territories of the Northern Uí Néill, venturing briefly into the Southern Half at the end of the Memoir. Perhaps Armagh decided not to contest claims with Brigit in this area.[3] Even so, Tírechán makes it clear that Armagh did not actually control all the properties which she claimed. He complains of those who 'hold the *paruchia* of Patrick because they have taken away from him what was his';[4] for one particular property he tells us that the community of Columcille and the church of Bishop Éógan of Ardstraw were competing with Armagh;[5] and on another occasion he laments that the *familia* of Ciarán of Clonmacnois had made many encroachments since the 'new mortalities' of 664.[6]

The temporary eclipse and subsequent revival of Armagh in the seventh century may have been due to political changes. In the pre-historic period the boundaries of Ulster, with its capital

---

[1] 'Patrick', p. 166.

[2] *Arm.* 11 a 2, *Tr. Life*, p. 312.

[3] See *infra*, p. 113. Her lawyers may once have prepared claims to property in this area (the *notulae*, *Arm.* 37 b, seem to refer to places in west Munster) which were omitted when the Book of Armagh was copied in the early ninth century.

[4] *quia video dissertores et archiclocos et milites Hiberniae quod odio habent paruchiam Patricii quia substraxerunt ab ea quod ipsius erat. Arm.* 11 a 2, *Tr. Life*, p. 311–12. These seem to be laymen.

[5] At Racoon in western Donegal. *Arm.* 11 b 2.

[6] *Arm.* 11 a 1.

at Emain Macha, stretched as far as the Boyne: probably at some time during the fifth century the kingdom of Ulster was thrust back to the north-eastern corner of Ireland. If Armagh was founded under the patronage of the royal house settled at Emain she may have suffered in the process of Ulster's contraction. Central and southern Ulster, the area in which Armagh was situated, became a collection of vassal peoples, known together as Airgialla, probably paying tribute to Niall king of Tara.[1] Niall's sons founded kingdoms in central Ireland and the central-east, and in the north-west and north (one of which, descended from Eógan, developed into the important kingdom of the Cenél Eógain with its capital at Ailech). The overlordship of these kingdoms passed among the descendants of Niall king of Tara.[2] In the later seventh century the biographer of Patrick was establishing a connexion between the saint and the Uí Néill. A fairly long part of Muirchú's narrative is taken up with a saga telling of the triumph of Christianity in Tara, and its acceptance by Lóegaire son of Niall.[3] The book, which was added to the Life of Patrick by Muirchú,[4] says that Patrick was buried at Dunlethglaise (Downpatrick in Ulster), but that the Uí Néill and the men of Airthir (the sub-kingdom in which Armagh was situated) disputed possession of Patrick's body.[5] According to the Book of the Angel, he rested at Armagh.[6] It would therefore appear that in the late seventh and eighth centuries Armagh writers were associating their church with the dominant Uí Néill dynasty, and that the tradition of his burial among the Ulstermen was something of an embarrassment.[7]

Armagh entered the field very late for the race for ecclesiastical precedence. The monastic *paruchiae* founded by Columcille,

[1] O'Rahilly, *Early Irish History*, pp. 223 ff.

[2] Binchy, *Congress 1959*, pp. 124–5, for a short exposition of the early political structure.

[3] Chapters 10–21.

[4] Book I closes with a statement of Muirchú's authorship. Book II appears to be an addition to the original Life.

[5] Muirchú laments the 'conflicting opinions' about Patrick, 'the very many surmises of very many persons', and the *incertis auctoribus*. *Arm.* 20 a 1.

[6] *Arm.* 21 a 2.

[7] For Armagh and the Uí Néill, see Binchy, 'Patrick', p. 61.

Ciarán, and others were already established. Kildare had already made claims to be a 'metropolitan church', with a prelate who was 'archbishop of the Irish bishops'. We know almost nothing of the early development of other churches, but what of Emly and Cork, the great churches of Munster, whose bishops (*ollam uasal eascub*) had the same honour price as the king of Munster?[1] These churches presumably also exercised overlordship over large *paruchiae*. Armagh was not the only church to attempt, or achieve, the transition from a small diocese of early type to a widespread overlordship. But she achieved the transition with outstanding success, and she is the only church which we can observe with any clarity.

By 700 most of the old sees had been absorbed into the new overlordships. A few themselves managed to change their constitution, inherited from the Roman Empire, to one in keeping with native political constitutions. Armagh was exceptionally successful in profiting, as we shall see, both from a native and a Roman inheritance.

[1] The Small Primer, *A.L.I.* v. 112.

CHAPTER 9

Ireland and the outside world

The Irish church, founded by the missionary efforts of men from Britain and Gaul, retained her contacts with the Continent in the sixth and seventh centuries. The organization of bishops established to rule territorial sees co-existed with monastic *paruchiae* (often under presbyter abbots) which had developed under native patronage. The influence of native law and custom in the end proved decisive in shaping the organization of the church, but during the seventh century influence from the Continent still seemed in the ascendant.

Whether Patrick received his training at Auxerre is a matter for dispute:[1] it is certain that from the later sixth century onwards Irishmen were travelling to Gaul and Italy. When the church ceased to be only for the insignificant minority and won prestige and endowment ardent spirits looked around for some further asceticism. At home in seventh-century Ireland the clergy were protected by law: ecclesiastical orders gave them an honour-price, the monks who belonged to the 'tribe of the church' enjoyed certain rights in common, and their property received certain immunities. They rested on the privileges of a legally recognized institution. Already, before about 570 in Ireland, there were monks who, fired with desire for a more perfect life, had fled to the deserts.[2] A man like Columbanus sought the abandonment of all earthly ties. For him, life was no homeland, where the Christian might dwell secure in his rights: it was a roadway, whereon none dwells, but walks.[3] The body, as S. Paul had written, was only a frail tent, which might at any moment be taken down, and the more man held to its protection the less he was aware of God's support. Such ideas did not allow men like

[1] *Supra*, p. 33.
[2] Walker, *Opera*, p. 9. 'Vennianus auctor' had consulted Gildas about them. For Vennianus see *supra*, pp. 44, 53–6.
[3] Walker, pp. 84–7, 94–5.

Columbanus to sit praying in their own monasteries, but drove them out, often overseas, in a pilgrimage which was perpetual exile.

But although Columbanus set up his hermitage at Annegray in the rocky wilderness of the Vosges, where he and his brethren lived on occasional gifts or starved on herbs, wild apples, even tree bark, he attracted disciples, and before long received endowments. The houses founded by him and his disciples, in particular Luxeuil, St. Gall, and Bobbio, became important and well-established monasteries. Similarly, the Irishman Fursey, abandoning all he possessed, came to England on pilgrimage and settled in East Anglia, but when he gained popularity there, longing to be free from all worldly affairs, he moved on to north-eastern Gaul. After his death he became patron saint of a new church at Péronne built by Eorconwald, Neustrian Mayor of the Palace, which was soon the head of a prosperous *paruchia*.[1] Other Irishmen came to Gaul on pilgrimage and remained there, like that Bishop Rónán 'a holy pilgrim of God of Irish race' whom Ansoald Bishop of Poitiers in the last quarter of the seventh century put in charge of the monastery at Mazerolles which he had restored,[2] or Kilian, martyred at Würzburg in the later seventh century.

Irish foundations in Gaul, Germany, and Italy kept open the communications between Ireland and the Continent. Irish pilgrims came out, sometimes in their old age, like that Bishop Cummian, who reached Bobbio when he was seventy-eight years old, and lived there for seventeen more years before his death; he was buried on 19 August, some time during the reign of King Liutprand, 712–35.[3] Other Irishmen joined the community at Bobbio and worked in the scriptorium, learning Italian scripts, but revealing their presence in their system of abbreviation, their restorations and additions, glosses and style of decoration, and sometimes writing whole manuscripts in Irish hands.[4] Manuscripts

---

[1] *Supra*, p. 82.

[2] Kenney, *Sources*, p. 499.

[3] See M. Stokes, *Six Months in the Apennines*, London, New York, 1892, pp. 171–6. The information is from an inscription.

[4] Lowe, *C.L.A.*, iv, pp. xx ff.

were brought from Ireland to the library there,[1] and probably books were taken back from Bobbio to Ireland.[2] Possibly some of those Irishmen who supported Roman usages in the Easter controversy made journeys to the Continent and secured books. In a letter which, in Dr Bischoff's opinion, was probably written in the seventh or eighth century,[3] a scholar named Calmanus (? *leg.* Colmanus) writes to tell his 'most dear and learned son' Feradad (? *leg.* Feradach) that his community has obtained a number of manuscripts from the *Romani*, as the sympathizers with a Roman Easter were called. These contain much better texts than Colmán and his pupil already possessed. He complains about the defects of the Irish manuscripts, of 'almost three pages left out by the scribes' in *De officiis ecclesiasticis*, and of the text of Sedulius' *Carmen Paschale*, of which he says that hitherto the first part had been corrupt and the second hardly known. Colmán's identity, like that of his pupil, is unsolved;[4] but the letter illustrates how improved recensions of works available outside Ireland must have been obtained and circulated.

The *paruchia* of Fursey in north-eastern Gaul was another lively Irish centre. Here we can trace Fursey's immediate successors: his brothers Ultán and Foílleán, and Cellán, Irish correspondent of Aldhelm, who died in 706. The earliest Life of S. Gertrude of

---

[1] The Antiphonary of Bangor is one of these. It was probably written at the end of the seventh century, though who brought it is unknown.

[2] The Gospels in the pre-Hieronymian version, now known as Codex Usserianus Primus, which Lowe dates to the beginning of the seventh century, may have been written at Bobbio, since the script is very closely related to that of Amb. C. 26 sup and Amb. D 23 sup, both written at Bobbio. See Lowe, *C.L.A.*, ii, 271. But cf. Bieler, *Amer. Jrnl. Phil.*, lxxxiii (1962), p. 103, note (1).

[3] Bischoff, 'Il monachesimo irlandese', p. 128. The text is printed in *Bull. de l'Acad. Royale de Bruxelles*, x (1843), 368.

[4] Colmán writes that the manuscripts 'have come to us from the *Romani*'. Could he have been Colmán abbot of Bangor, who died *A.U.* 680? Bangor had a *scriptorium* able to produce the Antiphonary of Bangor at the end of the century. Sillán, scribe and abbot of Bangor, had interested himself in paschal computation early in the century, and his pupil Mo-Chuaróc, who went to the south of Ireland, was called 'doctor of the whole world' by the *Romani*. See Grosjean, *A.B.*, lxiv, 215–20; Kenney, p. 218. Thus, Bangor, outside the area of Ireland where the *Romani* were most firmly established, had an active learned tradition and contacts with the *Romani* of the south.

Nivelles, one of the churches of this *paruchia*, was written about 670 by an Irish monk, while Suibne, another Irishman, was abbot of Nivelles some time before 684.[1] The cult of Patrick may have been disseminated on the Continent via the *paruchia* of Fursey: he was said to have brought relics of Patrick with him to the Continent,[2] and abbot Cellán composed verses on Patrick.[3] It seems likely that a manuscript of Patrick's confession was brought to Péronne (or one of the other houses of the confederation), where it was copied by a continental scribe of northern France in the late eighth or early ninth century.[4]

The churches of Fursey's confederation seem to have maintained contacts not only with Ireland but possibly with Irish foundations in Germany. The names of Fursey, Ultán, Foillán, and Cellán (whose notice is very rare) are found with other Irish saints in a ninth-century German pontifical now in the University Library of Fribourg-en-Brisgau.[5] Irishmen active in Bavaria must have introduced the names of Irish saints into litanies there: Orleans MS. 184, written in the first third or first half of the ninth century, invokes Columbanus, Fursey, Patrick, Columcille, Comgall, Adamnán, Ciarán, Brigit, Ita, and Samthann, who died much later than the rest, in 739.[6] At Salzburg before 784, during the period when the Irishman Vergil was bishop, the list of dead bishops and abbots who are to be commemorated contains the names not only of Patrick, Ciarán, and Columbanus but also of a series of Iona abbots from Columcille to Sléibéne the fifteenth abbot (obit. 767).[7] There seems to have been a union of prayers between Salzburg and Iona at least during the episcopacy of Vergil. Communications between Ireland and the Continent did not cease

---

[1] See Grosjean, *A.B.*, lxxv (1957), 397.

[2] The early ninth-century *Virtutes*, ed. Krusch, *M.G.H. Script. rer. mer.*, iv, 447. P. Grosjean, *A.B.*, lxxv, 398, cites other instances of interest in Patrick by Péronne and Fosses.

[3] Traube, 'Peronna Scottorum', pp. 107–8. Meyer, *Ériu*, v (1911), 110–11.

[4] Bieler, *Libri*, i, 17–18; Grosjean, *A.B.*, lxxvi (1958), 365.

[5] MS. 363. See Grosjean, *A.B.*, lxxv (1957), 419–20. The other Irish saints are Patrick, Columbanus, Columcille, Comgall, Cainnech, Ciarán, Brendan, Finnia, Brigit, Ita, and Darerca (i.e. Moninne).

[6] This MS. is the so-called *Libellus Precum* of Fleury. See Coens, *A.B.*, lxxvii (1959), 373–91.

[7] Grosjean, *A.B.*, lxxviii (1960), 92–123.

with the first generation of Irish founders, but were sustained throughout the seventh and eighth centuries.

Irishmen left their stamp on the monastic settlements and *scriptoria* of Merovingian Gaul, the Rhineland, and northern Italy: meanwhile their own literary tradition was profoundly influenced by Spain. In the seventh century, while northern Europe and Italy were still suffering from the general barbarization of culture which followed the invasions, Spain under the Visigoths enjoyed comparative security. The Visigothic church, in general sympathetic to ascetic ideals, held councils and passed legislation; the church in Galicia, the north-western part of the Iberian peninsula, was particularly favourable to monasticism of a type quite independent of the Benedictine rule. 'Much of what Roman Africa had left is gathered up and cherished' in the late-sixth- and seventh-century literature of Spain,[1] by none more successfully than by Isidore of Seville (c. 570–636).

Several of his works reached Ireland with such rapidity that close and frequent contacts between Ireland and Spain seem certain.[2] Laidcenn, one of the circle of scholars associated with Lismore,[3] who died in 661, less than a generation after Isidore, quoted from Isidore's *De Ortu et Obitu Patrum* in writing his abridgement of Gregory the Great's *Moralia on Job*, and a little later an anonymous grammatical treatise by an Irish contemporary of Aldhelm uses several of Isidore's works.[4] Other Spanish writings beside Isidore's were known to Irish authors,[5] and a Greek inscription on a seventh-century Irish cross slab gives a doxology which vividly illustrates the influence of Spain. In 633 the fourth Council of Toledo had sanctioned a peculiarly worded doxology, which passed into the Mozarabic liturgy: 'Glory *and honour* to the Father and to the Son and to the Holy Ghost'. The

---

[1] Raby, *Secular Latin Poetry*, i, 148.

[2] The transmission of Spanish texts to Ireland has been recently discussed by Dr Jocelyn Hillgarth, in two excellent and fully documented papers. See Bibliography. For early Irish references to Isidore, see also Ó Máille, *Ériu*, ix (1921–3), 71–6, and O'Rahilly, *Ériu*, x (1926–8), 109.

[3] See Grosjean, 'Exégètes', pp. 92–6.

[4] See Bischoff, *Archives d'histoire doctrinale et littéraire du moyen age*, xxv (1958), 5–20, and Hillgarth, *P.R.I.A.*, lxii, C. 187.

[5] Hillgarth, *Studia Patristica*, 448–9, and *P.R.I.A.*, lxii, C. 168.

same formula is reproduced in northern Ireland at Fahan Mura. Doubts have been cast on the authenticity of this inscription,[1] but there is support for it in the wording of the doxology which is recommended to be said at the conclusion of each psalm in an old Irish table of penitential commutations composed about 800.[2] In one manuscript[3] this reads 'Gloria *et honor* Patri et Filio et Spiritui Sancto'; in the other the doxology has been normalized.[4] It seems that the Toledan formula was known in eighth-century Ireland, and its presence on a seventh-century slab is therefore less startling.

Art historians have recognized the influence of east Mediterranean styles in the formation of Irish art. Manuscripts illustrating them may have reached Ireland via Italy and the Continent, or via Spain. The library at Bobbio possessed three uncial manuscripts which seem to have been written in North Africa in the fourth and fifth centuries. One of those, a pre-Vulgate version of the gospels of Mark and Matthew, is said to have been carried by S. Columbanus in his book satchel; and though the authority for this tradition is the eighteenth-century book catalogue, Dr Lowe comments that 'the survival of so unusable a book was probably due to its being regarded as a relic of the founder'.[5] This manuscript may have passed from Africa to Italy, and so to Bobbio; but equally well it may have been carried from Africa to Spain, from Spain to Ireland, and from Ireland to Gaul in the book satchel of Columbanus, and so, in the saint's old age, to the library at Bobbio.

Of the nine surviving manuscripts of Isidore thought to have been written in the seventh century, three were transcribed at Bobbio, and one either in Ireland or at Bobbio.[6] Isidore's influence is constantly to be seen in pre-Carolingian Irish scholarship. He encouraged and developed the tastes of Irish men of learning. He was interested in the 'three sacred languages' of

---

[1] R. A. S. Macalister, *J.R.S.A.I.*, xlix (1929), 90–8.

[2] Now ed. and transl. by Binchy, *Ériu*, xix (1962), 47–72.

[3] Rawl. B. 512, fourteenth to fifteenth centuries.

[4] *R.I.A.* 3, B. 23, fifteenth century. I owe this reference to Père Grosjean.

[5] *C.L.A.*, iv, 465. For the other two MSS. (texts of Cyprian), ibid., 458, 464. Hillgarth, *P.R.I.A.*, lxii, C. 172, draws attention to these.

[6] See Hillgarth, *P.R.I.A.*, lxii, C. 180.

Hebrew, Greek, and Latin: so were they, and they hunted through glossaries to track down the Hebrew and Greek equivalents of the familiar Latin.[1] He was interested in the etymological derivations of words: so were they, though, like their master's, their explanations were often philologically completely false. He liked to catalogue, arrange, and subdivide, and yet, at the same time, he loved the strange and fantastic: so did Irish scholars, combining with these characteristics a passion for the mystical use of numbers. Such tastes sometimes betray Irish writers of early homilies or grammatical works which are either anonymous or attributed to one of the Fathers.[2]

The intellectual attitude of an Irish scholar *c*. 700 can be seen in Adamnán's *De Locis Sanctis*.[3] Adamnán, as far as we know, travelled no farther east than Northumbria, but he was eager to know in detail about the holy places. He wanted measurements and maps; he looked up the Bible, Jerome, and other books in his library to set alongside the account of Arculf, the Gaulish bishop, shipwrecked off the coast of Britain, who was Adamnán's informant; he was interested in wonders like the Sicilian volcano and oddities like the locusts cooked in oil with leaves tasting of honey. A teacher with Adamnán's zest, his intellectual curiosity and pleasure in work could never have been boring.

Seventh-century Irish monastic schools set their pupils to learning Latin. They had a respect for grammar. The monks of Bobbio, in their poverty, though they 'deleted beautifully written texts of Cicero, Seneca, Pliny and Symmachus, in order to make room for church fathers and councils, spared the Latin grammarians'.[4] In the seventh century they were writing their own grammatical tracts, in Latin certainly, and possibly also in Irish. The first book of the vernacular *Scholars' Primer*, which is presented as a work of Cennfaeladh (died *A.U.* 679), is heavily indebted to Latin authorities. It discusses the origins of language (with apocryphal elaboration), the divisions of the Latin and Irish alphabets into vowels and consonants, contrasts between the two

---

[1] McNally, 'The *Tres Linguae Sacrae* in early Irish Biblical exegesis', *Theological Studies*, xix (1958), 395–403.
[2] B. Bischoff, 'Wendepunkte', pp. 207–11.
[3] Ed. D. Meehan.   [4] Lowe, *C.L.A.*, iv, xxiii.

languages, genders in Irish, and inflexion.[1] 'Ignorance is not good', the concluding phrase of this tract, might have been quoted as the schoolteacher's maxim.[2]

The Irish certainly had a taste for the fantastic and abstruse, which led some of them to adopt a Latin style weighed down with obscure words, now known as Hisperic Latin. The introduction of such words, sometimes of non-Latin derivation, seems to have been intended as a kind of ornament, and as a deliberate display of erudition.[3] But such Hisperic style is not typical of the seventh-century Irishman's Latin: Columbanus could turn an epigrammatic phrase, the author of the tract on the 'Twelve Abuses of the World' (c. 630-650) wrote a rather rhetorical style which is correct and even graphic,[4] while the direct simplicity of the Bangor hymns still invokes a response:

> *Sancti venite, Christi corpus sumite,*
> *Sanctum bibentes quo redempti sanguinem.*

The Irish venerated learning. When the Bangor poet of the late seventh century commemorated S. Patrick it was as 'teacher of the Irish'. The monks of Bobbio began very early to collect a library, for Attala, Columbanus' immediate successor, had his cupboard of books.[5] Too poor to buy all the new vellum they needed, they secured manuscripts no longer in demand and scraped them down for re-use.[6] Men like Columbanus, who had been Master of the Schools at Bangor before he came to the Continent, or Adamnán of Iona, had a fairly good knowledge of late-Latin Christian authors, and there are passages in Columbanus' writings which echo Vergil, Horace, Ovid, and Sallust.[7]

---

[1] Ed. G. Calder, *Auraicept na n-Éces*, Edinburgh, 1917. Cf. Grosjean, 'Exégètes', p. 95, and Calder, pp. xxxi ff., for debt to Isidore.

[2] Calder, p. 54. I have taken this phrase away from its context

[3] See Grosjean, 'Confusa Caligo', *Celtica*, iii (1955), 57-8, 66.

[4] Ed. Hellmann, see bibliography. The judgement is Laistner's, *Thought and Letters*, pp. 144-5.

[5] One of the oldest Bobbio MSS., Amb. s.45 sup., a Commentary of Jerome on Isaiah, has a note: *Lib. de arca domno Atalani*.

[6] Lowe, *C.L.A.*, iv, xxiii.

[7] Bieler, 'The Humanism of St Columban', *Mélanges Columbaniens*, pp. 95-102, Walker, *Opera*, and Meehan, *De Locis Sanctis*, indices; Brüning, *Z.C.P.*, xi, 213-304.

The seventh-century Irish commentary on the Bucolics and Georgics shows that Vergil was studied in Ireland,[1] and Irish scholars do not seem to have feared the lure of Apollo or the temptations of grammar as did some of their forerunners and contemporaries on the Continent.[2]

Throughout the seventh century Irishmen were in close touch with the Continent, and Irish Christian learning was deeply influenced by continental scholarship, in particular that of Isidore. But it was the stimulus of familiar contact with the Anglo-Saxons which helped to foster the art of illumination. Before Irish missionaries set out for Northumbria in 635 they had developed a distinctive style of writing: it can be seen in the Cathach (the 'Battler') of S. Columba, a Psalter written in the late sixth or early seventh century. They had, moreover, begun to evolve a peculiar style of ornamental initial, by which the capital does not stand out from the text in the normal late-antique manner, but is drawn into the text by a series of letters of diminishing size, and is decorated with a small repertoire of spirals, animal heads, and other patterns which are found in La Tène metalwork and which reappear on the contemporary Irish cross-slabs.[3] But the sudden wealth of illumination which appears first in the Book of Durrow and is developed subsequently in the Hiberno-Saxon manuscripts of Northumbria is best understood if we reckon that the art of the Anglo-Saxon goldsmiths was one of its sources of inspiration. The jewellery of the Sutton Hoo treasure and of other English finds contains designs which reappear in the Book of Durrow.[4] It is possible, also, that the art of Roman Britain, which could still

---

[1] Kenney, *Sources*, pp. 285–7.

[2] E.g. Cassian, whose memories of the poets distract his prayers, Paulinus of Nola, who thought that hearts dedicated to Christ must be closed to Apollo, Gregory the Great, who disapproved of bishops wasting time on grammar.

[3] Nordenfalk, 'Before Durrow', pp. 155 ff. For initials, see Plate IV.

[4] E.g. the cruciform step pattern of *Durm.*, f. 1ᵛ with the Sutton Hoo clasp; the animal interlace of *Durm.*, f. 192ᵛ with the animal interlace of the gold buckle and clasps of Sutton Hoo, with the sword-pommel of Crundale Down and with other Anglo-Saxon jewellery (see Bruce-Mitford, *Lind.*, pp. 110–11). The robe of the Matthew symbol (*Durm.*, f. 21ᵛ) is strongly reminiscent of millefiori work, while the roundels of f. 3ᵛ have their models in Celtic hanging bowls and Irish metalwork. See *Durm.*, Plates II and III.

be seen in England, may lie behind the man and eagle on the page of symbols at the beginning of the Book of Durrow (f. 2^r) and of the eagle which introduces the Gospel of Mark (f. 84^v), 'for which no satisfactory Mediterranean models can be found'.[1]

Both the provenance and date of the Book of Durrow have been disputed. The scribe was using a Vulgate text relatively free from the Old Latin readings which characterize the Irish family of Biblical manuscripts, but it was not the Italo-Northumbrian Vulgate text found in the Codex Amiatinus. Thus, the text of Durrow affords no argument for Northumbrian provenance, as it has previously been supposed to do.[2] Any of the Irish scribes concerned with exegesis might have wanted to possess a Vulgate text. Recent studies, moreover,[3] have proved conclusively that the Book of Durrow was written and illuminated in a *scriptorium* with an Irish background. The Vulgate text of Mark is preceded by an eagle, the text of John by a lion, as in the Old Latin version. Much of the prefatory material in the Book of Durrow belongs to the Old Latin, not to the Vulgate, tradition.[4] The colophon speaks of men with Irish names (Patrick and Columba); and Dr Luce claims that, under glass and with direct sunlight, it is possible to discern the Celtic tonsure on the head of the man-symbol (f. 21^v), where the front of the head is shaven and the long hair, parted high on the scalp, falls to the shoulders.

The Book of Durrow appears, then, to have been produced in an Irish-type *scriptorium*, which wanted a Vulgate text but clung to the architecture of the Old Latin version; by an illuminator

[1] Bruce-Mitford, *Lind.*, pp. 116–17. Cf, Henry, *L'Art Irlandais*, i, 239 f.

[2] The argument for dating the Book of Durrow after 674, because this is the date of the founding of Wearmouth (and the effective introduction of the Italo-Northumbrian Vulgate text presumably post-dates this), must also be discarded. Bruce-Mitford, *Lind.*, p. 110. In his review in *T.L.S.*, 22 February, 1963, Mr Bruce-Mitford revises his dating, and would be prepared to put the Book of Durrow 'back to 650, if necessary'.

[3] *Evangeliorum quattuor Codex Durmachensis*, 2 vols., Olten, 1960. See especially introductory section by Dr Luce.

[4] The 'Interpretationes nominum ebreorum' are a feature of the Old Latin version, and are in Durrow, but not in Amiatinus and Lindisfarne. The Durrow 'Breves Causae' are the Old Latin summaries, and reappear almost exactly in Kells, but show considerable differences in Amiatinus and Lindisfarne. The *Argumenta* of Durrow explain the sequence of the gospels, by which John follows Matthew in the Old Latin order. Luce, *Durm.*, pp. 9 ff.

familiar with the designs of Anglo-Saxon as well as of Irish metal-workers; one, moreover, who probably knew the animals inscribed on the stones of Pictland as well as the work of Irish stonemasons. The skill and excellence of the workmanship postulates an experienced scribe, and strongly suggests a well-established *scriptorium*. If the book was produced in Northumbria, and if Dr Luce's view of the Celtic tonsure on the man-symbol is accepted, it must have been written between 635, when the Irish mission arrived, and 664, after which the Celtic tonsure was abandoned in Northumbria. This allows a generation in which to establish a flourishing *scriptorium*, manned by scribes who must have been trained in Iona or some other Irish monastery. If, however, the book dates from *c.* 625 to *c.* 650, as Dr Luce argues, or as early as 650, as Mr Bruce-Mitford now allows, the possibility of its being written in the Northumbrian kingdom declines, though it is by no means eliminated. On the other hand, an Irishman who had spent some time in Northumbria and had travelled in Pictland could have returned to Ireland and written the book at one of the great *scriptoria* there, possibly at Durrow, as Dr Luce thinks most likely. Irishmen had been sent to Rome in 630, after the Synod of Mag Léna near Durrow, to obtain further information on the Easter question; and from Rome they might have brought back a copy of the Vulgate.[1] Nor should Iona, founded in 563, not long after Durrow, be neglected as a possible origin for the Gospel Book, for scribes of Iona must have been accessible to artistic influence from Ireland, Pictland, and England. But whether the manuscript was produced in Ireland, Iona, or Northumbria, it shows what a seventh-century scribe of Irish training could do, combining elements of east Mediterranean, continental, Celtic, and Germanic origin.

If Ireland was in close relations with the Continent throughout the seventh century, why was her ecclesiastical organization not

---

[1] The Paschal Letter addressed to Ségéne of Iona and Beccán the Hermit, which may have been written by Cummian abbot of Durrow and certainly after the return from Rome, uses the Vulgate in the majority of its quotations from scripture, but the Old Latin version in a number of well-known passages which would be read constantly in the Divine Offices. Luce, *Durm.*, p. 13. On the authorship of the letter see *infra*, p. 105.

H

more decisively affected by continental patterns? Possibly the eclecticism of Irish contacts may suggest part of the answer. In England Irish missionaries met a church founded under papal initiative, in Gaul they became familiar with the Benedictine Rule; but the Spanish church does not seem to have been in close touch with the papacy, and the Benedictine Rule had gained no popularity there. The Celtic church had earlier been the pupil of Gaul, but in the seventh century Celtic missionaries probably saw themselves as the teachers rather than the learners. The Irish inclination was towards independence and lack of universal authority, and the variety of their contacts probably served to strengthen as much as to combat their own tendencies. Relations with England and the Continent in the seventh century matured Irish scholarship and Irish art; as we shall see, they forced the Irish to consider certain liturgical peculiarities, and perhaps they strengthened some churchmen's support of episcopal authority; but they did not prevent the peculiar institutional development of the Irish church.

CHAPTER 10

Seventh-century controversies

When Irish clergy travelled abroad and made any stay in Gaul or England the Celtic peculiarity which was most troublesome to their hosts was their date for celebrating Easter. They were doctrinally orthodox, they were exceptionally devout: no fault could be found in the early seventh century on these grounds. Even their other oddities, such as a distinctive tonsure, episcopal consecration by one bishop, or bishops without jurisdiction, were less immediately important than the celebration of Easter at a time different from that observed by Christians elsewhere. So when conflict arose, it was on this issue.

This problem was no new one.[1] The Christian church had not found it easy to determine the proper date of Easter, and during the first centuries one new set of calculations after another was devised. The Gaulish Council of Arles (314) had enjoined unity, according to Roman direction;[2] the Council of Nicaea (325) seems to have preferred the Alexandrine to the Roman system of computation, although the church of Rome announced to the world the date ascertained by Alexandria.[3] The Nicene Council condemned the practices of the Quartodecimans, who kept Easter on the date of the Jewish Passover, but the controversy as to the correct date was by no means resolved.[4] The liturgical practices of the Christian church varied considerably from one area to another, and the Popes, though they normally followed the Alexandrine computists in their Easter reckoning, never gave formal approval to any one cycle. Even as late as the sixth century, the practice of the continental church in the west was not uniform. In 577, for example, the Victorian–Latin calculations gave 18

---

[1] See Hughes, 'The Celtic Church and the Papacy.'

[2] Hefele, *Histoire des Conciles*, I. 1. 280–1.

[3] Ibid., I. 1. 466.

[4] P. Grosjean, *Ciel et Terre*, lxxviii (1962), 1–11, and Jones, *Bedae Opera de Temporibus*, Chapters 4 and 5.

April as the date of Easter, the Dionysian–Alexandrine gave 25 April, while the Spanish church observed Easter on 21 March.[1] At the end of that century the Gallican bishops supported the cycle of Victorius, while Pope Gregory I seems to have been following Dionysian calculations.

The Celtic cycle differed from both of these, but until the seventh century Celtic clerics seem to have been untroubled by the diversity of practice. Why should they be? The church had endured such problems for centuries, and the popes had made no clear official pronouncement. 'Let Gaul, I beg, contain us side by side, whom the kingdom of Heaven shall contain,' writes Columbanus to the Gallican synod.[2] To him, even in the midst of the Easter controversy, there were matters which seemed of far greater importance in the life of the church than liturgical diversity.[3]

Yet in the late sixth and seventh century the attitude of the western church on this question was changing. At this time most of the western church based its Easter calculations on one of two sets of Easter tables, and both happened to give identical dates during much of that period,[4] while the Celtic calculations gave dates blatantly dissimilar from those practised elsewhere.[5] The Columban monasteries in Gaul, the *paruchia Fursei*, and, above all, the Iona mission to the English brought the Celtic church into close contact with continental practices. A party grew up within the church, which regarded diversity on the Easter question not as a matter of church discipline, but almost as a matter of faith. Nonconformity became a sin.

This, as far as we can judge, was not the attitude of the popes. Gregory I, to whom Columbanus appealed in his dispute with the Merovingian bishops, seems to have made no reply,[6] for the Papal Register records none. Gregory, caught between the Irish and Frankish systems, of neither of which he approved, may have

[1] C. W. Jones, *Speculum*, ix (1934), 412, note 3.
[2] Walker, *Opera*, p. 16.   [3] Ibid., pp. 12–24, 8.
[4] Jones, *Bedae De Temp.*, p. 103.   [5] Grosjean, *A.B.*, lxiv (1946), 203.
[6] The ninth-century *Vita S. Sadalbergae* (ed. B. Krusch, *M.G.M. Script. Rer. Merov.*, v. 52) claims that Gregory *melliflua remisit scripta*, but the author seems elsewhere to have mis-read Columbanus' letter, and his late and vague reference carries little weight against the silence of the Register.

deliberately decided on a discreet silence. Pope Honorius I (625–38) 'earnestly warned (the Irish) not to imagine that their little community isolated at the uttermost ends of the earth, had a monopoly of wisdom over all the ancient and new churches throughout the world; and he asked them not to keep a different Easter, contrary to the paschal calculations and synodical decrees of all the bishops of the world'.[1] Honorius' letter was thus one of exhortation and advice. John IV, writing as pope-elect in 640, seems to have been misinformed about the Irish, whom he mistakenly believed to be Quartodecimans.[2] Since Quartodeciman views had already been condemned, John speaks of their practices as 'heresy . . . contrary to the orthodox faith'.[3] This is the only known occasion when a pope condemned Irish Easter practice as heresy, and since John is condemning views which the Irish did not hold, his condemnation may be dismissed.

Irish and English *Romani* were less moderate. Cummian,[4] writing to Ségéne abbot of Iona and Beccán the hermit,[5] in an attempt to bring them over to the Roman observance, is much

---

[1] Bede, *H.E.* II. 19. Bede, writing a century later, had the texts of these letters.

[2] *H.E.* ed. Plummer, ii. 114.

[3] *H.E.* II. 19. Bede says that John went on to explain 'the proper calculation of Easter', but he omits this part of the papal letter.

[4] Cummian has usually been thought to be abbot of Durrow. Four of the five ecclesiastics whom he consults are from other North Munster houses (the fifth is from Clonmacnois); their place of meeting is Mag Léna, the plain on which Durrow stands; the abbot of Durrow, as a member of the *paruchia* of Columcille, would be a proper person to address the abbot of Iona on this controversy. But the identification is not certain. See M. Maloney, *N. Munst. Ant. Jrnl.*, ix (1964), 103, who points out that the names Cummene and Laidcenn appear on a slab four miles north-west of Cahir.

[5] The letter is edited by Migne, *P.L.*, lxxxvii, cols. 969–78. It has been studied by the late Canon Oulton, whose edition of it was never completed, but who has written briefly in *Studia Patristica*, i, Pt. 1 (1955), 128–33. The letter followed an Irish mission of inquiry, which internal evidence proves must have been sent to Rome in 631. Ségéne ruled Iona from 623 to 652 (*A.U.*). The Irishmen were in Rome at Easter, when their practice differed from that of other Christians by a whole month. The only two occasions when this occurred during Ségéne's abbacy were 631 and 642. Bede, writing a century later, tells us that in the time of Aidan bishop of Lindisfarne (635–51) the northern Irish kept Easter according to the Celtic usage, but the southern Irish had conformed (*H.E.* III. 3). It looks as if southern conformity had been achieved before 640, since the letter sent by the pope elect John in that year was addressed to a group of northern abbots (*H.E.* II. 19).

disturbed by a text which he has discovered 'excommunicating and expelling from the church and anathematizing those who come against the canonical statutes of the four apostolic sees (of Rome, Jerusalem, Antioch, and Alexandria) when these agree on the unity of Easter'.[1] It is on this decision, in particular, that he has sought the opinion of his fellow-ecclesiastics, the heirs of Ailbe of Emly, Ciarán of Clonmacnois, Brendan of either Birr or Clonfert, Nessan of Mungret, and Lugaid of Clonfertmulloe.[2]

He writes with bitterness of the abbot who betrayed the decision which the group first reached at Mag Léna, to keep Easter in the following year with the universal church. 'Not long after, there arose a certain whited wall, pretending that he maintained the traditions of the elders, who divided instead of making both one, and in part made void what was promised; whom God, as I hope, will smite in whatever way he wishes.'[3] When the Easter question was debated in Northumbria, according to Bede's account of the Synod of Whitby (663 or 664), the spokesman of the Roman party regarded conformity as a matter of belief. 'If you and your fellows, having heard the decrees of the apostolic see, nay, of the universal church, confirmed as they are by the sacred scriptures, if you scorn to follow them, without any doubt, you sin.'[4] The seventh-century *Romani* were treating the Celtic peculiarities of liturgical practice as the church had once treated the Quartodecimans.[5]

[1] *P.L.*, lxxxvii, col. 972 B.C. Had he met some condemnation of the Quartodecimans? I have not identified his source.

[2] *quid sentirent de excommunicatione nostra, a supradictis sedibus apostolicis facti.* col. 977 A.

[3] Col. 977 B. The 'whited wall' may be the abbot of Clonmacnois (or his representative, as not all the abbots were present in person), since the abbot of Clonmacnois, who was represented at the Synod, was later among the northern recalcitrants addressed by pope-elect John in 640.

[4] *H.E.* III. 25. This point is reiterated by Aldhelm in his letter to Geraint, Haddan, and Stubbs, *Councils*. iii. 272.

[5] If much later sources can be trusted, the violence was not confined to the *Romani*. *A. Tig.*, s.a. 635, speak of the 'flight of Carthage (*alias* Mochuda) from Rahan *in diebus pasce*'. A twelfth-century saga-type narrative describes how Mochuda was driven from his monastery at Rahan on the borders of Munster and Meath by a group of northern abbots, and fled southwards to found a new house at Lismore in southern Munster. There may be some tradition here of Easter quarrels.

Cummian's main concern was with the unity of the church. He fears to be 'cut off from the universal catholic church, to whom has been given by God the power of binding and loosing'.[1] The Hebrews, Greeks, Latins, and Egyptians are agreed; only the Britons and Scots stand out, these peoples 'who are almost at the ends of the earth, and, as I might say, a pimple on the chin of the world'.[2] 'What thing more perverse,' asks Cummian, 'can be felt of the church than if we say, "Rome is wrong, Jerusalem is wrong, Antioch is wrong, the whole world is wrong: only the Scots and the Britons know what is right?" '[3]

Cummian did not succeed in persuading Ségéne of Iona to join the Roman observance. The churches of southern Ireland seem to have come over in the 630s, but northern Ireland did not conform until shortly before Adamnán's death in 704,[4] while Iona and the *paruchia Columbae* in Scotland and Ireland held out until 716,[5] approximately the time when Roman practices reached the Pictish kingdom. When Bede wrote his Ecclesiastical History in 731 all Ireland, Scotland, Pictland, and the kingdom of the North Britons had conformed; Wales held out until 768, the most obdurate of all the Celtic areas.

The dispute over the date of Easter was not the only controversy which troubled the seventh-century church. Celtic clerics were also distinguished from Roman usages by their tonsure. But this matter caused less bitterness than the paschal question.[6] The tonsure received comparatively little publicity in Ireland, though the Roman tonsure was enjoined in the synods of the *Romani*.[7] In England after 664 the Celtic manner of consecration was discontinued; Wilfrid went to the Continent for consecration, and Chad was reconsecrated. The *Collectio Canonum Hibernensis* quotes continental authorities forbidding the consecration of a bishop by only

[1] Col. 974 A.
[2] Col. 972 D. Cummian seems to be paraphrasing Honorius' letter, *H.E.* II. 19.
[3] Col. 974 D.   [4] *H.E.* V. 15.
[5] *A.U.*, possibly based on Bede, *H.E.* V. 22. But the same chapter may suggest that the dispute was not settled at Iona until shortly before Ecgberht's death in 729.
[6] For discussion see Gougaud, *Christianity*, pp. 204–5.
[7] *Coll.* L. 11.

one bishop;[1] and the Book of Armagh records Patrick's anger at the ordination of clergy without his sanction,[2] but this question would be of less importance in the Irish church, where bishops had no powers of jurisdiction, than it was in England.

In Ireland the Easter controversy was active for almost the whole of the century. What was its significance in society? First of all, it should be clearly understood that Bede is in no way typical of Irish opinion on the Paschal controversy. Bede had a scholarly passion for accuracy, and a high regard for order and uniformity, while computation as a branch of chronology was his own field of study. Such a combination of qualities makes for dogmatism. No Irishman had comparable knowledge, or a comparable attitude to evidence, while the Irishman's background led him to expect diversity rather than uniformity. Monastic practice differed from house to house; in church organization the territorial bishop still survived in the seventh century beside the monastic *paruchia*; there was no metropolitan see to secure unity of observance. The Irish attitude is expressed by Columbanus' plea for the toleration of divergent practices,[3] or by the words attributed to Fintan Munnu, the Celtic spokesman at another synod held on the Easter question in south-eastern Ireland at about the same time as that of Mag Léna, 'Therefore let each of us do what he believes, and as seems to him right.'[4] Tolerance of liturgical diversity was already a rather old-fashioned attitude in the seventh-century continental church.

Some Irishmen, as we have seen, campaigned for uniform observance. Nevertheless, it took about a century before all the Scotti had come into the Roman unity, whereas in Northumbria the matter was settled in one generation. A powerful royal authority hurried on the decision in Northumbria: the absence of such authority among the Irish is yet another indication of their natural acceptance of division. There is no evidence that the controversy, long-drawn-out as it was, raised anything like the same bitterness in Ireland as it did in England. If the later record con-

[1] *Coll.* I. 4b, 5a.
[2] *Arm.* 9a, 1. Cf. MS. Cotton Otto E xiii, transl. Bieler, *Works*, p. 48.
[3] Walker, p. 16.
[4] *Acta SS. Hib. ex Cod. Sal.*, col. 411. Synod of Mag Ailbe.

tained in the *Cáin Adamnáin* is correct it did not prevent responsible ecclesiastics from getting together in 697 and agreeing to a law aimed at the protection of non-combatants and church property from acts of violence,[1] a law which is not concerned in any way with the Easter controversy, and which was reputed to have been signed by clerics who had been *Romani* for decades, those who joined the Roman observance round about this time, and those who held to Celtic practices for another twenty years.[2] The clarity and dogmatism of English views on the Easter question may be fairly represented by Bede and Aldhelm, but Irish views are represented by the Litany of Pilgrim Saints, compiled about 800, where the *Romani* are invoked, along with anchorites, voyagers, Gauls, Britons, and 'dogheads', in a document which could never have come from the pen of an Englishman.[3] It is worth noting also that when Suibne King of Uí Bairrche (a supporter of the Roman party) speaks at the south-eastern Synod of Mag Ailbe against Munnu, the Celtic leader, he is rebuked by Laisrén, Munnu's opponent and leader of Suibne's own group.[4] This is not a contemporary account, but it serves to show the spirit in which the dispute was remembered in Ireland, at least in some circles.

There is in fact no early evidence whatever of bitterness among the conservative party.[5] The Anglo-Saxon Ecgberht, firm

---

[1] The tract is not older than the eighth century. The list of attendant prelates and kings must be based on older records, but there are a few anachronisms.

[2] It is often claimed that the northern Irish churches (except for the *paruchia* of Columcille) came over to Roman practice at the Synod of Birr (697). This may be so. All we *know* is that Adamnán celebrated Easter in northern Ireland in 704 according to Roman practice. *H.E.* V. 15: 'He corrected their ancient error and restored nearly all those who were not under the jurisdiction of Iona to catholic unity, teaching them to observe Easter at the proper time. Having observed the canonical Easter in Ireland, he returned to his own island', where he died 'before the end of the year came round' (on 23 September, 704). This does not suggest to me that a final decision was made in 697 at a big ecclesiastical synod, though the matter may have been aired then.

[3] Hughes, *A.B.*, lxxvii (1959), 305–31.

[4] *AA SS. ex Cod. Sal.*, col. 410.

[5] Cf. Mrs Chadwick, *Age of the Saints*, p. 141: 'A new situation had arisen as the result of the Roman challenge. A "literature of the subject" was needed by the "case for the defence", both for the information of the adherents of their

supporter of the Roman party, spent most of his life among the
Scotti. He was one of those Anglo-Saxon nobles who went to
Ireland for study, supported by Irish generosity;[1] as a young man
of twenty-five he almost died there in the plague of 664. He remained in Ireland until his old age, 'indefatigable in teaching',[2]
and moved to Iona some time before 715, where he succeeded in
converting the *paruchia* of Columcille to the Roman observance.
Even the community of Iona, the most conservative of all the
Irish on the Easter issue, 'had not lost the fervent grace of
charity'.[3]

The only evidence of bitterness in Ireland which we have comes
not from the conservatives but, as might be expected, from the
reforming *Romani*; and even Cummian's thrusts are mild when
compared with the strictures of Aldhelm. In Ireland the Easter
controversy was nothing like so sharp and decisive as it was in
England. The conformity of the Northern Half was probably
generally achieved during the second half of the seventh century,
without dramatic flourishes. And whereas in England the effects
of the dispute were immediate and obvious, in Ireland the effects
were indirect and ill-defined, though of far-reaching importance.

own party and also for propaganda against the Romanizing party, which was
felt to be threatening cherished traditional usages with annihilation.' I do not
know of any such literature.

[1] H.E. III. 27. Chad was another (ibid., IV. 3); Chad, who humbly offered
to resign his bishopric when told by Theodore that his Celtic consecration
(in which two British bishops of the Roman party had taken part, III. 28)
was invalid. (IV. 2).

[2] III. 27. Mrs Chadwick, *Celt and Saxon*, pp. 203–4, makes the interesting
suggestion that Ecgberht may have spent some of his time at Mayo, in the
Anglo-Saxon community there, and that his presence may partly account for
the reputation of the monastery.

[3] H.E. III. 4. The report of Bede, writing as a convinced Roman adherent
in 731, of events which took place in 716.

Armagh's claims to archiepiscopal authority

Throughout the seventh century foreign and native influences were both at work in the church. The original diocesan bishops had been established according to the continental pattern, and the Easter controversy ended with the apparent triumph of 'Roman' opinion; yet in the seventh century the monastic *paruchiae* were flourishing, with their Irish notions of overlordship and their quite different arrangement of jurisdiction. As we have already seen, Armagh was making strong efforts in the later seventh century to build up for herself a *paruchia* of monastic type, with the coarb of Patrick as overlord.

Yet Armagh was not satisfied that her coarb should be one of many: her lawyers were claiming precedence for the heir of Patrick, and expressing their claims according to the concepts of native law. The highest status is accorded to Patrick and his heirs in the Book of the Angel, a claim with far-reaching implications, for in Irish law a man's status conditioned his obligations and duties, the amount of protection he could offer, the extent to which he could act as surety, the degree of hospitality or compensation he could expect. Patrick was *dux principalis omnibus Hiberionacum gentibus*,[1] while the status of his heir is indicated by the fact that he 'overswears all churches and their rulers',[2] since the oath of a man of higher rank is deemed in Irish law to override a contradictory oath by any inferior person.[3] The church of Armagh was to be *summa*, and to take precedence (*praeest*) over all the churches and monasteries of the Irish.[4]

As the over-king in Irish society exercised his authority by claiming tribute from his subordinate kings,[5] so the saint's heir had the right to tribute from the monasteries of his *paruchia*. Armagh, however, claimed a special tax (*peculiare censuum*) on all

[1] *Arm.* 21 a 1, *Tr. Life*, p. 353.   [2] *Arm.* 21 a 2.
[3] Binchy, *C.G.*, p. 99.   [4] *Arm.* 21 a 2, *Tr. Life*, p. 354.
[5] Binchy, *Early Irish Society*, p. 54.

the free churches and all the monasteries of the land.[1] She was asserting ecclesiastical suzerainty as 'highbishop' much as the Uí Néill kings of Tara were claiming suzerainty over other provincial kings.[2]

The Armagh lawyers were concerned with the honour due to the coarb of Patrick as ecclesiastical overlord when they tried to determine the amount of hospitality due to him. It was customary for members of the upper classes of Irish society to be accompanied on their journeys by a retinue suited to their rank. *Crith Gablach* lays down that a bishop conducting a visitation in the interests of church and polity (*tuath*) is to be accompanied by twelve men, who have the right to hospitality: the petty king commands a similar retinue, and the number is so limited because 'the *tuath* cannot bear the retinues of a king or bishop if they are always battening on it'.[3]

The Book of the Angel gives two discordant statements on the coarb's right to hospitality. In the first, he is to have 'worthy and suitable hospitality' for himself and his company 'to the number of fifty'.[4] This number is already considerably higher than the retinue of the bishop or petty king in *Crith Gablach*. The second, and much longer statement, gives the coarb's retinue as a hundred, to whom 'suitable hospitality' is to be provided, with fodder for their draught-beasts. Should anyone refuse hospitality, he will be liable to a fine of seven *ancillae*, or to seven years of penance.[5] In Irish law the refusal of hospitality which was rightfully demanded led to a fine equivalent to the honour-price of the person refused.[6] Hospitality for a retinue of a hundred must have been almost impossible to obtain, and it is worth noting that whereas there is a wide difference between the demands made for the petty king in *Crith Gablach* and those made for the coarb of Patrick in the *Book of the Angel*, the fine for refusal in the *Book of the Angel* is equal to the honour price of a petty king in *Crith Gablach*.[7] One wonders

---

[1] *Arm.* 21 a 1.   [2] See Binchy, 'Patrick', p. 61.
[3] Binchy, *C.G.*, lines 598–602. A later gloss on one of the tracts in the *Senchas Már* (*A.L.I.* i. 48) shows that even the 'brewy' with the ever-full cauldron does not have to entertain a company of more than twelve.
[4] *Arm.* 21 a 1.   [5] *Arm.* 21 b 1.
[6] Binchy, *C.G.*, p. 77.   [7] *C.G.*, p. 104.

whether the Armagh lawyers made their excessive claims to hospitality mainly for show, to demonstrate the superior dignity of Patrick's heir over all other ecclesiastics.

The Book of the Angel elsewhere suggests that Armagh lawyers recognized that the claims to authority which they were making were not entirely in accordance with the contemporary facts. Although the angel grants to Patrick 'all the tribes of the Irish by way of *paruchia*', Patrick foresees that many Christians will follow him who will need dioceses; so he offers to 'share in common the gift of abundance indisputably given to me by God with the perfect religious of Ireland, so that both I and they may enjoy in peace the riches of the bounty of God'.[1] Thus, the scribe establishes Armagh's original rights, while recognizing that they have been regranted to others. Tírechán, we have already seen,[2] made it clear that Armagh did not in fact hold all the properties she claimed: in his work Iona and Clonmacnois appear as her major rivals. The Book of the Angel shows that Brigit also held her independent *paruchia*.

> Between S. Patrick and Brigit, the pillars of the Irish, such friendship of charity dwelt that they had one heart and one mind. Christ performed many miracles through him and her.
> The holy man therefore said to the Christian virgin: 'O my Brigit, your *paruchia* in your province will be reckoned unto you for your monarchy: but in the eastern and western part it will be in my domination'.[3]

Presumably this means that Armagh recognized Kildare's claims to *paruchia* all over the central part of Leinster. There were churches connected with Patrick's fellow-missionaries and later supporters in west Leinster, Killashee (with Auxilius), Kilcullen (with Iserninus and Mac-Táil), and Sletty (with Aed), while Patrick was said to have founded churches in Uí Garrchon on the eastern seaboard of Leinster.[4] Armagh would not forego her claims to sovereignty in these areas, but she recognized the area

---

[1] *Tr. Life*, p. 353, *Arm.* ff. 20 b 2, 21 a 1.

[2] *Supra*, p. 88.

[3] *Arm.* ff. 21 b 2 and 22 a 1. Cf. Bieler, 'The Celtic Hagiographer', *Studia Patristica*, v (1962), 252.

[4] Known from later sources, *Tr. Life* and the glosses to Fiacc's Hymn.

of central Leinster as under Brigit's authority and exempt from Patrick's universal claims.

Thus, the Armagh lawyers were attempting to define an authority for their own *princeps* over the Irish church which was analogous to the authority exercised by the highest overlord over his subordinate kings. Yet Armagh was able to profit from Roman as well as from native ideas of ecclesiastical government. The claims of Armagh to superior honour are partly based on the presence of relics which may well have come from Rome – relics of 'Peter and Paul, Stephen, Lawrence et cetera'[1] and the Irish church had never forgotten that it was Pope Celestine who had dispatched their first bishop.[2] From early times Rome had claimed to act as an appeal court for Christendom, a claim to which, in the seventh century, Armagh gave explicit legal recognition. The Book of the Angel envisages a hierarchy of courts, with Rome as the apex: if disputes cannot be settled at home they must be referred 'to the apostolic see, that is, to the chair of the apostle Peter, which has authority in the city of Rome'.[3]

The hierarchy thus established, Armagh lawyers place their own church court immediately beneath that of the pope and above all other Irish courts.

> Whatever difficult cause shall arise, one unknown to all the judges of the tribes of the Irish, it shall rightly be referred to the *cathedra* of the Irish archbishop, i.e. Patrick, and to the examination of that bishop.[4]

Only if the case cannot be settled there is it to be referred to Rome. Moreover, any action against Patrick's *familia* or *paruchia*, or any insult to his *insignia*, is to be tried by the bishop of Armagh, 'all other judgements notwithstanding'.[5] The legal position of Armagh, as stated in the Book of the Angel, is an amalgam of native and Roman concepts, in which the claims of the native lawyers are supported by the authority of Rome. The bishop of Armagh is called not only *pontifex* and *praesul*, but *archiepiscopus*,[6] a title accorded, Bede tells us, to the bishop of Canterbury, who was granted authority by Pope Gregory over 'all the bishops of

---

[1] *Arm.* 21 a 2.
[2] Walker, *Opera*, p. 38.
[3] *Arm.* 21 b 2.
[4] *Arm.* 21 b 2.
[5] *Arm.* 21 b 2.
[6] *Arm.* 21 a 1, 21 b 2.

the Britains'.[1] And Armagh's jurisdiction over the church on earth is merely the image of her patron's authority in heaven, for Patrick is to 'judge all the Irish in the great day of terrible judgement in the presence of Christ'.[2]

Armagh's claims to a Roman-type jurisdiction seem to have been made (or possibly revived) during the period of the Easter controversy. Historians have for long seen a significant connexion between the two developments. There were seventh-century Irish churchmen of the party of the *Romani* who regarded Patrick as one of themselves. Cummian, propagator of the Roman Easter in the 630s, in his letter to Iona speaks of Patrick as *papa noster*[3] and the scribe of the *Book of Armagh* copied down some rather cryptic phrases (probably dating from the period of the controversy) which seem to urge the church of the Irish to identify herself with the church of the Romans.[4] It is most likely that Aed, Bishop of Sletty in the Southern Half of Ireland (which had conformed to the Roman Easter in the early 630s) was already one of the *Romani* when he inspired his disciple Muirchú to write the Life of Patrick. It would therefore appear that some, at least, of the *Romani* were eager to recognize Patrick as their patron before Armagh conformed on the Easter question.

The date when Armagh conformed is obviously of importance. In 640 she was still following the old Celtic practices, for in that year John, pope-elect, wrote to a group of Irish bishops, priests, masters, and abbots urging them to conform to the Roman Easter, and Tómméne bishop of Armagh headed the list.[5] The pope-elect was able to address these conservative churchmen by name, and it is not likely that his informant made any mistake about the sympathies of the bishop of Armagh. All the churches of northern Ireland, with the exception of the *paruchia* of Columcille, had certainly conformed to the Roman Easter before the death of Adamnán in 704.[6] Armagh must therefore have changed

---

[1] *H.E.* I. 27, *Brittaniarum . . . omnes episcopos.*
[2] *Arm.* 21 b 1. [3] *P.L.,* lxxxvii, col. 975 C.
[4] *Arm.* 9 a 1. [5] *H.E.* II. 19.
[6] In *HE* V. 15, Bede speaks as if the conformity of the 'majority of the Scotti' was not secured until shortly before 704. But elsewhere he had said that the southern Irish conformed much earlier, and he had mentioned the long residence of Ecgberht in Ireland. It seems likely that the process of

her position between 640 and 704. Muirchú wrote his Life of
Patrick during the lifetime of Aed of Sletty, who died, according
to the Annals of Ulster, in 700. Aed belonged to the Southern
Half of Ireland, which had conformed in the 630s, and he was
almost certainly one of the *Romani*: his disciple Muirchú had
access not only to a copy of S. Patrick's Confession but also to a
considerable amount of material on the founding of Armagh and
on Patrick's activity in the north-east. Such material would most
probably be supplied by the Armagh authorities, and suggests
that Armagh and Aed of Sletty were in sympathy. Moreover, Aed
joined the *paruchia Patricii* while Ségéne was bishop of Armagh.
Ségéne's death is recorded in the year 688. It is hardly likely that
Aed, a southern bishop and therefore of the *Romani*, would attach
himself to Armagh if the two churches differed on so important
an issue as the dating of Easter. It would therefore seem that
Armagh had conformed before 688.

Zimmer suggests that Aed's 'bequest' may have been intended
as a bribe to encourage the bishop of Armagh to join the *Romani*,
an aim which was finally achieved in 697.[1] Moreover, he sees the
Patrick legend as invented by an Irish member of the Roman
party: Muirchú and his master Aed, both southern *Romani*,
intended that the new Life of Patrick should win over the north
to the Roman observance. The bishop of Armagh was finally
persuaded into the Roman unity by 'the prospect of rising to the
rank of a metropolitan in the Irish church'. Thus, the relationship
between the Easter controversy and the growing claims of
Armagh becomes that of direct cause and effect.

Was the purpose of Muirchú's Life to provide propaganda for
the Roman unity? If so, we should expect the author to give
prominence to the question of conformity to the Roman Easter.
A long section of Muirchú's Life is taken up with an account of
Patrick's contests with the representatives of paganism. This

---

conversion was a gradual one, and that the culminating events in Ireland did
not take place until Adamnán's time. Bede was not intimately concerned with
the details of Irish affairs, and such a view is consistent with the evidence he
gives.

[1] H. Zimmer, *The Celtic Church in Britain and Ireland*, transl. A. Meyer, London, p. 82.

section seems to hang together: it is rather rhetorical in style, and may be influenced by some native saga.[1] It brings Patrick to Tara, *caput Scotorum*, in the reign of Lóegaire, *imperator barbarorum*, the son of Niall, 'who is the ancestor of the royal stock of almost the whole of this island'.[2] The narrative is dramatic, and fire is a feature of it,[3] but the central incident concerns the triumph of Patrick's Easter fire over the fire lighted by the druids at Tara. Professor Binchy has shown good reason for believing that the setting of this story is completely artificial: that the pagan fire ritual to which it refers was associated with the feast of Beltaine (Mayday), and that there is no evidence that any fire cult was practised at Tara.[4] The author was determined to show Patrick in triumph at Tara; he was also determined to place his tale in the time of Easter.

The theme of the story is the conquest of paganism. It starts with a prophecy which

> foretold the coming of a certain foreign religion, in the manner of a kingdom, with a certain strange and harmful doctrine, brought from a long distance across the seas, proclaimed by a few, accepted by the many, and honoured by all; one that would overturn kingdoms, slay kings that resist it, lead away multitudes, destroy all their gods, and, having cast down all the resources of their art, reign for ever and ever.

Patrick's purpose in coming to Tara at Easter time is to drive 'the unconquered wedge' (i.e. the celebration of Christ's resurrection) into 'the head of all heathenism and idolatry'. There is nothing in this whole episode about the only point in dispute among seventh-century Christians, the *date* of the festival; it is the place, as the

---

[1] Edited by J. Gwynn, *L.A.*, 3–16, 39–40, *Tr. Life*, pp. 269–300, 494–8. Transl. N. J. D. White, *St Patrick his Writings and Life*, London, 1920. The relevant section in White's translation is cc. x–xxi.

[2] *Arm.* 2 a 2.

[3] Episode 1, the burning of Miliucc; Episode 2, the druid's fire versus Patrick's paschal fire; Episode 3, the death of a druid; Episode 4, the escape of Patrick, first by supernatural darkness, then by shape-shifting; Episode 5, the conversion of the poet Dubthach; Episode 6, contests of Patrick and the druid, by the cup, by snow, by water, and by fire; Episode 7, Patrick's prophecy concerning Lóegaire's race.

[4] *Ériu*, xviii. 128–30.

I

heart of heathenism, that is emphasized. This sequence contributes nothing to the paschal controversy, and had Muirchú intended it to do so, he would surely have inserted some phrase defining on which day of the moon Easter was held, or which cycle Patrick used to determine the festival. The moral is the downfall of the old druidical order at Tara, and the victory of the new *magus*.

This does not mean that the setting of the saga was accidental. Muirchú had a good story to tell, rather similar in some ways to the story of Elijah on Mount Carmel defeating the prophets of Baal. The May-day feast, and the sites of Uisnech and Tlachtga which are associated with fire ritual in Irish traditions will not suit Muirchú's purposes. He (or his original) set the story at Tara because he wanted to show the source of the Uí Néill power recognizing the authority of Patrick. And he set it at Easter rather than Beltaine because Easter was a subject of topical interest. The intrinsic dramatic quality of the story must have been heightened by the political and ecclesiastical undertones. But the story was not created as direct propaganda for the *Romani*, to advocate their paschal dating. It is, rather, a popular echo of a highly technical subject which was being discussed at high levels in the church at that time.[1] It tells us nothing about the Easter controversy except that it was a matter of current interest.

Thus, an essential part of the evidence to support Zimmer's argument is missing. The purpose of Muirchú was not primarily to write propaganda for the Roman Easter, though his Life was composed during the period of the controversy. In the central chapters he was concerned to show Christianity triumphing over the old order of the druids, and S. Patrick accepted by the Uí Néill dynasty of Tara. Whereas Armagh had at first been part of Ulster, her future development was to be closely associated with the growing power of the Uí Néill. The Book appended to Muir-

---

[1] Kenney, p. 333, n. 137, says that 'the prominence given to Easter reflects the controversy on the observance of that festival'. Bury, *St Patrick*, p. 262, makes exactly the same point. Binchy, *Ériu*, xviii, 130, says the story has been 'built around the victory of the paschal fire over its pagan congenor'. Zimmer, *Celtic Church*, p. 81, seems to be making a much more far-reaching claim than any of these.

chú's Life of Patrick emphasizes Muirchú's concern with the Uí Néill by the contrast it provides, for the interests of Ulster are given more attention in the second book, where the scribe attempts to reconcile the various traditions of the saint's burial. Muirchú reflects both the contemporary controversy over Easter and the changing political allignments of the period.

Although we cannot accept Zimmer's suggestion that Muirchú wrote his Life and his master Aed made his 'bequest' primarily to draw Armagh into the party of the *Romani*, these events may be less directly connected. In the later seventh century the Armagh lawyers were rethinking their position in accordance with current ecclesiastical and political developments. Armagh had been founded as a bishop's seat near to the ancient capital of Ulster, and although it is almost impossible to believe that she could have received any formal authority over other Irish bishoprics, her proximity to Emain Macha suggests a position of acknowledged eminence. But the western boundaries of Ulster shrank, and Armagh came within the orbit of the Uí Néill tribes: meanwhile monastic *paruchiae* were established and rapidly expanding. Armagh therefore needed both to assert a connexion with the Uí Néill and to build up a *paruchia* of monastic type. The triumph of the *Romani* in southern Ireland and in Northumbria, and their willingness to acknowledge bishop Patrick as their *papa*, provided Armagh with an opportunity to re-assert her claims to leadership. In the hierarchy of Roman courts Armagh could place herself directly beneath the papal curia, and in a Roman-type organization her bishop might secure the authority of a metropolitan.

Such questions must have been constantly debated at Armagh, at least from 640 onwards, and both the 'Irish' and the 'Roman' legal traditions are reflected in the Book of the Angel. Armagh lawyers were determined to extend the authority of their church, by using any arguments which circumstances offered; yet although they were prepared to urge archiepiscopal claims and recognize Rome as an appeal court, the main emphasis of the Book of the Angel is upon an ecclesiastical overlordship which is much closer to native than to Roman traditions. Perhaps the *Romani* sought in the heir of S. Patrick a metropolitical authority which the church of Armagh was happy to encourage. But some of the Armagh

lawyers understood the strength of native governmental traditions, and were anxious to establish a native-type overlordship.
Events were to prove the victory of the *Romani* more apparent
than real, for a Roman-type archbishop remained a theory, while,
by the eighth century, the ecclesiastical superiority of Armagh
was beginning to secure wider recognition.

III. MATURITY

CHAPTER 12

Irish canonists and the secular law

The title of 'archbishop' accorded to the bishop of Armagh in the Book of the Angel was, in fact, interpreted as though it meant overlord, 'bishop over bishops', and corresponded to the Irish *rí ruirech*. All the same, many Irishmen of the late seventh and early eighth century must have understood the position of the contemporary continental or English bishop, and have compared it with Irish practices. While the *Romani* were persuading their countrymen to adopt Roman Easter observances, would they not also consider the difficult question of episcopal jurisdiction?

There is reason to believe that they did. So much is suggested by a collection of canons drawn up in the early eighth century, which is sorely in need of re-editing and further study.[1] It was compiled from both foreign and native enactments; from patristic writings, early church councils and papal decretals, and from rulings of the Welsh and Irish churches. The authorship of the collection is suggested by a colophon copied into one ninth-century manuscript, *Hucusq; nuben cucuiminiae du rinis*, which Thurneysen rendered, *Hucusque Ruben et Cú–Cuimine Iae et Dairinis*, 'Thus far Ruben of Dair-Inis and Cú-Chuimne of Iona'.[2] Since Ruben's death is recorded s.a. 725 and Cú-Chuimne's s.a. 747, and since no authors later than Theodore and Adamnán (died 704) are quoted, we may say that the collection was begun between 704 and 725 and finished before 747.

A number of the canons specifically legislate for a church governed by bishops. The bishop bears the image of Christ[3] and

---

[1] *Collectio Canonum Hibernensis* (abbreviated *Coll.*), ed. H. Wasserschleben, *Die irische Kanonensammlung*, Leipzig, 1885. See Kenney, pp. 247–50, H. Bradshaw, *The Early Collection of Canons Known as the Hibernensis*, and P. Fournier, 'De l'influence de la collection irlandaise sur la formation des collections canoniques', *Nouvelle revue hist. de droit français et étranger*, xxiii (1899), 27–78.

[2] 'Zur irischen Kanonensammlung', *Z.C.P.*, vi (1908), 1–5.

[3] *Coll.* I. 15.

123

is to be judged by God, not by men.[1] He is to be consecrated by more than one bishop with the consent of the clergy and laity,[2] and to be constantly with his own clergy, making judgements in their presence.[3] He administers church property, but as a trust and not as a private possession.[4] The bishop is responsible for affairs within his own diocese, and is not to intrude on the diocese of another bishop;[5] none of his own clergy may refer a case to secular judgement without his permission.[6] If a cleric thinks that his bishop has dealt with him unjustly he may refer his case to the synod.[7] Monks must be either cenobites living in a community under rule and in poverty or hermits or *inclusi*; *vagabundi* are condemned, who go running around among women, telling stories, living under no rule, and occupied with secular affairs.[8] All these rulings are quoted from foreign authorities, but they are consistent with the canons attributed to Patricius, Auxilius, and Iserninus. The *Collectio* also quotes a canon of this group forbidding the newcomer to build a church or exercise orders without the bishop's permission, and declaring anyone who looks for permission from laity or heathen to be himself *infidelis*.[9] Moreover, it attributes to Patrick a canon similar to that in the Book of the Angel, recognizing Rome as a supreme court.[10] The *Collectio* therefore includes a number of canons, most but not all from foreign sources, which relate to a church under episcopal jurisdiction.

But the administration of the Irish church in the early eighth century no longer conformed to this pattern. The monastic *paruchiae* of Columcille, Ciarán, and other saints were firmly established, and claims had been made on behalf of Patrick and Brigit to *paruchiae* similar in type. Much of the legislation on the bishop which is contained in the *Collectio* is thus inconsistent with Irish developments of the seventh century. In one case the *Collectio* repeats a canon of the Synod attributed to Patrick, Auxilius, and Iserninus, but with a significant verbal change. The canon, as it is written in *Pa.* I, reads:

[1] *Coll.* I. 16 a.
[2] *Coll.* I. 46, 5.
[3] *Coll.* I. 10 m.
[4] *Coll.* I. 10 o.
[5] *Coll.* XLIII. 2, I. 22 a, c.
[6] *Coll.* XXI. 27 b.
[7] *Coll.* X n.
[8] *Coll.* XXXIX. 3.
[9] *Coll.* XLIII. 4: *ab infidelibus aut laicis et non ab episcopo.* Cf. *Pa.* I. 24.
[10] *Coll.* XX. 5 b; *Arm.* 21 b 2.

If anyone has sought (anything) for captives in the tribe on his own authority, without permission, he deserves to be excommunicated.[1]

The other canons in the group make it absolutely clear that permission must come from the bishop.[2] A similar canon in the *Collectio* reads:

Patricius: if anyone has sought the redemption of a captive in the tribe on his own authority, without permission of the *abbot*, he deserves to be excommunicated.[3]

Though the canon entered in the *Collectio* is still attributed to Patrick, a scribe has altered it, perhaps without noticing, to conform with later conditions.

Yet the compilers of the *Collectio* were not completely antiquarian in their aims. The preface explains that they have tried to produce a brief and clear exposition of the canonical authorities from 'a great forest of writings', adding, omitting and editing, and inserting chapter headings for easy reference. This looks as if they intended their collection to be of practical use. The *Romani*, or the acts of the *Synodus Romana*, which they quote, also imply the existence of an episcopally administered church,[4] and nowhere suggest that the church is governed by abbots, though monasteries are flourishing. Bury argued convincingly that the acts attributed to the *Romani* were passed in Irish synods of the seventh century held in the interest of the Roman reform, though some of the canons were adopted from continental sources.[5] Some of the acts are specifically those of Romanizing Irishmen: for instance, the compilers not only forbid that cases shall be referred to other provinces but warn specifically against the Britons, 'who in all things are contrary, and cut themselves off from Roman custom and the unity of the church';[6] after discussing the origins and significance of the Petrine tonsure, they attribute to Gildas a similar insulting statement about British contrariness in the matter of the tonsure, and add that 'the Romans say' that the

---

[1] *Pa.* I. 1.

[2] E.g. *Pa.* I. 4–5. The whole group insists on the bishop's authority.

[3] *Coll.* XLII. 25 c. Cf. XLII. 26 a, also attributed to Patrick, which refers to the permission of the bishop.

[4] *Coll.* I. 8 b, XX. 3.

[5] *Life of S. Patrick*, pp. 237–9.   [6] *Coll.* XX. 6.

Britons derived their tonsure from Simon Magus, while in Ireland the native tonsure was first worn by the swine-herd of king Lóegaire.[1] Such canons give a clear indication of the sympathies of the men who passed them, and it may be significant that the *Romani* of the canons appear to have enacted no legislation which directly conflicts with the conception of an episcopally governed church. Could episcopal government and Roman liturgical practice have been two sides of the same coin in the eyes of some of the Roman supporters?

It is, however, clear from the *Collectio* that other Irish legislators of the seventh century belonged to the world of monastic *paruchiae*. The acts of the 'Irish Synod' (*Synodus Hibernensis*) which it quotes, acts which far outnumber those of the *Romani*, nowhere imply that they were drawn up for a church administered by diocesan bishops. On the contrary, there are many indications that the abbot controls the property of the church and directs its affairs. The bishop is mentioned once or twice, and commands the highest dignity;[2] nevertheless, it is the abbot who is regarded as the normal administrator. Even the word used to describe him would indicate this, for the *Synodus Hibernensis* often calls him not *abbas*, but *princeps*.[3] It is the abbot who controls church property and rights of burial.[4] One very interesting ruling shows that it is the abbot who governs affairs, even though the presence of bishops, dead or living, enhances the legal status of a church.[5] In the section *De locis* the quotations from the continental Synod of Orange (held in 441) and from the Canons attributed to Patrick,

[1] *Coll.* LII. 6.

[2] *Coll.* XLVIII. 5. For a theft committed upon a king or bishop, the penalty is 7 *ancillae* or 7 years of penance with a bishop or scribe. This repeats the ruling of *Canones Hibernenses* IV. 9, which adds the scribe to the protected class.

[3] *Si quis commendaverit animam suam . . . Deo et principi, id est abbati suo . . .* XVIII. 6 a. *Si qua contumacia inter principem et monachos ejus . . . orta sit,* XXXVII. 37. Cf. XXXVII. 35. *Omnes heretici, quamvis magnarum urbium principes sint . . . a cathedris suis consensu sinodi ejecti sunt.*

[4] *Coll.* XVIII. 7, XLIV. 20 b.

[5] *Coll.* XLII. 22. *Quicumque infantes in ecclesia Dei projiciunt ignorante abbate, si in ea episcopi sunt sepulti, aut praesentes sint, III annis et dimidio peniteant. Si vero homicidium in ea fecerint, VII annis peniteant. Unde hoc sumptum est, quod episcopus VII gradus habet et ecclesia septiformis est, si vero non habuerint episcopos, sed parva sit ecclesia, anno et dimidio peniteant.*

Auxilius, and Iserninus speak of the man who builds an *ecclesia* and insist on the administrative rights of the bishop in whose territory it lies;[1] while the *Synodus Hibernensis* speaks of the new-comer who receives a place *inter monasteria*[2] and of the property arrangements to be made when the abbot (*princeps*) is expelled or wishes to resign.[3] The ecclesiastics who attended the *Synodus Hibernensis* thought in terms of a monastic church, governed by abbots.

Their rulings show a much greater concern with native legal institutions than do those of the *Romani*. In Irish law the execution of contracts was guaranteed by the surety system. The surety might be of different kinds: one (the *ráth*) kept the memory of the transaction and undertook to discharge the obligation with his own property should the principal default,[4] another (the *aitire*) pledged his own person and freedom, and, according to one text, might not go surety for any amount exceeding his own honour price,[5] a third (the *naidm*) acted as the enforcing surety. The *Synodus Hibernensis* lays down how long the surety (*rata*) may wait before he discharges the debt,[6] and how much the debtor ought to pay to a surety who has met obligations on his behalf, encouraging the surety to be more lenient than secular legislation required.[7] The same synod gives a list of those persons who are not qualified to act as surety, this time using the word *fideiussor*.[8] The slave, the pilgrim, the fool, the monk without his abbot's consent, the son without his father's will, the woman unless she is a virgin abbess (*domina, virgo sancta*) are all incompetent. This compares with the list given in a secular law tract, *Córus Béscna*, of those unable to make valid contracts, though the secular tract adds the thief and the captive.[9] Every major purchase must have its *stipulatores* and *testes*, and anyone who resists them is to be

---

[1] *Coll.* XLIII. 1–4. *Arausicana* I. 10. Hefele-Leclercq, ii. l. 441.

[2] *Coll.* cap. 5.

[3] *Coll.* cap. 6 *infra*, p. 159.

[4] Binchy, *C.G.*, pp. 102–4, or a more general statement in *Early Irish Society*, pp. 63–4. For Thurneysen on Irish sureties, see *Z.C.P.*, xviii, 364–72 and 'Die Bürgschaft im Irischen Recht', pp. 35–74.

[5] *C.G.*, pp. 74–5.   [6] *Coll.* XXXIV. 4.

[7] *Coll.* XXXIV. 5.   [8] *Coll.* XXXIV. 3.

[9] *A.L.I.* iii. 58. On women as sureties see Binchy, *St. Ir. Law*, pp. 232 f.

excommunicated.[1] Irish law recognized a pledge (*gell*) given to indicate willingness to meet a claim or to submit the affair to adjudication. The man who gives a pledge on behalf of someone else who has failed in his obligations is entitled to pledge-interest, a subject on which there is a special tract.[2] If the debtor delays to discharge his obligation the pledge becomes forfeit. The Irish Synod orders that a fifth part of the debt should be given as a pledge (*pignus*), and that the pledge be forfeit after 'a certain time'.[3]

The *Collectio* includes a separate section on legal evidence. No catholic is to dare to overswear on any matter of which he is ignorant or doubtful.[4] This refers to the Irish practice of fastening liability by oath on a particular person or body (*for-toing*) or of exculpating from liability (*as-toing*).[5] Irish law distinguishes eye-witness evidence (*fiadnaise*) from evidence as to character (*teist*), and refuses to accept the eye-witness evidence of certain persons who may obviously be prejudiced, or of men degraded from holy orders, or of women.[6] The Irish Synod refuses the evidence (*testimonium*) of the sinner (*peccatoris*) or of a woman.[7] Perhaps the men who drew up this canon knew Irish law better than biblical study, for they provide a very lame reason for classing the woman with the sinner. 'The *testimonium* of a woman is not to be accepted, as the apostles did not accept the testimony of women concerning the resurrection of Christ.' The fact that the women on this occasion happened to be right does not seem to matter. It is worth noting that in the New Testament example which is quoted the women's *testimonium* was eye-witness evidence (*fiadnaise*), the type of evidence which the secular law refused to accept from women.

When a woman inherited family land she gained only a life interest, giving legal guarantees that she would not alienate the land, which later had to be restored to the kin.[8] The Irish Synod endorses this position: 'The authors of the church add many things here: that female heirs should give sureties and guarantees

---

[1] *Coll.* XXIV. 8 a. Cf. Thurneysen, *Z.C.P.* xviii. 364 ff.
[2] *A.L.I.* v. 376 ff. See *C.G.*, p. 94.   [3] *Coll.* XXXIII. 9.
[4] *Coll.* XVI. 6.   [5] *C.G.*, p. 99.
[6] *A.L.I.* v. 284.   [7] *Coll.* XVI. 3 a.
[8] M. Dillon, *St. Ir. Law*, pp. 164, 178–9.

not to transfer the inheritance to strangers.'[1] In secular law an illegitimate child begotten on a chief wife (*cét muinter*) belongs to the wronged husband until the father pays the child's price. He must also pay for its fostering according to the normal fees; but the harlot has to nurse her own child without any support from its father.[2] The Irish Synod gives a somewhat similar ruling.[3] In all these cases the canons of the Irish Synod are reflecting principles of the secular law which were not concerned exclusively with the church. These seventh-century Irish ecclesiastics were much more concerned to fit the church into the structure of the native legal institutions than to bring it into line with continental practices. The harmony of spirit between such Irish canonists and the secular lawyers may be seen in the *Senchas Már*. One of the tracts explains that there are many things in customary law which do not come into the canon of scripture. 'Dubthach showed these to Patrick; what did not disagree with the word of God in the written law, and with the consciences of the believers, was retained in the brehon code by the church and the *fili*.'[4]

Other canons not included in the *Collectio*, but which were promulgated by 'Irish' synods, show a similar concern with the church's position *vis-à-vis* the native law. Such concern may be seen in the third, fourth, fifth, and sixth sections of the *Canones Hibernenses* (*Hi.*),[5] in canons similar to *Hi.* IV contained in MS. Cambridge C.C.C.279 and in the *Tres Canones Hibernici* (*Ca.*) of MS. C.C.C.C.265. *Hi.* IV is mainly interested in the compensations to be paid for injuring a bishop, a great abbot (*excelsus princeps*), or scribe. C.C.C.279 repeats these rulings and adds the price for killing a bishop, which is fifty *ancillae*. *Ca.* gives the penalties for insulting, wounding, or killing anyone attached to a bishop, or

---

[1] *Coll.* XXXII. 20.

[2] *A.L.I.* v. 200–2.

[3] *Coll.* XLVI. 30 c: If anyone corrupts the legitimate wife of another, and has sown his seed so that the woman becomes pregnant, the son will be of the body from which he was born, yet he shall give the price of the son and his education as the judges shall judge. If he has inseminated an adulterer the corrupter returns nothing, nor shall an adulterer give anything to an adulterer, unless by chance on the confession of the son, the price of education.

[4] *A.L.I.* iii. 30–2.

[5] See Bieler, *Penitentials*, 160–75, 182. The first two sections of *Hi.* have a different manuscript tradition from *Hi.* III–VI.

for theft from a holy shrine or treasury. *Hi.* V describes the compensation due to various clerical grades for refusal of hospitality: seven *ancillae* for a bishop, eight and two-thirds for an *episcopus episcoporum.* It would seem that the Book of the Angel, in demanding only seven *ancillae* (or seven years of penance) for refusing hospitality to the bishop of Armagh, was not making an exorbitant claim.[1] *Hi.* III defines the tithes due to the church: there is some clash of opinion, but it is clear that tithes are to be offered on livestock, on the fruits of the earth, and on human beings[2] as well as first fruits. *Hi.* VI, 'on dogs', is not even specifically ecclesiastical. These canons should be considered alongside the canons of the Irish Synod contained in the *Collectio.* The ecclesiastics who attended the *Synodus Hibernensis* were concerned primarily with legal responsibility for misdeeds and compensation due, with arrangements over debts and contracts, and with church income and property. They were seeking to define the church's position in native society.

The clerics who attended the 'Roman Synod' passed legislation somewhat different in emphasis. Here we must consider the canons in the *Collectio* which are attributed to the *Romani* or the *Synodus Romana,* and also the Canons of the alleged Second Synod of S. Patrick (*Pa.* II), twelve of which the *Collectio* quotes as enactments of the *Romani.*[3] The *Romani* occasionally legislated for the monastic life,[4] passed canons on church property,[5] and accepted (with reservations) the church's right of sanctuary.[6] But, unlike the *Hibernenses,* they are concerned with the organization of an episcopal diocese: bishops are not to invade other bishops' *paruchiae,*[7] strangers are to bring letters of recommendation,[8] priests and clerics are not to take cases overseas, but are to have them tried at home, and if agreement cannot be reached, then cases should be referred to the synod.[9] They are anxious to keep the clergy separate from heretics,[10] they order priests to be content

[1] *Arm.* 21 b 1. Cf. infra p. 112   [2] *Infra,* p. 140.
[3] *Pa.* II is edited by Bieler, *Penitentials,* 184–97. See Bury, *Life of St Patrick,* pp. 236–9.
[4] *Coll.* XLI. 6; XLV. 13, 14; LXVI. 16.
[5] *Coll.* XVII. 8; XLII. 7.   [6] *Pa.* II. 9.
[7] *Coll.* I. 8 b.   [8] *Coll.* LVI. 4.
[9] *Coll.* XX. 3, 5, 6.   [10] *Coll.* XL. 13 ab, XX. 6.

with food and clothing and to reject the gifts of the wicked.[1] They pass regulations on excommunication,[2] penitents,[3] and on fasting.[4] They are concerned with the marriage law: a man may not take his dead brother's widow;[5] if he had a virgin wife before Christian baptism, and has lived with her, he may not discard her after baptism;[6] a man may accuse his wife of adultery (though a wife may not accuse her husband),[7] and may be divorced from a harlot;[8] the Irish customs of forbidding marriage within only four degrees is deprecated.[9] Occasionally they insist on a foreign custom: a man contracting a debt needs not only witnesses and sureties but a written record,[10] and business transactions must be confirmed 'by signature, in the Roman manner'.[11] Whereas the canons of the *Synodus Hibernensis* have notable parallels with the Irish law tracts, the 'Romans' do not identify themselves with the secular lawyers to anything like the same extent.

If we compare the whole *corpus* of seventh-century canons with the canons of the Synod ascribed to Patrick, Auxilius, and Iserninus (= *Pa.* I) we may observe some significant differences. In the early group (*Pa.* I) we see a church within a still pagan society: in the seventh-century canons the church holds an established legal position in a society which had become nominally Christian. The early canons never mention any secular penalties for misdeeds. They discuss penance and excommunication,[12] on one occasion, 'if possible', they require the restoration of stolen goods,[13] but there is nowhere any hint that the church could exact any secular penalty, and there is a clear statement that the wronged Christian must not resort to secular (and presumably pagan) judgement.[14] The seventh-century canonists discuss other punishments beside penance and excommunication, they lay down scales of restitution for theft and compensation for injury, for which

[1] *Coll.* II. 23.   [2] *Coll.* XL. 1 c.
[3] *Coll.* XLVII. 20.   [4] *Coll.* XII. 15 c, LXVI. 19.
[5] *Coll.* XLVI. 35 b.   [6] *Coll.* XLVI. 29.
[7] *Coll.* XLVI. 38 a.   [8] *Pa.* II. 26, 28.
[9] *Pa.* II. 29: 'What is observed among us, that they be separated by four degrees, they say they have never seen or read.'
[10] *Coll.* XXXIII. 4.   [11] *Pa.* II. 30: *Subscriptione ⟨more⟩ Romanorum.*
[12] *Pa.* I. 14, 16, 17, 31; 11, 19, 22.   [13] *Pa.* I. 15.
[14] *Pa.* I. 21. *Christianus cui dereliquerit aliquis et provocat eum in judicium et non in ecclesiam ut ibi examinetur causa, qui se fecerit alienus sit.*

there must have been consent from society as a whole.[1] The eighth-century *Collectio* attributes to *Patricius* one canon not found in the earlier code and quite out of accordance with its spirit. It describes the penalties for theft from a church where the bodies of saints and martyrs are buried: the lot is to decide whether the culprit shall lose a hand or foot, or whether he shall be imprisoned and return what he has taken, or whether he shall be forced to go on pilgrimage and restore two-fold, becoming a monk on his return.[2] This type of penalty occurs elsewhere in the seventh-century canons,[3] and indicates a church with a protected and privileged position. The earlier canons forbid the church to accept alms offered by heathens, or by excommunicated Christians:[4] seventh-century *Romani* forbid the church to take the alms of the wicked (*iniquorum*)[5] or of excommunicated clerics,[6] but churchmen now legislate on payment of tithes and offerings by a society no longer heathen.

The seventh-century *Romani* whose legislation is recorded in the *Collectio* could still think of a church governed by bishops,[7] with a hierarchy of ecclesiastical courts.[8] The eighth-century compilers of the *Collectio* put in numerous excerpts from continental sources about the bishop's authority and duties, statements by no means consistent with contemporary Irish conditions. It is interesting that the two men whose names are given in one of the early manuscripts, and who were probably its compilers, came from Dairinis and Iona. Ireland has several places named Dairinis,[9] one of them an island on the Blackwater, north-west of Youghal, about ten miles south of Lismore. This was one of the first areas in Ireland which we know to have been interested in the Easter controversy. A note (probably of the ninth century) in an eighth-century Gospel at Würzburg tells us that the first Irishman to learn 'the computus' by memory from a Greek was the scribe and

---

[1] Though *Pa.* II. 6 thinks it improper to demand restitution. The majority of the seventh-century canons are in no doubt that the church should insist on its proper rights.

[2] *Coll.* XXIX. 7.

[3] *Hi.* IV, in the section on compensations for injury to the clergy.

[4] *Pa.* I. 12, 13.   [5] *Pa.* II. 2; *Coll.* II. 23.

[6] *Coll.* XL. 8 repeating *Pa.* I. 12 about the alms of excommunicated *christiani.*   [7] *Coll.* I. 8 b, XX. 3 a, XLII. 23.

[8] *Coll.* XX. 5 a.   [9] Hogan, *Onom. Goed.*, p. 329.

abbot of Bangor, Mo-Sinu maccu Min, to be identified with Sintán or Sillán, abbot of Bangor, whose death the Annals of Ulster record at 610.[1] His pupil Mo-Chuaróc maccu Neth Semon 'whom the *Romani* style doctor of the whole world' recorded it in writing. This Mo-chuaróc came from a branch of the Dési, and his church is at Cell-Cuaráin (Kilcoran) near Youghal. Lismore, a little farther up the Blackwater estuary, was a centre of seventh-century Irish scholarship. Ruben of Dairinis is described in *A.U.* as 'scribe of Munster'. Thus the elder of the compilers[2] was from an area which had contained the pioneers of the Roman Easter, and which had long been a centre of learning and in touch with the Continent. His younger colleague, described in the annals as *sapiens*, was from Iona, the last of the Irish churches to come over to the Roman Easter in 716. These two men, and others like them, must have recognized the differences in the government of the monastic church in Ireland, and the episcopally governed church which many of their sources described. Their collection, arranged for easy reference, may be a final statement by the *Romani*, setting out canons advocating a Roman-type government as well as a Roman-type tonsure.[3]

But if this was part of the compilers' intention, it had little effect in Ireland. Monastic government had developed too far to be superseded. Seventh-century ecclesiastics had secured a recognized place for the church in the legal framework of Irish society, and a monastic church with its respect for kindred and its ideas of overlordship fitted far more readily into that framework than the Roman-style bishop. Men who had attended church councils which termed themselves 'Irish', in distinction from the 'Roman' councils, had striven, with success, to bring the church into line with the native law. The adjustments made by the Christian church in the later sixth and seventh centuries to the Irish machinery of government had become the facts on which the eighth-century church must build.

---

[1] Kenney, *Sources*, p. 218; Grosjean, *A.B.*, lxiv (1946), 215 ff. The Antiphonary of Bangor gives the name as Sinlan.

[2] An assumption only, based on the fact that he died twenty-two years before his colleague.

[3] The fact that no section is given to Easter suggests that the collection post-dates 716.

K

CHAPTER 13

Monastic establishment

By the eighth century the church held a firmly established place in society. The legal value of her clergy had been fixed, her learning accepted, the rights due to her from the people and her reciprocal obligations towards them had been laid down. The detailed rulings on these matters are to be found in the secular law tracts and in the ecclesiastical canons, in particular the *Canones Hibernenses* and the canons of the *Synodus Hibernensis* contained in the *Collectio*. Patrick's own fifth-century writings show us an apostolic church; in Vinnian, Columbanus, Columcille, and Cummean we are overtaken by the ascetics in the church; in the seventh- and eighth-century laws we settle down with the establishment.

Three secular law tracts on status define the legal value of the clergy. Their rulings are not as clear as one would like, but they allow us to draw some firm conclusions. *Uraicecht Becc*, probably drawn up in the seventh or early eighth century,[1] gives an honour-price (*díre*) to the ecclesiastical orders comparable to those it grants to the secular nobility,[2] ranging from seven *séts* for the *lector* in the lowest grade to an honour-price of three and a half *cumals*[3] for a priest, equal to that of a petty king, while the bishop had the honour-price of an over-king.[4] The most important bishops[5] were the equals of the highest grade of king, with an honour-price of fourteen cumals. This tract, after according legal

---

[1] Translated by MacNeill, *P.R.I.A.*, xxxvi (1923), C 272–81; see Binchy on 'The date and provenance of *Uraicecht Becc*', *Ériu*, xviii (1958), 48, 53–4.

[2] *A.L.I.* v. 52.

[3] In a society where there was no coinage units of value were measured in *séts*, often translated 'chattel', and in *cumals*, meaning female slave. Normally 6 *séts* = 1 *cumal*. *Ancilla* is the Latin rendering of *cumal*.

[4] The MS. reads *rí ruireach*, the king of over-kings, i.e. the highest of the three grades of kingship. MacNeill (op. cit., p. 274) would read *ruiri*, 'over-king'.

[5] *ollam uasal-eascub* (*A.L.I.* v. 112). *Ollam* here means 'supreme', *uasal* means 'noble, lofty'. See Binchy *Ériu*, xviii, 49.

status to those in holy orders, provides for the abbot[1] who is a layman,[2] and whose honour-price is to be determined by the rank of the church which he governs. Presumably the *díre* of abbots in orders was determined by the ecclesiastical order which each held.

A second secular law tract, *Críth Gablach,* dating from the 'opening years of the eighth century' and from a different law-school, gives a different scheme of classification.[3] Here the grades of ecclesiastical orders are said to correspond with the grades of secular society,[4] but the tract gives seven secular grades, culminating in the petty king *(rí)* with an honour-price of seven *cumals,* adding the over-king of three or four *tuatha,* whose *díre* is eight *cumals,* and the king of over-kings, whose honour price is fourteen *cumals.* Presumably the bishop corresponds to the petty king.

A third tract, which is part of the text known as *Miadshlecta,* and was compiled in the first half of the eighth century,[5] gives yet another classification. To the question: 'What *díre* is the highest in Ireland?', it makes answer: 'The *díre* of a celibate bishop',[6] a value reckoned at eight *cumals,* with seven *cumals* as the honour-price of a celibate priest.[7] This tract is more detailed than either of the others: it makes provision for each clerical grade, down to the clerical student and the layman who has entered religion; it divides each into three classes, the celibate, the man of one wife, and the penitent; for the bishop and priest it gives in detail the penalties for wounding and insult.

The rulings on compensation for celibate bishops and priests show similarities with those laid down in the *Canones Hibernenses* (*Hi.* IV. 1–8) and to the version of these rulings in MS. C.C.C.C.279 (pp. 156–7). The canons, however, do not legislate for the married or penitent cleric, and together with the bishop they class the great abbot and the scribe.[8] In spite of minor divergencies, the combined legislation shows that bishops, scribes, abbots, and

---

[1] *comarba,* literally 'heir'.   [2] *A.L.I.* v. 54.
[3] See Professor Binchy's edition and introduction.
[4] Binchy, *C.G.,* lines 487–8.   [5] Binchy, 'Patrick', p. 63, note 166.
[6] *A.L.I.* iv. 362.   [7] *A.L.I.* iv. 366.
[8] *Sanguis episcopi vel excelsi principis vel scribae.*

priests held positions of dignity at the apex of an aristocratic society.[1] They were the equals of kings.

The high rank of the *scriba*, or *suí* (sage, *sapiens*), is indicated in the secular as well as in the ecclesiastical laws. His presence indicates a school of Latin learning, and his prestige was analogous to that of the *fili* who professed secular learning. Secular law divides the 'classes of wisdom' in the church into seven, and *Uraicecht Becc* gives the master of wisdom the same honour-price as the petty king.[2] In *Miadshlecta* the master of the second grade has an honour-price of seven *cumals*, like that which the same tract assigns to the celibate priest. All seven grades are distinguished, down to the pupil with a *dire* of half a *cumal*. These divisions may be to a large extent artificial, but they show the seriousness with which learning was regarded. The scribe and bishop need not humble themselves before princes. According to one of the tracts in *Senchas Már*, they were among the very few persons whose eye-witness testimony a king could not overswear, for their legal value was equal to his own.[3]

The abbots, bishops and clergy, and the orders of learning did not comprise the total population of a monastery. In the legislation of Columbanus and Cummean and in Adamnán's Life of Columcille we see monks under strict rule. Early monks were not necessarily in orders, but they lived in communities under the control of an abbot, in chastity and poverty. The standard of austerity might vary,[4] but the principles of personal poverty, chastity, and obedience were constant. In the secular law tracts, however, we meet men who are called *manaig*, monks, but who seem to be more like monastic tenants than monks under religious rule. Their relationship with the abbot is discussed in terms similar to those which the law tracts use to describe the clients of a secular lord. Irish clients were of two kinds, 'free' (*sóer-chéle*) and 'base' (*dóer-chéle*). The free client was an honoured figure, one of those folk who were fitting company around a king;[5] he

---

[1] In C.C.C.C. 279 the fine for killing a bishop is fifty *ancillae* (defined as seven *ancillae* for each ecclesiastical grade) or fifty years of penance.

[2] *A.L.I.* v. 112.

[3] *A.L.I.* i. 78. The other class was the *deorad Dé*, on whom see Binchy, *Ériu*, xii, 58 f.

[4] *Supra*, pp. 57 ff.   [5] *C.G.*, line 594.

formed part of his lord's retinue and gave him personal service, but retained his legal independence. From the lord he received a fief of stock on which he paid rent, but which became his own property in seven years, after which the lord must grant a new fief, or the clientship terminated. The base client received from the lord a payment equal to his own honour-price together with a fief of stock, and in return paid a rent in kind, with a fixed amount of manual service to the lord, who also received part of the compensation for certain injuries committed against his client. The secular laws regard the *manaig* as clients of the church, men who held land and stock of the abbot, having rights and duties in a contractual relationship. In the case of finds, glosses lay down that the *sóer-manach* pays his church a quarter, the *dóer-manach* a third, in the same proportions as the noble and base clients of a secular lord.[1] A gloss on the 'seven binding contracts' allows the abbot five days in which to invalidate a compact made without his knowledge by a *sóer-manach*, though after this time, if the abbot takes no action, the contract is binding; a month must pass before a contract made by a *dóer-manach* becomes valid. The monks in their turn, have some control over the abbot's contracts: the contract of an abbot made without the knowledge of the *manaig* becomes valid only after ten days, to allow time for a sufficient number of monks to assemble and make the necessary decision.[2] Abbot and *manaig* form a kind of corporation in which the monks have definite rights over property and some independent control. The dying monk has property to leave: if he dies away from his own church the church in which he dies may perversely try to secure control of it.[3] The monks of the secular laws are not vowed to personal poverty as are the monks in the Rule of Columbanus. Nor is their obedience like that of Columbanus' monks, though the abbot controls their actions as head of the tribe of the church.

But are the monks of these secular laws identical with the monks of the ecclesiastical legislation? The monks of Columbanus, as we have already seen, were very different. Cummean's monks are under obedience to the abbot and steward of the monastery,[4] they are not to speak alone or to spend a night under

---

[1] *A.L.I.* iv. 196; *A.L.I.* v. 332.   [2] *A.L.I.* v. 356.
[3] *A.L.I.* v. 430.   [4] *Cu.* VIII. 17.

the same roof with a woman.[1] This is in accordance with the
legislation of *Pa.* I,[2] and of *Pa.* II, which defines *monachi* as those
who dwell in 'solitude without worldly resources, under the
power of a bishop or abbot'.[3] Cummean's monks may be in orders,
but need not be. He is writing for bishops, priests, deacons, monks
in higher orders (or priests and deacons under monastic vow),
monks *inferiori gradu*, and layfolk. The laity are subject to a severe
régime of sexual abstinence,[4] and both the monk without orders
and the layman are given a three-year penance for the sin of
fornication. Yet for Cummean, though the monk may be a layman, he is living in celibacy and under rule, and the men who
preside over the churches are not laymen but priests.[5]

The Old Irish Penitential, of a date 'certainly not later than the
end of the eighth century,[6] provides some paraphrases in Irish of
passages from Cummean, with instructive Irish parallels of
Cummean's Latin terms. Cummean's 'vow of a monk' becomes in
the Old Irish Penitential either a 'vow of perpetual monkhood' or
the 'vow of a *dóer-manach*'.[7] This Penitential also provides a severe
sexual régime for the layman.[8] Those who would reach the peak
of perfection must be in complete poverty, either going on pilgrimage or living in a communal church,[9] and the people mentioned as living in such a church are clerics or nuns.[10] The monks
of the old Irish Penitential are celibate[11] and under the abbot's
rule; but the term *dóer-manach* occurs here, the term which in the
secular laws implies a relationship between lord and client.

---

[1] *Cu.* VIII. 23.   [2] *Pa.* I. 9, 34.

[3] *Pa.* II. 17. Cf, 21, Wandering is discouraged in both *Pa.* I and *Pa.* II.

[4] *Cf.* Vinnian's Penitential, *supra*, pp. 53–4.

[5] *Cu.* Epilogue 3.   [6] Binchy, *Penitentials*, p. 258.

[7] *Cu.* II. 2. *Presbiter ant diaconus faciens fornicationem naturalem praelate ante
monachi votu.* Cf. *O. Ir. Pen.* II. 3, 'If he be a priest or deacon who has taken a
vow of perpetual monkhood' (*bith-manchai*), or *O. Ir. Pen.* II. 10, 'they vow
perpetual monkhood'. *Cu.* II. 4, *Si vero sine monachi voto presbiter aut diaconus
sic peccaverint, sicut monachus sine gradu peniteant.* Cf. *O. Ir. Pen.* II. 8, 'If it be a
priest or deacon not having taken monastic vows (*cen erchoiliud dóer-mancha*),
the penance of a monk not in orders (*pennind manaich cen gra*) is what he
performs.'

[8] *O. Ir. Pen.* II. 36.

[9] Ibid., III. 6, *ind eclais oentath*.

[10] Ibid., III. 10, *Cleirech nó caillech bis ind eclais oentath*. . . .

[11] Ibid., II. 3, 6, 8, 10.

The Old Irish Metrical Rule belongs to much the same period as the Penitential.[1] The tone of this rule is admonition rather than command: the man to whom it is addressed is advised to cultivate the love of God because love determines piety, to hate wealth, and to follow certain ascetic practices. The rule is concerned with the individual's pursuit of holiness, and there is no direct reference to community life; but guests are entertained[2] and the religious life is to be practised under the guidance of a holy and learned man.[3] The ascetic is either celibate, or has separated himself from his family, thinking of them no more.[4] *Manaig* are mentioned at the end of this Rule, in a section which may have been added to the original text, and which begins: 'If you are a shepherd to monks (*do mhanchaibh*)'. The next stanza refers to *manchuine*, the labour services which would be paid by the *manaig*. Here again, monks appear in the terminology of the secular laws.

The most interesting and instructive correspondence with the secular laws comes from the canons passed by the *Hibernenses*, those 'Irish' as distinct from 'Roman' supporters who attended seventh-century church councils. Here the abbot and his monks form a kind of corporation, as they do in the secular laws. The monk (*monachus*) is under the abbot's jurisdiction and has no *libertas* apart from the abbot;[5] he cannot act as surety without his abbot's command.[6] Living under tribute (*sub censu*) to the abbot, who is his lord (*dominus*), he may make no bequests at his death without the abbot's permission.[7] If, however, anyone under tribute to either abbot or king has made a bequest, if his lord has heard of it and kept silent for two days, his silence is taken to imply consent.[8] Here the principle is the same as in the secular laws, that the abbot may repudiate contracts made by his *dóer-manaig*, though the timing is different.[9] The monk here is similar to the client-monk or *manach* of the secular lawyers. The abbot is his *dominus*, he owes tribute (*sub censu*), he has no legal

---

[1] Ed. J. Strachan, *Ériu*, i (1904), 191–208. 'It can hardly be put later than about 800.' The phrase *diamba chéle Maic Maire* (§ 22) may indicate the culdee movement in the later part of the eighth century.

[2] O. Ir. Met. Rule, 18.   [3] Ibid., 15, Ecnaid cráibthech dot airli.
[4] Ibid., 26.   [5] Coll. XVIII. 3 b.
[6] Coll. XXXIV. 3.   [7] Coll. XLI. 8.
[8] Coll., XLI. 9.   [9] A.L.I. iii. 10, and supra, p. 137.

independence; but he is not completely poor like one of Columbanus' monks.

The *Synodus Hibernensis*, legislating on tithes,[1] suggests that these monastic clients not only had the management of flocks and lands but were married. Tithes and first fruits were offered on agrarian produce, on animals and human beings, and whereas first fruits were once offered at Jerusalem under Jewish law, now in the new dispensation each person pays them 'to the monastery of which he is a monk'.[2] The secular law tract on Customary Law (*Córus Béscna*) clarifies these regulations. The tithes in human beings, mentioned twice by the church *sapientes*,[3] are there explained. The first-born son was given to the church to receive an ecclesiastical education: he inherited his share of the family land on his father's death and farmed it as a *sóer-manach* of the church. After ten sons had been born, another son with his inheritance was set aside for the church.[4] This means that the *sóer-manaig* were married men with families, holding property of the church, which they farmed as her clients, the eldest son inheriting his father's liabilities. The system is confirmed by a tract on the reciprocal obligations of church and tenants which probably belongs to the ninth century. It exists in two versions, one incorporated into the Rule of the Céli Dé,[5] the other known as *Ríagail Pátraic*.[6] According to this statement, the church had to provide baptism, communion, and intercessory prayer for her *manaig*, and in return the free clients of the church (*sóerad eclaisi*) provided their material support.[7] The priest in charge of the church had to hear the confessions of its *manaig*, men, boys, women, and girls.[8]

Thus, it is clear that before the eighth century the church had clients, known to the Irish lawyers as monks (*manaig*) who held property of the church and paid tribute to the church, passing on

---

[1] *Hi.* III. Bieler, *Penitentials*, p. 166–9.

[2] *Hi.* III. 5, *ad monasterium cui monachus fuerit.*

[3] *Hi.* III. 1, 3.   [4] *A.L.I.* iii. 38–40.

[5] Ed. E. J. Gwynn, *Hermathena*, Second Suppl. Vol. 1927, § 57–65, pp. 78–87.

[6] Ed. J. G. O'Keefe, *Ériu*, i. 216–24.

[7] Rule of Céli Dé, § 57; Ríagail Pátraic, §§ 5, 8, 9.

[8] Rule of Céli Dé, § 64.

their obligations to their eldest sons, who had been educated in the monastery. They were subjected to a rigorous code of sexual abstinence and were part of an ecclesiastical society. In certain cases the 'tribe of monks' had the right to select a new abbot. Do such monastic tribes go back to family lands made over to the church, where the existing landholders accepted the new ecclesiastical lordship? Some of the characteristics of a family monastery seem to appear in the Englishman Aethelwulf's Poem on the Abbots, written between 803 and 821.[1] It concerns a cell of Lindisfarne founded between 704 and 716.[2] Of the six abbots whom the author names, Eorpwine and Aldwine were brothers, and so were Sigebald and Sigewine. One monk, Merchdof, had been twice married, and would seem to have been still living with his second wife, since he had opportunity for repentence and improvement.[3] Yet the monastery seems by no means degenerate: it had a distinguished Irish illuminator and teacher, Ultán, it had its own smith, a very holy man, its lands were prosperously farmed, and charity was dispensed, while some of its members, at least, were noted for their piety. It may be some such mixture of ecclesiastical and family interests that we should expect to find in eighth-century Irish monasteries.

But religious life in Ireland was not entirely made up of the monastic clients, who appear as *manaig* in the secular laws, and sometimes as *monachi* in the canons of the *Hibernenses*. There were those *in habitu religioso* on whom complete chastity was enjoined;[4] there were clerics and nuns living in complete poverty in a communal church;[5] there were men under the guidance of a religious senior following an ascetic régime. In the early seventh century Columbanus legislates for clerics and monks together, separating them from the laity, though not all his monks were in

---

[1] I am indebted to Professor Alastair Campbell for drawing my attention to this poem and for supplying the chronology. It is edited by T. Arnold, *Symeonis Monachi Opera Omnia* (Rolls Series), 1882, i, 265–94. Professor Campbell is re-editing it.

[2] Shortly before Bede complained to Egbert of York in 734 about the practice of founding family monasteries in England. See Whitelock, *E.H.D.* i. 741.

[3] Pp. 277–9.

[4] *Coll.* XLVI. 11 d.   [5] *O. Ir. Pen.* III. 10.

orders: it seems likely that, by the eighth century, those following a religious rule were usually in orders. Christianity was introduced into Ireland through an episcopally governed church, but the monastic institutions which became popular in the sixth century probably expressed from the beginning the familial structure of society. Our sources suggest that at first religious life under strict rule was followed in Irish monasteries. By the seventh century some monks were still following a communal life in celibacy and personal poverty; there were also 'monks' educated by the church, sometimes having a voice in its government, but married, holding land and stock as clients of the church. As time went on, it is likely that under such a system the difference between monks without orders and monastic clients would decrease, and that fewer and fewer men would follow the religious life.

The monastic clients gave the church an assured income whose continuity was guaranteed. They paid tithe, first fruits, and firstlings to the church. Fees were also paid for burial in a church: canons of the *Synodus Hibernensis* define them as a cow, a horse, the clothing and bed-trappings of the dead man, or, if he were of higher rank, two horses with a chariot, his bed-trappings, and the cup from which he drank.[1] Both ecclesiastical and secular lawyers take account of occasions when a man might be buried away from his own church, and disputes over his property might arise in consequence,[2] and the secular law tract *Córus Béscna* lays down a scale of bequests to be made by the noble grades of society.[3] By the seventh and eighth centuries the church's legal status and economic position was assured. Her higher clergy compared in dignity with kings, her men of learning commanded as much esteem as secular poets and lawyers. She had land and clients under her lordship, she received rents and grants. Kings were weak and political authority divided, and had the church been united in a hierarchical organization she would have been the most powerful institution in the country. What use did she make of her privileges?

[1] *Coll.* XVIII. 6. Are these the possessions which might once have been buried with a pagan?
[2] *Coll.* XVIII. 7 a. Cf. *A.L.I.* iii. 64–6.
[3] *A.L.I.* iii. 42.

CHAPTER 14

The uses of power

The Christian church had in many ways been fortunate in its reception by the Irish. Though society was not civilized in the Roman sense, neither was it brutish. Though there were no towns, the magnificent natural pasture gave considerable economic prosperity, and though royal authority was weak, the family group gave protection and support, the surety system existed to enforce the law, and the practice of compensation mitigated some of the effects of violence. Above all, the traditional recognition accorded to a professional learned class provided a natural place for the church in the structure of society. Though the Roman administration of the church which was originally established had been profoundly modified, Christian teaching had taken firm root, and in time affected the standards of pagan society. For, once established, the church, with its status and wealth, had considerable opportunities to influence the lay world.

Latin learning had been a new technique with which Irishmen could grapple, the Scriptures provided a vast new field of study. Much as the secular men of learning expected to master the knowledge of their class, so seventh-century monastic scholars turned their attention to knowing, understanding, and interpreting the Scriptures. The Latin language was their tool and they spent time on grammar, but they would have regarded exegesis as their most important activity.[1] A considerable number of their commentaries survive.[2] The Antiochan school of Biblical exegesis, with its stress on the literal and historical interpretation of the text, and the Alexandrine school, with its emphasis on the moral or allegorical meaning, were both familiar to Irish scholars. One commentator on S. Mark's Gospel (who may be that Cummean who advocated the Roman Easter c. 632) explains that he will try

[1] See Bischoff, 'Wendepunkte', pp. 207–11.
[2] Bischoff, 'Wendepunkte', pp. 212 ff., lists exegetical works by early Irish scholars.

to show the mystical meaning of his text.[1] He is following the
Alexandrine method. A contemporary who calls himself Augustine, addressing the monks of Lismore somewhere about the
middle of the seventh century Concerning the Miracles of Holy
Scripture, deliberately rejects this aim:

> In this work we have tried to explain the reason and order of actual
> events, excluding, at this stage, figurative interpretations. . . .We
> have thought fit to omit this aspect particularly because all those
> authors who have taken care to expound these passages have clung
> to spiritual understanding of allegories, that is to figural exposition,
> which has been found in them.[2]

Sometimes commentators combine the two exegetical methods.
The Old Irish Treatise on the Psalter requires a discussion of the
circumstances under which the Psalms were composed and subsequently recited (this is the 'history'), their Messianic significance,
and their moral application.[3]

All of them aim to teach first of all the contents of the Scrip-
tures. These are the cleric's authority, and he must familiarize
himself with them. The commentator often sets passages from the
Old Testament alongside the New. Writing on S. Mark's Gospel,
when he comes to the words 'They led him out and crucified him',
Cummean provides a list of the Old Testament types of Christ.
There are opportunities for displays of ecclesiastical learning, and
Greek and even Hebrew words are not infrequently introduced.
But much of the exegetical writing is straightforward teaching of
Christian ethic, sometimes of moving simplicity. Cummean com-
ments on the words *Et condempnavit eum reum esse mortis*:

> So that with His cross He might cancel our own crucifixion, and by
> His death He might destroy our death. With the form of a serpent
> He slays the serpent (this is an allusion to the serpent lifted up in the

---

[1] The identification is Bischoff's, 'Wendepunkte', pp. 199–201. For the
text see *P.L.*, xxx, 592.

[2] On Augustine and other members of the Lismore group, see Grosjean,
'Exégètes', pp. 73–96, and Esposito, *P.R.I.A.*, xxxv (1920), 189–207. For
text of *De Mirabilibus*, *P.L.*, xxxv, cols. 2151–2. Augustine may here be paraphrasing the words of his contemporary Cummean. Cummean says: *De
Marci Evangelistae historia, vel mystico intellectu . . . intimare curabo.* Augustine
says: *Quoniam quicumque auctores haec loca explanare curaverunt mystico allegoriarum
intellectui, hoc est, figurali expositioni quae in his reperta est, adhaeserunt.*

[3] Ed. K. Meyer, *Hibernica Minora*, Oxford, 1894, p. 30.

wilderness by Moses, the sight of which healed the children of Israel from their snake bites. Num. 21 6–9, Cf. John 3. 14), because by the serpent made of wood (i.e. the cross) other serpents are swallowed up. Whence He said through the prophet: 'I will be your death, O Death, and your destruction, O Hell.' (Hosea 13. 14). His reproach has removed our disgrace. His chains have set us free. By the crown of thorns on His head we have gained the diadem of the kingdom. With His wounds we are healed. By His burial we are resurrected. By His descent into hell we rise to heaven. Foreseeing all this the prophet said, 'What shall I render unto the Lord for all his benefits toward me?' (Ps. 116. 12)[1]

Priests trained on such teaching themselves preached in the vernacular. The secular laws clearly recognize that the church is responsible not only for performing the sacraments but for instructing the laity in the Christian faith:[2] a gloss on *Córus Béscna* defines the church's duty to tell out the word of God to everyone who will hear as 'preaching to everyone who is a listener to it', and a gloss to *Cáin Lánamna* provides a list of obligations from the church to her tenants: preaching, mass, requiem, education (of the sons of tenants), penance.[3] The commentaries written and studied in the monastic schools must have had their effect on popular preaching. One homily, composed in the later seventh or eighth century, takes as its theme the text: 'If anyone wishes to come after me, let him deny himself and take up his cross and follow me.' This sermon is not providing displays of erudition or referring to Old Testament types; it is a call to repentance, and a clear statement that repentance means that a man turn away from himself and identify himself with the needs of his fellows. Speaking of S. Paul, the preacher says:

> Everyone's sickness was sickness to him, offence to anyone was offence to him, everyone's infirmity was infirmity to him. Even so it is meet for each one of us that he suffer with everyone in his hardship and in his poverty and in his infirmity. We see from the words and wisdom of the sage that fellow-suffering is counted as a kind of cross.[4]

Of course, Irish teachers were well aware that the preaching and practice of self-denial and charity are not necessarily the same

---

[1] *Thes. Pal.* i. 490–1.   [2] *A.L.I.* iii. 32–5.
[3] *A.L.I.* ii. 344–5. Cf. Thurneysen, *St. Ir. Law*, p. 9.
[4] R. Thurneysen, *Old Irish Reader*, pp. 35–6; *Thes. Pal.* ii. 246.

thing. Monastic life had been founded on a realization that discipline is required. They were aware, moreover, of the force of pagan tradition and of hostile powers: they had to remind themselves that it was their God who had created the world, it was He who expressed himself through it. The Old Irish hymn attributed to Patrick starts with a declaration of faith in the power of the Trinity, and in Christ's baptism, crucifixion, resurrection and reign. Then the poet joins himself with the heavenly hosts, with the patriarchs, prophets, apostles, and saints and with God's earthly creation. He recollects the power of God –

> I buckle on today
>> God's strength to pilot me,
>> God's might to uphold me,
>> God's wisdom to guide me –

to protect him

>> against incantations of false prophets
>> against black laws of heathendom
>> against false laws of heretics

and he summons Christ to surround him, before, behind, beneath, beside, above, in the hearts, eyes, ears, mouths of all whom he meets, instead of spells and curses. The last stanza reasserts his confidence:

> I buckle on today
>> a mighty strength, invoking the Trinity.[1]

This poet does not underrate the forces of paganism even while he rejoices that his salvation is in God.

These early evidences of Irish Christianity which I have just quoted are singularly attractive, for they go directly to the heart of the Christian faith in emphasizing God's love for men and man's response. The contemporary saints' Lives are different in character. They are concerned not so much with the saint's teaching as with establishing his reputation, so they stress the qualities which were best appreciated in a heroic society. Patrick's Confession reveals a saint toiling, insulted, persecuted even unto bonds: Muirchú shows us the same saint worsting his heathen opponents, cursing his enemies sometimes to the death, able to

---

[1] For translation, see Professor Binchy's discussion in the forthcoming number of *Ériu* xx.

detect falsehood and mete out justice, perform miracles, and protect his followers. Cogitosus, in his Life of Brigit, gives a picture of a saint so completely in harmony with nature and in control of it that she can hang her cloak upon a sunbeam, a woman hospitable and generous, circumventing wrongdoers, healing and performing miracles. Except for its opening and concluding sections, Cogitosus' entire text is made up of a series of miracles performed by Brigit. Some of these fantastic stories have considerable charm, and they are intended to demonstrate not only her power but her generous charity: nevertheless, others are puerile and repetitive.[1] Such works teach much less about the Christian faith than do the homilies and commentaries, and should probably be regarded as providing popular entertainment rather than serious instruction.

The popular attitude to Christianity is further revealed in spells, where the new faith has been fitted to the age-old practices of magic. The principle here seems to be the invocation of holy words and holy names. The charm for headache in the eighth- or ninth-century St. Gall fragment goes (in Latin)

> Head of Christ, eye of Isaiah, forehead of Elijah, nose of Noah, lip of Job, tongue of Solomon, neck of Matthew, mind of Benjamin, breast of Paul, grace of John, faith of Abraham, blood of Abel: Holy, holy, holy, Lord God of Sabaoth.[2]

This does not suggest that the speaker attached much meaning to what he recited, and it degrades the intellectual content of Christianity. Yet the charm implies prayer and faith, and its complete absence of scientific thinking is the inevitable background of contemporary Irish life.

Thus, Christian teaching was being disseminated at various levels during the seventh and eighth centuries, and in spite of defects it was having some influence on the ethic and institutions of Irish society. The monasteries added to the amenities for which secular law had already taken thought, and in some cases extended

---

[1] Some people have thought that Vita Cog. 12 (*A.A.SS.* 1 February 1658, p. 136, where Brigit relieves a lapsed virgin of her pregnancy) is dubious in its ethics. The writer obviously regarded this as an act of charity, whereby the nun was restored to penitence.

[2] Ed. R. I. Best, *Ériu*, viii (1916), 100.

their scope. They provided hospitality. The Rule of Ailbe, which may go back to the eighth century, requires the steward to provide

> Blessing and welcome for everyone who comes to him.
> A clean house for the guests and a big fire,
> Washing and bathing for them and a couch without sorrow.[1]

Several of the miracles told of S. Brigit show her entertaining guests, and demonstrate clearly that good entertainment was expected from a saint with a reputation to maintain. But perhaps the most important contribution of the church was that it added to the security of society. Population was often more concentrated in the monasteries than elsewhere, so that the monastic inhabitants were able to defend themselves. As we shall see, they sometimes used their power to attack, but on the whole they were among the peacemakers.

The church was able, in the first place, to benefit from the native law of precinct, for each Irish lord had an inviolable area surrounding his house, its size depending upon the owner's rank. A church similarly had its precinct or *termon* (from the Latin *terminus*), the area depending upon its rank. Seventh-century church legislators decreed that the *termon* of a holy place must be consecrated by king, bishop, and people[2] (presumably to secure public acknowledgement of its inviolability) and that it must be clearly marked out by crosses. They seem to recognize different degrees of sanctity within the area of *termon*, at least two, possibly three or even four.[3] The most explicit of the canons on this subject is corrupt, but the areas are called *sanctus, sanctior*, and *sanctissimus*: the most holy seems to have contained the relics of the saints, into another only clerics might enter, while a third accommodated laymen and women,[4] with penalties for violation differing according to the area.[5]

---

[1] *Ériu*, iii. 106–7.

[2] *Synodus Hibernensis, Coll*. XLIV. 3 c.   [3] *Coll*. XLIV. 5, 8.

[4] Another canon, attributed to Origen in the *Collectio* (XVII. 4), distinguishes between grants which are made to a church: first, the place containing the relics of saints, which ought to be occupied by saints alone and not left without a priest; second, land near the monastic city, which should be occupied by men only, the *familia ecclesiae*; third, land farther off, where the laity of both sexes dwell. A fourth gift might be in flocks or other moveables.

[5] *Coll*. XLIV. 8.

It is possible that the plan of crosses in the seventh-century Book of Mulling may indicate some such distinction. An outer circle of crosses to Luke, Mark, Matthew, and John stands east, south, west, and north. Within this lies another circle of crosses to the four prophets Isaiah, Jeremiah, Daniel, and Ezekiel. Then comes a double circle, on and within which are eight crosses, mostly with indecipherable inscriptions, though one is the Cross of Christ with his Apostles and another the Cross of the Holy Spirit. This diagram is usually taken to be a plan for an ecclesiastical city, the double circle perhaps representing the *rath*, the crosses within it stationed at the chief buildings, the crosses outside to put the holy sign on its approaches.[1] But it would be possible to set this plan alongside the canons of the *Synodus Hibernensis*, which are of the same date, and suggest that the plan might illustrate the separate areas of sanctuary of which the canons speak. Whether or not this interpretation is correct, it is certain that the *termon* of monastic cities added to the areas of sanctuary throughout the land.

So far the church had merely appropriated the means of peace already indicated by the native law. But she did more than this, for she introduced and secured the acceptance of new laws designed to protect non-combatants from violence. The evidence for this statement concerns the series of 'laws' of various saints enacted between 697 and 842. We need to know by whom these laws were imposed, how they were put into effect, and above all, what was their purpose. The clues to these questions lie in the annal entries, in the secular law tracts where they are mentioned, and in a treatise known as the 'Law of Adamnán'.[2]

A common type of annal entry is: 'The law of such and such a saint over such and such an area,' *Lex Ciaraini for Connachta* (*A.U.* 788) or, in Irish, *Cáin Ailbi la Mumain* (*A.I.* 784). Often the law is to be imposed over a considerable territorial area, Connacht or Munster or Leth Cuinn (the Northern Half); occasionally, by

---

[1] See H. J. Lawlor, *Chapters on the Book of Mulling*, Edinburgh, 1897, pp. 167–85.

[2] For a discussion of the laws and references to texts in which they are cited see Thurneysen, *Z.C.P.*, xviii (1930), 382–96. The Law of Adamnán is edited by K. Meyer, Oxford, 1905, and discussed by J. Ryan, *St. Ir. Law*, pp. 269–76.

L

agreement between kings, over a wider area, as in 737, when, after a meeting between the king of the Northern Half and the King of Munster, 'the law of Patrick held Ireland'. The Annals sometimes also give the names of persons in connexion with the law: these are the provincial kings and the coarbs of the saints to whom the laws are attributed. An entry of this type reads in this way:

A.U. 778 –

The law of Columcille by Donnchad (i.e. king of the Southern Uí Néill and overlord of Leth Cuinn) and Bresal (i.e. abbot of Iona).

or *A.U.* 823 –

The law of Patrick over Munster by Feidlimid son of Crimthann (i.e. king of Cashel) and by Artrí son of Conchobar (i.e. abbot of Armagh).

Thus, it is clear that the coarbs and the kings were both concerned in the imposition of the law. *Críth Gablach* bears witness to the king's share when it names the Law of Adamnán among the kinds of government which it is proper for a king to bind on his people.[1] The saints' laws seem to have been deliberately introduced and enacted by consent, their validity depending mainly on will.

The text known as *Cáin Adamnáin*, 'The Law of Adamnán', gives information about how one saint's law was to be put into effect. Adamnán's law, the first in the series, was promulgated at the synod of Birr in 697: the tract, however, is a composite document, the oldest section probably going back to a date not earlier than the eighth century.[2] This section lays down the penalties for violation of the protection afforded by the law, describes the legal procedure of pledges and sureties needed to enforce it, requires that judges for the law are to be chosen in every church and tribe, and demands hospitality for those who levy its dues. Details concerned with the administration of the fines connected with various saints' Laws are also laid down elsewhere.[3] All this suggests that

[1] *C.G.*, lines 521–4. Cf. p. 104.

[2] §§ 34–53 in Meyer's edition. Here I am indebted to Professor Binchy, whose opinion on the date I have given. Professor Ryan, *St. Ir. Law*, p. 269, regards this section as 'the original law in its strict legal form as drafted by the professional *brehons* and adopted by the assembly' (i.e. of Birr).

[3] Thurneysen, *Z.C.P.* xviii. 383–4.

the laws were applied by methods familiar to secular legal practice.

The purpose of the laws is a question as controversial as it is important. It is usually assumed that the laws were intended to raise income for the churches concerned:[1] the Irish word *cáin* which is normally used to translate the Latin *lex* has the double sense of 'law' and 'tribute', and medieval rights of jurisdiction were profitable, since they brought in fines. It is also clear that the *cáin* was often imposed on a circuit which was accompanied by the relics of the saint, for the annals occasionally read in some such way as this:

A.U. 734 –
Commotatio martirum Petir ocus Phoil ocus Phatraicc ad legem perficiendam.

A.U. 836 –
Dermait do dul co Connachta (went to Connacht) *cum lege et vexillis Patricii.*

But the presence of the relics does not prove anything: it would have been equally suitable had the purpose of the *cáin* been to apply a law or to exact a tribute.[2] The oldest part of the text *Cáin Adamnáin* states in its opening sentence that it aims to secure exemption from violence for the church, her household, clients and property, clerics, women, and children under the age of armed combat. Later the law of Adamnán confined itself to the protection of women. A gloss on Colmán's hymn defines the purpose of the law of Adamnán as 'not to slay women'; of the law of Patrick as 'not to slay clerics'. This same gloss defines the law of Dáire as 'not to steal cattle' or, in another version, as 'not to kill cattle',[3] a measure possibly directed against the wanton killing of cattle which could not be driven off in raids. The Law

[1] Ó Briain, 'Hagiography of Leinster', p. 458: 'the alleged juridical title under which the tax (imposed during the circuit of the saint's relics) was claimed was termed the *lex* of the saint'. Kenney, *Sources*, p. 237 says: 'It is probable that the chief feature of many of these enforcements, or promulgations, of "laws" was the levying of a cess.'

[2] In the annal entries of the later tenth and eleventh centuries, when the circuit is definitely aimed at raising tribute, the *lex* is not mentioned, and the word used for the visitation is *cúairt* (*A.I.* 973); but by this time conditions had changed and it is dangerous to read back the later facts into the earlier period.

[3] Colman's Hymn, *Thes. Pal.* ii. 306, *M.O.*, p. 210.

of Dáire is mentioned on several occasions in the annals, most explicitly in the Annals of Inisfallen as the *bo-shlechta*.[1] All these references very strongly suggest that the original primary purpose of the laws was to secure peace and order. The wording of the annals supports this impression with entries such as these:

A.U. 697 –

> *Adomnanus ad Hiberniam pergit et dedit legem innocentium populis* (similarly in *C.S.*)

A.U. 721 –

> *Inmesach religiosus legem cum pace Christi super insolam Hiberniae constituit* (similarly in *C.S.* and *A.Tig.*)

The fines derived from such jurisdiction must have been an important source of ecclesiastical income to those monasteries which succeeded, with the help of the provincial kings, in imposing their patrons' laws, and perhaps as time went on the tribute became the decisive factor. Nevertheless, the original legislators seem to have been aiming at 'the peace of Christ', and their laws, proclaimed on at least thirty-three occasions between 697 and 842, must have done something to increase the stability of society.

They may also have helped to change its warlike ethic. Ecclesiastical story-tellers followed secular tradition in admiring courage, generosity, wit, and powers of repartee. But in the secular tales those qualities are often accompanied by savage violence. 'Since I took spear in my hand I have never been without slaying a Connachtman every day and plundering by fire every night, and I have never slept without a Connachtman's head beneath my knee' is the boast of an Ulster hero, but by the eighth century fines awaited the warrior who murdered innocent clerics, women, and children in the process. The reiterated exhortations of church legislators urged that the heart of the true churchman must be without revenge for evil, without hatred of enemies, without arrogance, that he must not speak with a loud, proud voice, that he must be modest, 'gentle his countenance'.[2] Church leaders did

---

[1] *A.I.* 810: 'The law concerning cows in Munster by Dáire and by Aduar son of Echen.'

[2] Rule of Ailbe, stanzas 4, 6, 8, 12, 15.

not always live up to these precepts, but their constant repetition may have tended to mitigate the old standards of boasting and physical prowess.

The general effect of Christianity upon Irish law was to modify it without dislocating it: its rigidity was reduced, and the result was a strengthening of native institutions. Thus, the *cána* provided in effect an extension of the old law of inviolability. They did nothing to weaken the existing methods of maintaining peace in society. Similarly, although the church, as we have seen, was fitted into the law of status which lay at the foundation of secular order, the clerical order provided a means of traversing the hierarchy of classes in Irish society. 'The unfree in the seat of the free,' says the *Small Primer*, quoting a legal maxim, and explains its meaning as 'The man who buys land or rights or franchise by his art or by his husbandry or by his talent that God gives him. From this comes 'A man is better than his descent'.[1] Thus, the son of the free client (*manach*) was educated in the monastery, and though he might remain a layman he might, if he wished, take orders, and become a master of learning, a priest or bishop. Sometimes the authorities were prepared to press the boys to receive orders: 'It is the duty of everyone in orders with whom these boys study to correct and chastise them and to press them to take ecclesiastical orders forthwith, because they are being bred up for the church and for God with a view to receiving orders.'[2] Thus, it was possible to rise through the church from the middle classes of society to its peak.

Was it possible to rise from the lowest classes? The genealogies of saints are almost all aristocratic, but they may not be altogether trustworthy evidence. The canons attributed to Patrick and his coadjutors had recognized the cleric who was 'held under the yoke of servitude'.[3] All the same, it is worth noting that the seventh-century church tried to protect herself from those who abandoned infants on the church. The person who had committed the misdeed, if he or she could be identified, had to perform a penance, the severity of which depended upon the honour-price

---

[1] *A.L.I.* v. 20.
[2] Rule of the Céli Dé, pp. 82–4.
[3] *Pa.* I. 7: but *Pa.* I. 8 implies clerics who are of the noble grades.

of the church involved.[1] The child brought up without any fosterage fee, to whom the church had no legal obligation, seems to have been the slave of the church.[2] Transition from the lowest to the highest rank of society was probably very rare; the normal relationship between church and laity was a contractual one, in which each side profited.

Through the medium of education, the church provided opportunity unknown in pagan society. The learning which it gave was not the exclusive prerogative of those destined to take orders: it was also given to those sons of laymen who would inherit their share of the family lands and remain free clients of the church. In eighth-century Ireland the proportion of literate laymen must have been abnormally high when compared with the rest of northern Europe. It is no coincidence that the Irish church was extraordinarily tolerant in her attitude to native secular learning, for the number of boys from the world being educated in the monastery, and of adults in the world who had received a clerical education, would tend to narrow the gap between the church and lay society. Each could sympathize with the other. The Irish church did not attempt to suppress pagan classical literature or Irish secular learning, and, though the theologians knew well enough that grammar and philosophy, literature and metrics would not suffice to get a man into heaven,[3] everybody recognized that they brought him honour in both the church and the world.

By the eighth century the more important monasteries had well-established *scriptoria*, with a special official in charge.[4] Books were copied – gospels, psalters, liturgical books, commentaries and homilies, extracts from the Fathers, canon law texts, grammars.[5] They hung in leather book satchels from the walls of the clerics' huts, and were taken by the pilgrim on his travels. Sometimes the manuscripts were illuminated, large, richly decorated, to lie upon

---

[1] *Coll.* XLII. 22, *Synodus Hibernensis.* Seven years' penance for a church of high rank, three and a half years for a church of lower rank.

[2] *Coll.* XLII. 24. *De infantibus in ecclesia projectis: Filius allatus servus est eiusdem.* . . .

[3] *Auraicept na nÉces*, ed. Calder, p. 6.

[4] Hughes, 'Irish *Scriptoria*', pp. 249 ff.

[5] Hughes, 'Irish monks and learning', pp. 61–86.

some altar; sometimes they were little pocket-gospels, to be carried around by the priest.[1] By the eighth century Ireland had a great scribal tradition, a beautiful hand, experience in illumination, and an abundance of vellum. She also had men able to read what her scribes had written, laymen with Latin learning, and clerics sympathetic to the secular lore.

Irishmen were not distinguished by any originality in the content of their Latin learning, but by their enthusiasm for it. Masters were determined that their pupils should understand a language with a strange syntax and word-order, not merely copy and learn by rote. They sometimes prepared their texts carefully for the classroom, glossing them with a system of marks connecting one word with another so that Irish students might learn more easily,[2] annotating words and phrases with Irish equivalents or references. It was their eagerness to learn and to teach which fused their contribution with that of English men of learning, and led them to take so active a part in the Carolingian renaissance.

The most clear and obvious use which the church made of her wealth in the later seventh and eighth centuries was in the exercise of artistic patronage. Earlier the great patrons had been the warriors. Whether or not the splendid metal-work objects which adorned the ceremonial of eighth-century churches were made within the monastic city, they were made for the church. Relics were now enshrined, not in simple cases, but with a variety of techniques, the metal cast or beaten, overlaid with a filigree of twisted gold threat, inlaid with enamel, inset with precious stones. The texture was varied, the patterns intricate and delicate. A church might be small and dark, but its altar must have gleamed with reliquary, hanging bowl, chalice, or book-cover. In stone-work the contrast between the simplicity of the early crosses, incised on dressed slabs of stone, and the elaborate beauty of the later, free-standing crosses with their panels of ornament, vividly illustrates the transition from an apostolic and ascetic to an established church.[3]

[1] P. McGurk, *Sacris Erudiri*, viii (1956), 249–70. See Plate V.
[2] M. Draak, *Mededelingen der Koninklijke Nederlandsche Akademie van Wetenschappen, aft Letterkunde*, Nierve Reeks, xx, No. 10, 1957, pp. 261–82.
[3] See Plates II and X.

The church had brought Irish art and learning into close touch with continental developments, and had widened the repertoire of the craftsmen without stamping out the old forms. The native schools of law and poetry continued to flourish, but the land had accepted Latin learning and the native schools had learned the art of writing. The smiths, who had once been patronized exclusively by the warrior class, now produced their most exquisite work for the church. Pre-Christian society, with its institutions of sick-maintenance, fosterage, and the care of the old, had already some concept of social responsibility: the church, with its rights of sanctuary and laws of protection, attempted to increase public security. The Christian church had embraced all that was congenial in heroic society, its honour and generosity, its splendour and display, its enthusiasm, its respect for learning: in so doing, she had shed some of her classical trappings, and had become a Celtic church. Her strength and weakness lay in her full adjustment to her environment.

CHAPTER 15

The 'abuses' of power

The eighth-century church, respected, powerful, and wealthy, was not subject to any hierarchy and not uniform in its discipline. Although the Easter controversy had been settled, there was still considerable difference of opinion on the degree of ascetism which should be required from churchmen, and no one over-riding authority existed to announce and enforce a fixed standard. Thus, the dangers of prosperity were enhanced. In such a situation the manner of life practised by the leaders of the church was of vital importance. The abbot, who might be in episcopal orders, was head of the tribe of the church; he had legal responsibilities towards the tribe and administered the church's property. In the words of an early-ninth-century Rule:

If you are the leader (*toísech*) of a church, noble is the obligation;
Preservation of the rights of the church from the small to the great.

. . . . .

Yours to judge each one according to grade and according to deed.

. . . . .

Yours to rebuke the foolish, punish the hosts, turning disorder into order . . . [1]

In addition, the abbot was father of his church, head of the monastic family, and, if he were in orders, responsible for their spiritual instruction. We have already seen how Columcille cared for both the temporal and spiritual welfare of his monks, and there are stories in the saints' Lives, though most are later in date, which show the abbot entering into the problems of some monk with imaginative sympathy.[2] Moreover, he was accessible to the laity, and must act as their adviser and protector. The tract on the Monastery of Tallaght, originally written in the Old Irish period,

[1] From the section on the abbot in the Rule of S. Carthage, ed. Mac Eclaise, pp. 498–500.
[2] E.g. the homesick Leinsterman in the monastery of S. Comgall of Bangor, *V.S.H.* ii. 16.

tells how Duiblitir of Finglas, importuned by a poor old beggar woman as he came 'out of the garden, over the stile into the field', at first cursed her impatiently ('Be off with you then! Misfortune take your face!'), but later made provision for her,[1] while both earlier and later saints' Lives praise the shrewdness or the loving kindness of their heroes. The words commonly used to describe the abbot's office in the pre-Viking era indicate his many-sided activity: *abb* or *abbas*, 'father', with its feminine equivalent, *abbatissa*; *comarba*, 'heir' to privileges and property; *princeps* 'prince', or the feminine *dominatrix*. The leaders of the early Irish church not only held positions of authority but also were frequently exposed to worldly influences.

One of the most disputed questions of early Irish church history is this: Were the holders of high ecclesiastical office in the pre-Viking era in major orders, or were they sometimes laymen? Patrick describes himself as bishop; the canons attributed to 'Patrick, Auxilius and Iserninus the bishops' emphasize episcopal authority within the hierarchy of the church, and demand letters of introduction from British clergy, who may not minister without them. We know that many of the leaders of the sixth-century church were priests and that some were bishops, and it is generally assumed from this that all were in major orders. The Additions to Tírechán name eight men who are the 'ecclesiastical progeny' of Feidlimid, concluding with the words: 'These men were all bishops and abbots (*principes*) venerating Patrick and his successors.'[2] In the seventh century Cummean speaks of 'the priests of the Lord, who preside (*praesunt*) over the churches',[3] and both ecclesiastical canons and secular laws leave no doubt that the layman commanded less honour than the bishop or priest. Some of the evidence thus shows clearly enough that church leaders were often in major orders.

Nevertheless, there is other evidence, probably from the seventh century and certainly not later than the eighth, which shows that the abbot was not always obliged to be in major orders. The *Synodus Hibernensis* legislates for the *princeps* who is a priest, and, by implication, for one who is not. The canon reads as follows:

[1] *P.R.I.A.* xxix. 130.   [2] *Arm.* 16 b 2, *Tr. Life*, p. 336.
[3] *Cu.* Addenda 3.

Placuit, ut princeps, qui se ipsum non dedit aut sua, sed tamen servabit ecclesiae, si ejectus fuerit, aut voluerit abscedere, dimittat dimidium seminis in pecoribus ecclesiae, et quod ei datum, relinquat intactum, nisi quod necessitas loci illius exegerit ab eo, et quod secum intulit, tollat. Si ipse dominatricem aut ministros conduxit, in sua parte erunt, si vero causa loci conduxit, cum parte loci exibunt, et omnes oblationes alienorum inter principem et ecclesiam dividentur in separatione; sed si princeps sacerdos catholicus sit, omnes autem labores, quos ille fecit, et omnia loci ornamenta, loci erunt, et quidquid ipse laborans impenderit, de substantia loci non reddet, exceptis rebus maximis et propriis, id est, specialibus ecclesiae vasis. Aliis vero placuit, quod in primo anno sparsit, quando egenus fuit, in separatione non reddet.[1]

I take this to mean that the departing abbot has to leave half his own herds to the church, that whatever was granted to him as abbot he must leave intact unless he has legitimately dispensed it in fulfilling his office, but that if he himself has added anything to the church's substance he may take it away. If he hired[2] *ministri*[3] or an abbess (*dominatrix*) they leave with him. All the offerings made by outsiders (*alieni*) during his tenure of the abbacy are to be divided between him and the church. The canon then goes on to consider what happens *si princeps sacerdos catholicus sit*, in which case his activities will have been more closely identified with the interests of the church. This must imply that the preceding regulations apply to the *princeps* who is not a priest or, by implication, a bishop:

> But if the *princeps* be a catholic priest, all the labours which he did and all the ornaments of the place belonged to the place; and whatever he, labouring, expended from the substance of the place he shall not return, except the outstanding and exclusive things, i.e. the special vessels of the church.

The way in which these regulations worked is by no means clear, but it can hardly be denied that the men who framed the canon

[1] *Coll.* XLIII. 6.

[2] A possible meaning of *conduco*. The contingency by which a lay abbot engages men in orders to perform ecclesiastical duties seems to be envisaged in the commentaries, *A.L.I.* v. 54, 126.

[3] In late Latin *ministri* might mean 'any church official below the rank of presbyter, especially deacon' (Souter, *Glossary of Later Latin*, p. 253). In MS. C.C.C.C. 279 a ninth- or tenth-century collection of Irish canonical texts, *ministerium* is quite clearly used to mean the office of deacon. The sense here would seem to suggest 'priests'.

regarded the 'abbot' and the 'abbot who is a priest' as two different persons.

The succession to the coarbship of Druim Lias, as it is described in the Additions to Tírechán, also suggests that under certain circumstances the abbot could be a layman. Féth Fio seems to have been the landowner here, for it is he who, two years before his death, made the confession and bequest governing the succession:

> That there is not a family right of inheritance to Druim Lias, except [in] the race of Féth Fio if there be any member of the clan, who shall be good, shall be devout, shall be conscientious. If there is not, it is to be seen whether such a person can be found from among the community of Druim Lias or of its monastic clients (*di muintir . . . no diamanchib*). If one is not found, a pilgrim of the household of Patrick is put into it.[1]

It is possible that the good, devout, and conscientious candidate of Féth Fio's family or the candidate from the community of Druim Lias would have been in major orders, but likely that the monastic client would not. The precedence for succession contained in this extract has some general similarities with that laid down in *Córus Béscna*. Here the original text, as printed in the edition of 1873, is so laconic as to be incomprehensible without its gloss.[2] Text and gloss taken together require that the succession rests, first, in the family of the patron saint, secondly, in the family of the landowner, though these may be one and the same. The gloss says that the patron's family has the prior claim, provided it can produce a fit candidate; 'even though there should be but a psalm-singer of them, it is he that will obtain the abbacy'. The psalm-singer would not have been in major orders. If neither of these families has a suitable candidate the coarbship passes to one of the monastic client class; failing this, to the chief church of the monastic confederation (the *annóit* church). Three more types of church are then given, in descending order, until, in the last resort, a pilgrim may assume the abbacy. This gloss suggests that under certain circumstances an abbot who is not in major orders

---

[1] *Thes. Pal.* ii. 239, or *Tr. Life*, pp. 338–41, emending *décrad dimuintir Patricc* to *deorad* (see E. Gwynn, *Hermathena*, xxxii (1911), 384–5). On the pilgrim, see *supra*, p. 136.

[2] *A.L.I.* iii. 72–5.

may be the legitimate successor, and that kindred was a most important condition governing ecclesiastical inheritance.

As we have already seen, family connexions were from early times an important element in Irish abbatial succession. This does not necessarily mean that abbots were originally non-celibate and that sons succeeded their fathers. Claimants to the abbacy were probably often descended from a common ancestor, and a man might be succeeded by his nephew, or by a more distant relative. At Iona Columcille's successor was his cousin, Baíthéne; the next abbot, Laisrén, was the son of another cousin of Columcille, then the succession passed to a different branch of the family before it returned, in the fifth abbot, to Laisrén's nephew Ségéne. Until the death of Adamnán in 704 all the abbots except one were descendants of Conall Gulban, though some of them were only distantly related to their immediate predecessors. Throughout this period there was a high standard of ecclesiastical discipline at Iona, and the hereditary principle had no apparent ill effects on the quality of candidates for the abbacy. Abbot and monks would appear to have been celibate.

By the eighth century there is evidence that not all abbots of Irish monastic churches were celibate, and that abbatial succession was sometimes passing directly from father to son. Eighth-century secular law recognized the celibate bishop or priest, the bishop or priest of one wife, and the bishop or priest undergoing penance, all of whom had a differing honour-price.[1] It may, of course, be argued that the married bishop had a wife before he took orders, and then ceased to cohabit with her, but though the fifth-century church needed such mature converts, by the eighth century, when the church was established with monasteries full of boys receiving a clerical education, this argument sounds somewhat forced. Another law tract mentions the bishop with sons.[2]

The Annals for the pre-Viking age provide a number of examples of abbots whose sons succeeded them in abbatial office.

[1] *A.L.I.* iv. 364. For examples of *óg(a)e*; 'chastity', see *Contribs. to a Diction-ary*, N-O-P., Cols. 111–12.

[2] *A.L.I.* v. 234. Neither king nor bishop paid for the legal liabilities of their sons.

Sometimes the son immediately follows his father, sometimes the reigns of other abbots intervene. This is not surprising, for succession to secular kingship was not governed by primogeniture: any man whose father, grandfather, or greatgrandfather had reigned was himself eligible for royal office. In many cases it is impossible to tell the antecedents of abbots named in the annals, but often the patronymic is given, and if the name of the father of one abbot occurs a few years earlier as the name of a reigning abbot of the same house it seems likely that the two abbots are father and son. In cases where the family inheritance can be traced for three or more generations the likelihood becomes virtual certainty.

The houses of Slane and Lusk both provide clear examples of family inheritance. During the last three decades of the eighth century the church at Lusk was ruled by a series of men who traced their descent to Crundmáel, who died as abbot of Lusk in 736. One of Crundmáel's sons seems to have become abbot of near-by Duleek,[1] but that man's son was abbot of Lusk.

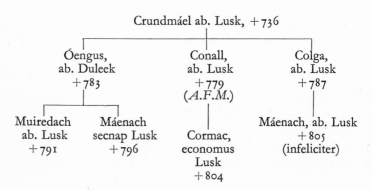

At Slane men of two families seem to have held the abbacy, one descended from 'Colmán of the Britons' abbot of Slane, who died in 751 *A.U.*, the other from Cormac of Slane. During part of the time descendants of Colmán held appointments at Slane together with the abbacy of the neighbouring house of Cill-Foibrich; while of the three sons of Cormac of Slane, one died as abbot of

---

[1] We have only his father's name, so cannot be certain. The entries shown in the table are from *A.U.*, unless shown otherwise.

Slane, another as abbot of Slane, Louth,[1] and Duleek, and another as abbot of Louth.

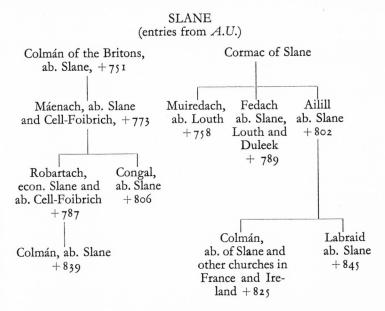

SLANE
(entries from *A.U.*)

Colmán of the Britons, ab. Slane, +751

Máenach, ab. Slane and Cell-Foibrich, +773

Robartach, econ. Slane and ab. Cell-Foibrich +787

Colmán, ab. Slane +839

Cormac of Slane

Muiredach, ab. Louth +758

Fedach ab. Slane, Louth and Duleek + 789

Ailill ab. Slane + 802

Colmán, ab. of Slane and other churches in France and Ireland + 825

Congal, ab. Slane + 806

Labraid ab. Slane + 845

There are other houses where succession within a family was less persistent, but where father and son would both appear to have held the abbacy: at Monasterboice Cormac died in 764, and his son Dub-da-inber seems to have succeeded him immediately; at Achad Bó, Scandal died in 782, after ruling his abbey for forty-three years, and his son Feradach after an intervening reign died in 813; at Trevet, a father, son, and grandson seem to have followed each other, ruling between 774 and 839; at Lann Leire abbot Máenach, who died in 721, was succeeded in turn by two grandsons, the latter dying in 781; at Armagh Dub-dá-leithe (*obit* 793) and his son Condmach (*obit* 807) both held the abbot's chair. In the poem of 'Advice to a Prince', parts of which seem to be old though the whole composition is hardly earlier than the tenth century,[2] the section which suggests that each man shall

[1] Some versions say Lusk, but *A.U.*, probably the most reliable for Meath affairs, reads Louth.

[2] I quote Professor Binchy's opinion on the date. The poem is edited and translated by T. O'Donoghue, *Ériu*, ix (1921), 43–54.

follow his father's calling begins: 'Let the abbot's son enter the church.' The eighth-century annals show that this advice was not infrequently followed, and annals, secular laws, and ecclesiastical canons together establish beyond reasonable doubt that married abbots were recognized in the pre-Viking era.[1]

The system of family inheritance was not universal. Professor Ryan has demonstrated that there is no evidence for it in the monastic succession of Clonmacnois during the pre-Viking age.[2] In many houses a hereditary system with celibate abbots like those of seventh-century Iona may have continued. Moreover, we should not exaggerate the degeneracy of a married abbacy and of direct abbatial succession from father to son. Ireland was not a democracy of equal opportunity for all, but an aristocratic society in which it was recognized that special skills often ran in particular families. The sons had almost certainly received a clerical education, whether or not they were in orders, and were sometimes learned men. Families like those which controlled the abbacies at Slane and Duleek must have been part of the tribe (*fine*) of the church, their family lands inseparably tied up with the property of the church. It may well be that some families genuinely did produce a series of able ecclesiastical administrators, whom churches were eager to appoint. Torbach, the abbot of Armagh, at whose will (or 'dictation' *dictante*) the Book of Armagh was written, was the son of Gorman, abbot of Louth, and his own son Áedagán was also abbot of Louth. Armagh, Trevet, and Lusk all had flourishing *scriptoria* during the period when sons were succeeding their fathers in the abbacies. Slane had her distinguished men of learning, Ailill, *sapiens et iudex optimus*, Congal 'wise man and celibate', and round about this period was supporting at least one anchorite.[3] The evidence does not suggest that in these churches either intellectual life or religious observance was in any way retarded.

Some of these abbot-sons-of-abbots held office in more than one church. Máenach was abbot of Slane and the neighbouring

---

[1] There are also cases of family influence, e.g. the Ua Suanaig at Rahan, the Ua Lugadon at Clondalkin. For Kildare see F.Ó Briain, 'The Hagiography of Leinster', pp. 454–64.

[2] 'The abbatial succession at Clonmacnois', pp. 490–507.

[3] *Infra*, p. 175.

house of Kilbrew, and his son was *economus* of Slane and abbot of Kilbrew. Fedach combined the abbacies of Slane, Louth, and Duleek, while his nephew Colmán was abbot of Slane 'and other churches in France and Ireland'. The custom by which one and the same man held office in two or more churches seems to have begun in the eighth century, though it becomes much more common later. It is not confined to monasteries in which there is a clear family interest. In 748 the annals record the death of a man who held the abbacies of Clonard and Kildare, in 778 another had been abbot of Connor and Lynally.[1] An abbot of Kilcullen, who died in 785, was also scribe of Kilnamanagh. Cormac (*obit* 782) had been abbot of 'Ardbraccan and other monasteries', Ciarán (*obit* 784) abbot of Ráith-maige-oenaigh and Tech-Mofinnu, Senchán (*obit* 796) abbot of Killeigh and Birr. How are we to interpret such combinations?

Most of the houses are geographically fairly near each other; but not all, for Clonard and Kildare, Connor and Lynally were in different kingdoms. The houses were not part of the same *paruchia*, and the combination seems to have been temporary and personal. Could the abbot have held his two, or three, appointments in succession? This seems unlikely. Very occasionally the annalists indicate, by using a word like 'previously', that a man has ceased to hold an office,[2] but normally there is no such indication, and, indeed, the annalists assume that the offices were held conjointly: if a reigning king could 'take' up an abbacy, or a bishop 'take' kingship,[3] as happened a little later, a double abbacy was surely not outside the bounds of possibility. But the chronological incidence of these double abbacies offers the best evidence that they were held concurrently, not in succession, for the number recorded rises very sharply from 837 onwards, reaching its greatest frequency in the 860s. The serious dislocation caused by the Viking settlements begins in 830, and most of the abbots appointed round about then would have been dying in the 860s. How, then, are we to account for the commencement of this

---

[1] All dates from *A.U.*

[2] *A.U.* 848 Fínsnechta of Luibnech died, an anchorite, and king of Connacht previously (*antea*).

[3] See *infra*, pp. 211 ff., 221.

M

practice in the pre-Viking era? A probable explanation seems to be that the monasteries concerned wanted to secure a good candidate, and found that they could do so better by arranging for the joint tenure of two abbacies. Shortage of candidates and troubled conditions may have encouraged the practice. The combination of the abbacies of Clonard and Kildare must have existed between 745 (when Forannán abbot of Clonard died) and 748. It is significant that in 742 and 743 there had been a serious outbreak of a disease called *bolgach*, which the annalist interprets as leprosy, but which is now identified with smallpox.[1] Apart from this forerunner, the practice of holding in plurality is not recorded in the annals until the 770s. Between 773 and 807 there are thirteen recorded instances, none in the second decade and two in the third decade of the ninth century, before the accumulation of the 830s and the subsequent period. During the 770s and 780s Ireland suffered a series of famines and plagues, and the difficulties of those years may have encouraged monasteries to appoint men of experience, often abbots of near-by houses, probably persons who already possessed some material provision. It is possible that the joint-tenure of abbacies came about owing to the need of the churches rather than the greed of the abbots.

Married clergy, lay abbots, sons succeeding their fathers in ecclesiastical appointments, offices held in plurality, all characteristics usually considered as abuses of the Viking age, were in fact all present in the Irish church before the Viking raids began. None of these customs were necessarily abuses: all were either continuous practices of early usages or direct developments from the social environment. There were many links between the monasteries and lay society, and laymen frequently entered the monastic enclosure. At Kildare in the seventh-century church, as we have seen, clergy and nuns were separated from the laity by a dividing wall; at Armagh the bishops, priests, anchorites, and other religious worshipped in the south church, while the virgins met in the north church with the penitents and those serving the church in legitimate matrimony.[2] Columbanus at Luxeuil was accused by the Gaulish king 'of violating the customs of the

---

[1] Sir William P. MacArthur; *I.H.S.*, vi (1949), 184.
[2] *Arm.* 21 a 1, 2.

country and of not allowing all Christians to enter the interior of
the monastery'.[1] But other sources show that strict segregation of
the monastery from the world was not practised. The *Synodus
Hibernensis* regulates the penalties for the violation of a holy
place:[2] seven years' penance is due for the public violation of the
relics of bishops or martyrs, presumably relics kept in the inner
enclosure. For any killing done within the boundary of a holy
place where laymen are entertained, one year's penance is demanded. The laity habitually came within the *termon* of an Irish
monastery. But even this does not go far enough, and the canon
concludes:

> We make indulgence, indeed, in the latter day, fifty days, because
> that place is not said to be holy in which enter murderers with their
> spoils, thieves with their thieving, adulterers and perjurors and
> *precones* (hawkers) and *magi*. And not only should every holy place
> be cleansed within, but its *termini*, which are consecrated, should also
> be cleansed.

This suggests that the outer precincts of a monastery were open
to all comers. Monasteries were cities, schools, places of refuge,
and penitentiaries as well as religious centres.

It was necessary that as the church gained property and privileges and assumed responsibilities it should take an interest in
material wealth. From the sources at our disposal it is difficult to
judge whether or not this interest was inordinate. The *cána* were
promulgated on twenty-one known occasions between the first
publication of the Law of Adamnán (697) and the end of the
eighth century. Originally the purpose of these saints' 'laws' was,
as we have seen, to maintain peace and order; but the Irish word
cáin means 'tribute', as well as 'law', and the text of the *Cáin
Adamnáin* shows that his community gained part of the profits of
jurisdiction. During the eighth century the communities of
Columcille, Patrick, Ciarán of Clonmacnois, Brendan, Ailbe of
Emly, Ua Suanaig of Rahan, and Comán of Roscommon must
have found that their *cána* brought in substantial gains.[3]

The promulgation of a saint's 'law' with its attendant tribute
must have had a double effect: to encourage peace and to add to

---

[1] Life by Jonas, c. 33.   [2] *Coll.* XLIV. 8.
[3] Hughes, 'The Church and the World', pp. 99–113.

the wealth of the patron. It seems to have been customary, when the *cáin* was applied, to take round the relics of the saint for exhibition. The word which the Annals use for this custom is *commotatio*. When Patrick's law was effected in 734 the annalist notes the *commotatio* of the precious relics of Armagh; 'Circuit of the relics of Peter and Paul and Patrick to fulfill the law'.[1] Sometimes the annals record a 'moving round' of the relics without mentioning any law. It has been maintained and is usually accepted that the purpose of such a circuit was the exaction of a tax.[2] But another explanation is possible. Examination of the Annals for the pre-Viking age suggests that the circuit of the relics, like the original promulgation of the *cána*, may at first have been genuinely intended for the help of society and have contributed only incidentally to the support of the monasteries. For the circuit of the relics seems frequently to follow or to be associated with natural disasters. The outbreak of smallpox in 742–43 was accompanied in 743 by the 'Circuit of the relics of Trian of Kildalkey'.[3] The calamitous period from 772 to 786 coincides with several relic-circuits. A great fair of 772 was interrupted by 'lightning and thunder, like unto the day of judgement', and 'fire from heaven', which so terrified the people that they fasted for two three-day periods separated by only one meal. 773 brought 'unusual drought' and famine, and the following year many people died from the disease which the annalists call 'the bloody flux'. In 777 and 778 the 'bloody flux' broke out again, with a 'mortality of cattle' in 778, and in the following year famine and smallpox (*bolgach*). Heavy snow in the April of 780 further reduced morale.

---

[1] *Commotatio martirum Petir et Phoil et Phatraicc ad legem perficiendam.*

[2] 'From an early period the custom had prevailed, as in continental countries, of holding processions of these relics for the veneration of the faithful. By the eighth century the practice seems to have deteriorated to a mere expedient for replenishing the coffers of the king and his monastic relatives. The relics, with their shrines, were taken on a tour of the country at frequent intervals, and a tax was imposed on the district thus visited with the concurrence of the ruling prince and of the abbot of the monastery possessing the shrine. The tour included the territories claimed as belonging to the *paruchia* or jurisdictional sphere of the monastery possessing the shrine. The annals use the term *commotatio* for this circuit of the relic-shrine . . .' F. Ó Briain, 'Hagiography of Leinster', p. 457. In previous publications of my own I have implied acceptance of Professor Ó Briain's view.

[3] *A. Tig. Commotatio martirum Treno Cille Delge et in bolgach.*

In 783 disease again broke out (*scamach*), with a further recurrence in 786, a year of storm and flood. During this disastrous time several churches brought their relics out on circuits: in 776 Clonard and Slane took round the relics of their respective patrons, Finnian and Erc. In 784 the relics of the son of Erc came to Tailtiu, the ancient hill of meeting,[1] and in 785 the church of Ardbraccan made a circuit with the relics of its saint, Ultán. The evidence does not allow us to say that the disaster and the relic-circuit were directly and closely associated, but it does suggest that during a period when society had been disturbed by plague or cattle murrain or famine, both church and people welcomed the relics of the saint. Further circuits were made in 790, 793, and 794, without the spur of natural disaster. Nevertheless, it may well be that at first the circuits were not dictated wholly by the grasping demands of the monasteries, but were partly remedial in character, having the same double nature as the early *cána*.

One practice of the church in the pre-Viking age can hardly be given any moral justification. The monasteries were already involved in physical violence. On a number of occasions it is impossible to say where responsibility lay. It seems likely that the ecclesiastics killed in 735 and 744 were not the aggressors,[2] and when a tribe destroyed a church we need not assume that the church had invited attack.[3] But there are fights initiated by clerics, sometimes each heading their own party, and pitched battles between monasteries, for which the churches cannot escape responsibility, while monasteries put armies into the field to take part in secular wars. The 'killing of bishop Echthigern by a priest at the altar of Brigit', recorded at 760 and 762 may well have been a personal quarrel ('From that time forward,' adds one annalist,[4] 'no priest performs mass at Kildare in the presence of a bishop'); but the battle (*bellum*) at Ferns in 783, between the abbot and the *economus*, sounds like a major split between two parties in the

---

[1] Is this a slip for Erc son of Daig, i.e. the Slane patron?

[2] *A.Tig.* = *A.U.* 735 Flann, abbot of Kilmore; 744 *A.U.* Laidgnén abbot of Seir, Colmán bishop of Lissan.

[3] E.g. The burning of Cell-mor-dithrib by the Uí Cremthainn 757 (the church whose abbot was murdered in 735).

[4] *A.Tig.*, which occasionally give details omitted elsewhere.

monastery. In 760 there was a pitched battle between the house-holds (*muintir*) of Clonmacnois and Birr, followed in 764 by a major battle between Clonmacnois and Durrow, in which two hundred men of the *familia* of Durrow fell and Clonmacnois was victorious.

Sometimes the monasteries were involved in secular wars. In 759 there was a battle at Emain Macha between the Ulstermen and the Southern Uí Néill in which the King of Ulster was victorious. The Annals of Tigernach say that the battle was 'at the will of Airechtach priest of Armagh through discord with abbot Fer-dá-chrích', and there seems no reason to doubt this statement. Céle-Petair, abbot of Armagh, died in 758 and his successor Fer-dá-chrích ruled until his death in 768, so the quarrel would have occurred at the beginning of his abbacy. 'Airechtach the priest' could be the man of this name who died as abbot of Armagh in 794; in 759 he would probably have been in his thirties, and he was of the Uí Bresail, the area from which Céle-Petair had come. He may have been disappointed at Fer-dá-chrích's appointment, and have tried to stir up trouble. This is not the only instance in which abbeys were involved in secular wars in the pre-Viking age. In 776 the *familia* of Durrow seem to have been fighting on the side of the Munstermen in a battle between the Uí Néill and Munster, and in 757, when the Munstermen were fighting each other, the abbot (*princeps*) of Mungret (near Limerick) was killed. It has been argued that the fighting forces of the monasteries did not include monks or priests, but the total evidence makes this very unlikely. In any case, the abbot must ultimately be re-sponsible for the decision to go to war.

Ecclesiastical synods are rarely mentioned in the eighth-century records. It had been the custom during the sixth and seventh centuries for church leaders to meet, discuss their problems, decide on policy, and pass legislation, a practice which had probably been encouraged by the differences existing between the 'Roman' and 'Irish' parties. But after the Synod of Birr in 697 we hear of no further meeting until 780, when 'several anchorites and scribes' under the leadership of Duiblitir abbot of Finglas attended a *congressio senadorum* of the Uí Néill and the Leinstermen at Tara. Ecclesiastical assemblies become less frequent, and abbots in the eighth century seem to have been looking increasingly to the kings for support, rather than to their fellow-clerics.

There are indications at Armagh, in the later eighth and ninth centuries, that political divisions lent strength to disputes over the abbatial succession. Armagh was situated within the sub-kingdom of Airthir and was part of the over-kingdom of Airgialla; during this period the Uí Néill of Cenél Eógain, on the northern frontier of Airgialla, were becoming the dominant power. In 827 the king of Airgialla was defeated at the Battle of Leth Cam by the Cenél Eógain, to whom the Airgialla now became tributary. During the decades preceding this battle some of the abbots of Armagh appear to have been on friendly terms with the Cenél Eógain. Abbot Dub-dá-leithe and his son Condmach were members of the Clann Sinaich, one of the leading families of Airthir. These two abbots were opposed by no less than three rival claimants. Dub-dá-leithe gained help from the north in opposing one of them;[1] another, Gormgal, had the support of the sub-kingdom of Uí Cremthainn, neighbour to Airthir.[2] It was a dispute between Eógan Mainistrech, abbot of Armagh in 827, and the king of Airgialla which touched off the Battle of Leth Cam; for the king of Airgialla drove Eógan from the abbacy and instead set up his own half-brother, Artrí. Niall Caille, king of Cenél Eógain, seized his opportunity, made war on the Airgialla, reinstated Eógan, and made himself overlord of the kingdom.[3] The abbots of Armagh had recognized and supported the growing power of Cenél Eógain. Abbot Eógan's troubles did not end with his reinstatement in 827. In 830 he was attacked by the king of the Southern Uí Néill (Conchobar son of Donnchad), his household was taken prisoner and his herds carried off. We do not know the immediate consequences of this, but king Conchobar died in 832 or 833, whereupon Niall Caille became overlord of his kingdom. Presumably he continued to support Eógan, for when Eógan died in 834 it was as abbot of Armagh and Clonard, one of the great monasteries of the Southern Uí Néill. The history

---

[1] Faendalach: 'it is he who fell by Dub-dá-leithe . . . Dub-dá-leithe, son of Sinach, is at hand with kings from the North'. Note and poem in the 'Ancient List of Coarbs', p. 322.

[2] *A.U.* 793. [3] *A.F.M.* 825.

of the abbots of Armagh in the pre-Viking period clearly illustrates the value to the church of royal patronage.

Armagh politicians seem to have been astute and active, and
were probably not altogether typical of Irish abbots; but the
association of kings and abbots in the promulgation of the *cána*
must have stressed the identity of secular and ecclesiastical
interests, and may have tended to emphasize any divergence of
interest which existed between monasteries. The church had been
founded as a religious force, and such it remained; but by the
seventh century it had become an institution accommodated to
secular law, and by the end of the eighth century certain churches
were beginning to play a more direct and decisive part in secular
politics. As we have seen, most of the so-called 'abuses' in the
church which are usually ascribed to the evil effects of the Viking
settlements were present before the Vikings arrived. Yet they did
not exclude the beneficial uses of power. An ambitious monastic
community, willing to fight for its own advantage, could also use
its wealth to encourage learning and art; abbots who succeeded
their fathers in office made efforts to maintain peace and order in
society; they saw to it that the sacraments were performed, that
Christianity was preached and hospitality provided. During the
eighth century ascetic discipline had become increasingly (though
not universally) relaxed, but the church still respected ascetic
practice and was still conscious of her spiritual mission. She was
ready for revival.

CHAPTER 16

Ascetic revival

Eighth-century Irish monasticism had adjusted itself to the world in a way which some sixth- and early seventh-century ascetics would have condemned. Columbanus, who had absolutely forbidden sexual relations to any man in orders, would have taken no lenient view of lapses; his autocratic concept of the abbot's authority would hardly have admitted the arrangements between abbots and monks for which the *Synodus Hibernensis* legislates; his austere standards of behaviour for monks were not consistent with lay intrusion. Yet ascetic practices were never completely neglected, and towards the end of the eighth century they achieved a powerful revival.

Asceticism in the Irish church had always commanded veneration. All the great saints are described as holding lightly to the good things of the world, like S. Brigit in the ninth-century hymn which begins:

> Victorious Brigit loved not the world.
> She sat the perch of a bird on a cliff.[1]

For centuries the Irish church had had its anchorites, men who withdrew from the life of the monastic city into asceticism and prayer: the canons speak of them with esteem in the same tone as they use when referring to bishops, scribes, and the great abbots.[2] During the latter part of the eighth century a new order of ascetics appears, men who call themselves *céli dé* (culdees), 'companions of God'.[3] Moreover, in the later eighth and more especially in the ninth centuries the number of recorded anchorites markedly increases. The fire of asceticism had never died out in Ireland, but now it once more burst into flame. The ascetics themselves were

---

[1] *Liber Hymnorum* i. 112, ii. 40. [2] *Hi.* I. 29, V. 11.

[3] Or perhaps 'clients' or 'vassals of God.' As Professor Jackson points out to me, the *céle* enters into a contract of *célsine* with a *flaith* or lord. The *céle Dé* was the man who took God for his *flaith*, who entered into a contract of service with Him.

no longer isolated individuals, but often groups of like-minded men. It is surely reasonable to apply the words 'reform' or, better, 'religious revival' to these developments.[1]

The culdees certainly regarded themselves as reformers. Máel-ruain (*obit* 792), founder of Tallaght and head of a community of culdees, was in touch with a number of like-minded ascetics. Their teaching has been recorded in three versions,[2] all going back to material put together in the ninth century. The original text was written by some disciple with a very puritanical cast of mind, who may have over-emphasized certain rather unattractive aspects of his masters' teaching. Nevertheless, we cannot escape observing that on several occasions the culdee leaders are shown as disparaging the laxity of the 'old churches', to which their own strict practices bore favourable contrast.

> Máel-díthruib [of the culdees of Terryglass] asked Hilary [of Loch Cré] whether it would be right to accept any of the fruits of the church from the clergy of the old churches who were known not to be leading a good life. Hilary replied that it was right, 'For,' said he, 'you have no responsibility for their evil ways if you had no hand in receiving or maintaining them in the degrees or orders which they occupy; and even though they are corrupt by reason of their own bad life, the fruits of the church, or of the saint who left his blessing there, are not corrupt. We have a better right to receive them, if we do receive them, than they have to own them, being evil as they are.'[3]

Another version gives this episode more succinctly, but leaves no doubt of what Hilary the Culdee thought of the old churches which supported him and his like:

> 'Though they be defiled, they defile not the patron's fruits. For that belongs to us rather than to them.'[4]

---

[1] Professor Binchy defines them as a 'reform movement'. *Ériu*, xix (1962), 53–4. Mrs Chadwick, *The Age of the Saints*, pp. 73, 85–8, rightly stresses the continuity of the later-eighth- and ninth-century anchorites with their predecessors in the earlier period, but in refusing to allow that these developments constituted a 'reform' in the church she neglects part of the evidence. It is true that the teaching of Máel-ruain and his friends grew out of the teaching of the saints before 650, but it is also true that ascetic practices had not been generally maintained in the eighth-century church.

[2] 'The Monastery of Tallaght', 'The Teaching of Máel-ruain', and 'The Rule of the Céli Dé'. There is also a section on 'The Culdees' in the early-ninth-century metrical 'Rule of S. Carthage'.

[3] 'Teaching', § 35.   [4] 'Monastery', § 4.

On another occasion Máel-ruain of Tallaght dealt with similar scruples voiced by Colgu, anchorite of Slane:

> 'But as to what shall be brought to you out of the patron's fruits, though all who bring it be impure, it is pure for him who is holy. . . . For the patron's fruit belongs to you rather than to them'.[1]

It is difficult to maintain, in the face of these and similar statements,[2] that according to one who knew of their views, Máel-ruain, Máel-díthruib, Hilary, and other culdees did not regard themselves as reformers, advocating a stricter life and condemning certain accepted practices.

It is partly strictures like these which have earned a bad name for the church establishment, with its lay abbots, wealth, and powers of jurisdiction. But ardent reformers are bad witnesses to the piety of their predecessors, and, in any case, though the views expressed in the tract are likely to be an accurate representation of the reformers' opinions, the self-righteous tone in which they are couched may not be typical of the whole movement. The evidence shows that the folk of the 'old churches' felt no bitterness towards the reformers: on the contrary, they often maintained the ascetics, giving them honour, sometimes appointing an anchorite as head of their *scriptorium* or as abbot. Even the reformers' own statements sometimes show that the less-severe attitude of monastic officials in the old churches might be dictated, not by laziness, but by a sensible appreciation of what their communities could understand. The Teaching of Máel-ruain quotes Muirchertach mac Olchobair, abbot of Clonfert, who required the recitation of the *Beati* twelve times rather than the culdees' practice of the whole Psalter, 'because he knew that there were more of the monks and penitents who knew the *Beati* by heart than knew the Psalms'.[3] This Muirchertach, who died in 802, was abbot of an old and rich house: none of the annals suggest that he was an anchorite, though the Teaching of Máel-ruain shows that he was sympathetic to the culdees and willing to adopt from their practices as much as he felt could be suitably applied in his own, different, monastic society. The old churches often seem to have shown

---

[1] 'Monastery', § 77.   [2] 'Monastery', § 26.
[3] 'Teaching', § 37: *dona manchaibh* could mean 'of the monks' or 'of the monastic clients'.

more charity and tolerance than the disciple who has given us the ascetics' views.

The reformers were, moreover, much less exposed to worldly influences. Anchorites maintained on the patrons' fruits while they meditated and prayed had no essential work to do among the laity. In the ninth-century Rule of S. Carthage the culdees are called 'the clerics of the enclosure', while Máel-ruain told his disciple Máel-díthruib to stay in his church, to avoid meddling with worldly disputes, never to accompany any man to a law court or assembly in order to plead for any one, but to continue in prayer and let people come to him for instruction.[1] Earlier ascetics had gone on pilgrimage and found themselves preaching to pagan Germans and half-converted Franks, but times had changed, and Máel-ruain forbade men to leave their own country on pilgrimage: such deserters would be 'deniers of Patrick in heaven and of the faith in Ireland'.[2] The new religious did not ask visitors for news of the world, 'since it might harrass and disturb the mind of him to whom it was told'.[3] Máel-ruain advised bishop Sechnassach that the good of his own soul was more important than his filial duty:

> This is what Máel-ruain said to Sechnassach the bishop from Cill Gulbin. His mother besought him to take care of her, and yet would not turn from her sins.[4] Then Sechnassach asked Máel-ruain, 'How shall I at all manage these two things?' This is what he said: 'Though you do not bring her with you to life, let her not carry you to death. But if she be converted, you are bound to take care of her.'[5]

The reformers felt the urgency of the predicament created by men's sin: they were like men at the gallows' foot, praying for deliverance.[6] In such a situation, no compromise with the world was possible.

A similar severity characterizes their standards of asceticism. Secular law recognized the bishop and priest of one wife.[7] The Old Irish Penitential had allowed the reinstatement of priests after

---

[1] 'Teaching', § 12.

[2] 'Monastery', § 17.   [3] 'Monastery', § 2.

[4] I think that this probably means that she would not enter the religious life, or adopt the ascetic practices of the reformers.

[5] 'Monastery', § 46.

[6] 'Monastery', § 1.   [7] *Supra*, p. 135.

the prescribed period of penance following the sins of lust.[1] But Máel-ruain did not approve of allowing any priest who had sinned against chastity to say mass, provided his offence was established:[2] 'he parted with his priests' orders when he committed the sin, and he never recovers them, even though he should do penance'.[3] The régime for married lay folk accepting spiritual direction is as severe as that laid down by the seventh-century ascetics. They are to practise strict continence for three, or according to some authorities, four days and nights in every seven, besides certain additional periods.[4]

The sayings of the reformers show that they thought of the flesh, including the natural functions of the body, as providing constant occasion for sin.[5] The body must therefore be kept in subjection. Lust and desire, as they believed, went with an abundance of blood, so the amount of blood in the body must be reduced by fasting. Women, in particular, were an added source of danger. The early saints had allowed the ministration of women, and some of the reformers' contemporaries in 'the old churches' still associated with them, but Máel-ruain's own attitude is expressed in a story about him and the woman saint Samthann.[6] The holy woman thrust her brooch pin deep into her cheek and after much effort managed to squeeze out a tiny drop of yellow liquid, saying: 'So long as there is this much juice in this body, let him (Máel-ruain) bestow no friendship nor confidence upon womankind.'[7] In their attitude to the body the reformers reacted violently against the practices of the established church. Women were not to be trusted, and with such views it need not surprise us to find that in the later Life of Máel-ruain woman is spoken of as man's 'guardian devil'.[8]

In their other ascetic practices the culdees continued and

---

[1] O. Ir. Pen. II. 3–10.   [2] 'Teaching', § 56.

[3] 'Teaching', § 69.

[4] 'Monastery', § 50; 'Teaching', § 63.

[5] 'Rule of Céli Dé', § 42; 'Monastery', § 59, and the morbid stories which illustrate this dictum in §§ 60 and 61.

[6] Samthann, foundress of Clonbroney, died in 739, and her Life shows a more enlightened attitude. The story expresses the views of Máel-ruain rather than the views of Samthann.

[7] 'Monastery', § 61.   [8] Silva Gadelica I. 37.

developed many of the austerities of earlier saints. The commutation of penance to shorter periods has been spoken of as an 'alleviation',[1] but it was intended to encourage the practice of penance. The Old Irish Table of Penitential Commutations composed in the second half of the eighth century is almost certainly to be associated with the culdees, for the manuscript tradition connects it with other tracts of that provenance, and texts of the 'Tallaght' group on a number of occasions use the word *arre* in its specialized religious meaning of 'commutation of penance'. It seems that the culdees were reviving and popularizing in this practice a form of discipline known to the early Irish church.[2] They performed asceticisms of cross-vigil, and vigils standing in water,[3] and flagellation was administered by another person.[4] Total abstinence was the rule at Tallaght: 'the liquor that causes forgetfulness of God shall not be drunk here,' said Máel-ruain; but his disciple Duiblitir pleaded for relaxation, at least during the three great feasts (Christmas, Easter, and Whitsun), and though Máel-ruain would not relent, Duiblitir did not follow him: '"Well," said Duiblitir, "my monks shall drink it, and they will be in heaven along with yours."'[5] Máel-ruain would allow no music. When Cornán the piper, an anchorite and a 'man of grace', asked if he might play to the saint, Máel-ruain sent him answer: 'These ears are not lent to earthly music, that they may be lent to the music of heaven.'[6]

The culdees also kept Sunday much as though it had been the Jewish Sabbath. No work was done on Sunday, not even the gathering or preparation of food. Bread must be baked and fruit and vegetables must be picked before Sunday began; not even a single apple might be lifted from the ground.[7] Food brought from a distance on Sunday night might not be eaten by the religious.[8] Journeys might not normally be undertaken, though short

---

[1] T. P. Oakley, 'Commutations and Redemptions of Penance in the Penitentials', *Cath. Hist. Rev.*, xviii (1932), 347–8.

[2] See Binchy, *Ériu*, xix (1962), 47–72, for discussion and edition.

[3] 'Monastery', §§ 8, 30, 61. For the practice of vigils in water see *H.E.* v. 12 or Anon. Life of Cuthbert c. 3.

[4] 'Teaching', § 1. Flagellation was practised by Columbanus' community.

[5] 'Monastery', § 6.   [6] 'Monastery', § 10.

[7] 'Monastery', §§ 13, 49, 'Teaching', § 62.   [8] 'Teaching', § 82.

distances (a thousand paces) were legitimate to watch over the sick, administer communion, attend mass, and other 'urgent matters', and some culdees occasionally went farther.[1] Sunday, the Lord's Day, was to be as free as possible from any worldly activity. One man, who 'happened to stay in the bath a while after vespers on Saturday', had to undergo a special fast.[2]

The strict enforcement of Sunday observance must thus be regarded as one of the practices of the reformers. A legend had arisen on the Continent which told how a letter of Christ had fallen from heaven ordering the religious observance of Sunday, with the cessation of all work. This legend seems to have reached Britain and Ireland in the ninth century, where it gained wide currency.[3] *Chronicon Scottorum*, a set of annals connected with Clonmacnois, relates a 'wonder' under the year 811 which may be one of the Irish versions of the legend. If so, it is significant that the letter is received and interpreted by a culdee:

> The culdee came over the sea from the south, dry footed, without a boat; and a written roll used to be given to him from heaven, out of which he would give instruction to the Irish, and it used to be taken up again when the instruction was delivered: and the culdee used to go each day across the sea southwards, after imparting the instruction.

Irish teaching on the religious observance of Sunday was embodied in the *Cáin Domnaig*, the 'Law of Sunday'.[4] Whatever the precise date of the tract, its instructions are in general accordance with the teaching of the reformers, who helped to propagate its teaching.

The culdees did not confine their religious observance to Sundays. Each of the canonical hours was celebrated in the church. When he heard the bell sounded the culdee bent his head, sang a *Pater* and a *Gloria*, made the sign of the cross and proceeded to the

---

[1] 'Monastery', § 71.   [2] 'Monastery', § 45.

[3] See Kenney, *Sources*, pp. 476–7; R. Priebsch, 'Der Sonntags-Epistel in der irischen *Cáin Domnaig*', Z.C.P., ii (1906–7), 138–54, and 'The chief sources of some Anglo-Saxon homilies', *Otia Merseiana*, i, 129 ff.; R. E. McNally, '*Dies Dominica*: Two Hiberno-Latin texts', *Mediaeval Studies*, xxii (1960), 355–61. Cf. Whitelock, *Eng. Hist. Docs.*, i, no. 214.

[4] A new edition with translation and notes by Vernam Hull is to appear in the forthcoming number of *Ériu* xx.

church, where he genuflected three times before entering.[1] In addition to the formal offices, each of Máel-ruain's culdees was expected to recite the whole Psalter daily, whatever the manual or intellectual work on which he might be engaged.[2] During the night-time, between the offices, two culdees remained in the church reciting the Psalms.[3] Individual prayer was encouraged. The Martyrologies of Tallaght and of Oengus the Culdee, both written about 800 to record the festivals of saints, were intended for private devotion rather than liturgical celebration. Litanies were composed, like the *Scúap Chrábaid* (the 'Broom of Devotion'), attributed to Colcu Ua Dinnechda, who died in 796. This Litany reflects the ideas of a learned religious: he prays by the evangelists who wrote the gospels, by the prophets, by all the men of wisdom and understanding who have ever received ecclesiastical orders. Later in his prayer he comes to those who had understanding of the law of nature, of the written law given to Moses, of the prophetic law, and of the law revealed by Christ; finally, he entreats 'by all the holy disciples who learned the spiritual sciences', by 'the perfect teachers who taught the spiritual meaning', that God will protect him from all harm, supernatural, natural, and moral, and kindle 'gentleness and love and affection and mercy' in the hearts of his enemies. In their return to prayer as the central duty of the religious, the culdees have much in common with the Carolingian reform associated with the name of Benedict of Aniane. Their concern with liturgy and ritual also suggests that in some of the old churches the liturgy may have been very casually performed, and prayer have been overlaid by other activities.

One other aspect of the Irish revival also seems to be paralleled by the continental movement. The monks of eighth-century Irish monasteries were, as we have seen, often laymen, but the reformers definitely encouraged boys to take holy orders,[4] and many of the mature men seem to have been able to celebrate mass, and to act as confessors. Some, however, were laymen. The culdees of S. Carthage, in the period before the hour of terce,

---

[1] Rule of S. Carthage, section on culdees.
[2] 'Monastery', § 16, 'Teaching', § 65.
[3] 'Teaching', § 30.   [4] *Rule of Céli Dé*, § 63.

were all required to watch, read, and pray 'each according to his strength', but between terce and none they went to more specialized work, 'those in orders to prayer, . . . the learned ones to preach, . . . the young folk to obedience, . . . work for the un-learned, stubborn work in his hand'.[1] Nevertheless, the number of men in orders must have substantially increased, as it did during the Benedictine reform on the Continent.

In other respects the reformers made little innovation in the underlying constitutional structure of Irish monasticism. The number of anchorites seems to have grown, but these were usually supported by the 'old churches'. Some new communities of strict life were founded, with independent resources, of which Tallaght was one. Such houses took tithes, as the old churches did, on flocks and on agrarian produce:

> Tithes are collected in this way (says the Rule of the Céli Dé). Every animal that a man owns is let out through a gap, and every tenth beast is given to God, except only oxen: because every tenth cartload [of the fruit] of their labour is taken.[2]

The great monastic house of the earlier period had often held a number of far-flung churches under its jurisdiction, and though the foundations of the reform seem to have produced nothing strictly parallel to the old large-scale monastic *paruchia*, individual men grouped themselves into 'unities' regardless of proximity. Thus, a tract on the 'Folk of the Unity of Máel-ruain' gives a list of twelve men,[3] of whom three are certainly from old founda-tions,[4] but others are from houses which appear to have been founded by the reformers.[5] The unity would appear to have been a personal association, not a *paruchia* under the jurisdiction of Tallaght. Each house appears to have been autonomous, following its own practices, as the great mother-houses had been. The re-formers tried to prevent lay intrusion[6] and to insist on the

---

[1] Rule of S. Carthage, section on Culdees.

[2] *Rule of Céli Dé*, § 54.

[3] Book of Leinster facs. 370 a; Flower, 'Two Eyes of Ireland', p. 70; Hughes, 'Irish *Scriptoria*', p. 263.

[4] Dairinis (a seventh-century Ruben was here), Terryglass, and Kilcullen.

[5] Tallaght, Dísert Diarmata, Dísert Maele-tuile, and probably others.

[6] Rule of the Céli Dé, § 65.

N

churches providing the services of religion, but they created no new machinery for making permanent the effects of their enthusiasm.

The list of 'Folk of the Unity of Máel-ruain' suggests that the culdees were especially strong in the Southern Half of Ireland. Three men whom it names are from Tallaght, one from Westmeath, one from Leinster, eight from the kingdom of Munster. Robin Flower, on the strength of a gloss in the Martyrology of Oengus, suggests that Máel-ruain may have had his own training in Munster.[1] Another list, of 'Folk of the Unity of Feidlimid', indicates a similar Munster concentration, for Feidlimid mac Crimthainn was King of Cashel and is described in the annals as *optimus Scotorum, scriba et ancorita*.[2] His activities hardly suggest piety,[3] but he must have been a powerful patron. The folk of his 'unity', the tract obscurely says, 'used to be together in Daire Ednech (in Munster) . . . practising devotion without extravagance, at cross vigil in Lent', and from Daire Ednech proceeded to Tallaght.[4] Munster, which provided the first support for the *Romani*, may have been good soil for a religious revival.

The reform brought a revived spirit into the church, but it brought no new constitution: its authority was moral and carried no powers of enforcement. Those holding positions of power in the church sometimes made confession to an ascetic leader, and received penance and instruction; but they did not always do what was advised and the ascetic 'soul-friend' could no nothing with such a man except send him away from confession 'gently and kindly'.[5] Laymen might also make confession but refuse penance: in such cases the ascetic could only refuse to receive confession. The reformers taught that confessors should take no gifts from any layman who failed to submit to their directions,[6] 'for as the sins of the thief fall on him who entertains a thief or gives him bed or harbourage, so the sins of worldly people cleave to those who accept from them fees or gifts'.[7] The reformers' method, both

---

[1] 'Two Eyes of Ireland', p. 71. *M.O.*, 15 August.
[2] *A.U.* 845.   [3] *Infra*, p. 192.
[4] Hughes, 'Irish *Scriptoria*', p. 263.   [5] 'Monastery', § 2.
[6] 'Monastery', § 35; Rule of S. Carthage, section on Confessors.
[7] 'Teaching', § 30.

necessarily and by choice, seems to have been persuasion, the tone is that of exhortation rather than command. When persons 'older or more venerable' came to confession, the 'soul-friend' was to hear them, but 'not to lay upon such persons strict injunctions', merely to read to them the relevant passages from the penitentials.[1]

Each reformed house determined its own standard of asceticism, and even within the same house there was no common level of discipline. 'Different is the condition of everyone,' says the Rule of Carthage, 'different the nature of the place, different the law by which food is diminished or increased.' The fasts observed by one saint were not identical with those of another.[2] Even within one community, 'everyone should regulate his pittance for himself . . . as much as suffices him, and does not induce sickness'.[3] Máelruain refused to receive the anchorite Colcu into his community at Tallaght because his diet was so scanty that he would be unable to perform his share of the monastery's work. Perseverence in a regular, measured austerity was considered to be of more value than extreme abstinence, but no man was forced, only advised.

Irish ascetic practice lacked the discipline of the Benedictine Rule or the uniformity of Carolingian reform. Anchorites might meet for discussion, but there was no emperor to enforce their decisions, not even a metropolitan to keep them in mind. Diversity of custom characterized this phase of Irish monasticism, as it had stamped the earlier phases. Yet through all the diversity there shone the central fact of religious revival. Two ninth-century poems on the anchorite's life well illustrate both the diversity and unity of the movement.[4] In both, the hermit has renounced the world, one escaping the strife of a princely family, the other making 'an end to fighting and visiting', perhaps retiring from some worldly monastic house. One feasts on salmon, trout, eggs, honey, beer, and strawberries ('good to taste in their plenty'),

[1] 'Monastery', § 79.
[2] 'Monastery', §§ 68, 80. See also *supra*, p. 178, for different attitudes to beer-drinking.
[3] 'Monastery', § 63.
[4] Murphy, *Lyrics*, pp. 10 ff., 18 ff.

while the other confines himself to 'an unpalatable meagre diet' of bread and water; both are content and of pure heart. One rejoices in God's creation, while the other prays with tears, trampling on the body; both have their minds stayed on God. The awareness of the presence of God was the root of the reform.

CHAPTER 17

The influence of the ascetic revival

The influence of the ascetic revival was moral and spiritual rather
than constitutional, and nowhere can it be seen more clearly than
in the poetry of the ninth century. The hermit retreated to the
woods, living under the forest trees, regarding the seasons advance, listening to the birds, watching the wild beasts as they
played or came to drink;[1] or he built himself a hut at the lakeside,
or within sight of the sea, perhaps on one of the many islands
which surround the coast, where he might meditate and pray. A
man might come to such a cell after a long period of training in
the monastic schools, so that a scholar sophisticated in taste and
subtle in expression might enjoy without interruption the beauty
of his surroundings at a time when his imagination, stirred by
religious emotion, was peculiarly sensitive: hence his delight in
the blackbird whistling from a yellow-heaped branch above
Belfast Loch,[2] or his exultant exclamation, 'Let us adore the Lord,
maker of wondrous works, great bright heaven with its angels,
the white waved sea on earth.'[3]

The earlier Irish saints had shown sympathy with created
things, and control over them. Columbanus would call the beasts
and birds in his wilderness, to play about him 'as cats frisk about
their mistresses', and the squirrel would climb about his shoulders:[4]
Columcille sent a monk to the western shore of Iona to await an
exhausted guest, due to arrive from northern Ireland about the
ninth hour, a crane, which was nursed back to health on the island
before it terminated its pilgrimage and returned home;[5] a raven
stole and returned Columbanus' gloves and a bear obediently
left the stag on which he was feeding so that the monks might
have its hide to make their shoes.[6] So the affection and sympathy

[1] Murphy, *Lyrics*, p. 10.   [2] Ibid., p. 6.
[3] Ibid., p. 4. For a discussion of the hermit poetry, see Jackson, *Early
Celtic Nature Poetry*, pp. 80–109.
[4] *Life* by Jonas, c. 30.   [5] Adamnán, I. 48.
[6] Jonas, *Life*, c. 25, 27.

which existed between ascetics and the natural creation was no new thing.

The manner of its expression, however, was new. In the wake of the anchoritic revival came lyric poetry, expressed in new metres, with an elaborate system of rhyme (both internal and end rhyme) and alliteration. For the lyrics are the poems of scholars on holiday from the *scriptorium*, of men nurtured on the rhymed syllabic metres of the Hiberno-Latin hymns, but now producing something in the vernacular which was at once novel and sophisticated.

> A hedge of trees overlooks me; a blackbird's lay sings to me (an announcement which I shall not hide);
> Above my lined book the birds' chanting sings to me.
> A clear-voiced cuckoo sings to me (goodly utterance) in a grey cloak from bush fortresses.
> The Lord is indeed good to me: well do I write beneath a forest of woodland.[1]

So wrote an early-ninth-century scribe, and later glossators continued to associate the culdees and anchorites with the 'nature' theme. Máel-anfaid of Dairinis, one of the men listed in the 'Unity of Máel-ruain' and the 'Unity of Feidlimid' one day saw a bird lamenting the death of Mo-lua mac Ocha[2] because Mo-lua 'never killed any creature, small or great'. And it was a glossator of the Martyrology of Tallaght who later brought the birds into that festology: on the feast of Ciarán in January (5th) 'the birds of the world . . . to welcome the sun', on 25 March 'the swallows arrive', on the feast of Ruadán in April 'the cuckoo calls from the pleasant wood', on 9 September 'wild geese come over the cold sea', and finally, without any festival date, the dawn chorus:

> the ocean will burst over every place
> at the end of the night, at the call of the birds.[3]

The influence of the ascetic revival in Ireland penetrated far beyond the desert hermits. The names of Máel-ruain of Tallaght

---

[1] Murphy, *Lyrics*, p. 4.

[2] *M.O.*, p. 56. Mo-lua moccu Óche, founder of Clonfertmulloe died *A.I.*, 612 or 615. Mac-oiga, abbot of Lismore (died *A.U.* 753) is mentioned in 'The Monastery of Tallaght'. Cf. the white horse at Iona grieving the impending death of Columcille. Adamnán, III. 23.

[3] *M.T.*, pp. 94–6.

(*obit* 792), Duiblitir of Finglas (*obit* 796), Hilary of Loch Cré (*obit* 807), and Máel-díthruib of Terryglass (*obit* 840) are associated with the movement, and the Teaching of Máel-ruain quotes the practices of various eighth- and ninth-century saints. A number of monastic rules date from this period of revival,[1] though they are ascribed in several cases to earlier saints. One is attributed to Comgall,[2] another to Columcille, though neither of these contains the regulations quoted from them in the Teaching of Máel-ruain. These contemporary rules, however, give teaching similar to that of Máel-ruain and his friends: the need to observe the *opus dei*,[3] to recite the Psalter daily[4] and to perform prostrations,[5] to preserve personal poverty[6] while practising charity to the poor[7] and sick,[8] to work, pray, and study,[9] to avoid women,[10] and to keep separate from the world.[11] All this must be performed with moderation[12] and perseverance,[13] all must be inspired by the love of God.[14]

These rules were not intended for men in identical situations. The Rule of Columcille is addressed to the anchorite, who is told to 'be alone in a separate place near a great monastery'[15] under

---

[1] Kenney, *Sources*, pp. 474–6.

[2] This, with the 'Testimony of Cóemán', is the earliest: 'it can hardly be put later than about 800'. It is advising the man who calls himself Céle Maic Maire, 'gillie of the Son of Mary'.

[3] Testimony of Cóemán, pp. 41–2.

[4] Rule of Comgall, § 13.

[5] Ibid., 13a requires three hundred per day with three at every canonical hour; 13b requires only two hundred daily. Cf. the same practice for Confessors in the Rule of S. Carthage.

[6] Rule of Columcille, p. 119. But note that the anchorite of this rule, though he may have nothing without his senior's permission, will be allowed a servant.

[7] Rule of Columcille, p. 120, Rule of Comgall, § 21.

[8] Testimony of Cóemán, p. 42.

[9] Rule of Céli Dé, § 55, and Rule of Columcille, p. 120, in identical phrases.

[10] Testimony of Cóemán, p. 41–2.

[11] Rule of Comgall, § 19; Rule of Columcille, p. 119.

[12] 'Advance a step every day, practice not the ways of a charioteer', Rule of Comgall, § 24. Cf. 'Monastery', § 68.

[13] 'Make not a fire of fern', Rule of Comgall, § 4; Cf. 'Monastery', § 76, for persistence as the most excellent quality of the culdee.

[14] 'Love determines piety', Rule of Comgall, § 9.

[15] *prim cathrach*. This seems to be the *cathair ataig* of the Laws, *A.L.I.* v. 54

spiritual direction, working for part of each day to help his neighbours, by teaching, writing, sewing, or whatever work is needed. Such a man was presumably maintained by the great monastery. The Rule of Comgall, however, might apply to those who had direct responsibility for the church's lay clients (*manaig*) and who received their service. Thus, as we have already seen, some monasteries were supporting anchorites, others were trying to revive religion throughout the monastery.

Some ninth-century ascetic rules were probably produced under the influence of anchorites who held positions of authority in the old churches. A gloss on the Small Primer says that a church, in order to hold the highest honour-price, must have a bishop, a man of learning (*fer-léginn*), and an erenagh (i.e. abbot), though the three offices may be combined in one man.[1] The anchorites were often learned men. The Rule of the Céli Dé regards learning as a most excellent labour of piety, when it declares that 'the kingdom of heaven is granted to him who directs studies, and to him who studies, and to him who supports the pupil who is studying'.[2] Anchorites were often (though by no means always) appointed as masters of the *scriptoria*.[3] As we have seen, they were usually in major orders, and sometimes they held the office of abbot with distinction. Duiblitir was abbot of Finglas, a bishop and a man of learning who led the scribes at the Synod of Tara in 780. The reformers remained a minority in the church, but their positions often gave them opportunities to propagate their concept of the religious life.

Nevertheless, in Irish monasteries much depended on the man available at the moment, and while some houses appointed ascetics to offices of responsibility, others chose the sons and grandsons of former abbots. At Slane the practice which had already been established by the mid-eighth century continued in the ninth, and can be traced with certainty until 845.[4] At Trevet a father, son, and grandson ruled from 774 until 839.[5] Domnach-Sechnaill

---

[1] *A.L.I.* v. 54.   [2] § 63.

[3] Flower, 'The Two Eyes of Ireland', pp. 67–9; Hughes, 'Irish *Scriptoria*', pp. 249–66.

[4] *Supra*, p. 163, for genealogical table.

[5] Daimtech (died *A.U.* 793), his son Conall (died *A.U.* 813), and Conall's son Cormac (died *A.U.* 839).

(Dunshauglin) retained the abbatial succession within the same family for most of the ninth century, though the last two abbots of the series both suffered violent deaths. The following genealogical tree shows their relationship:

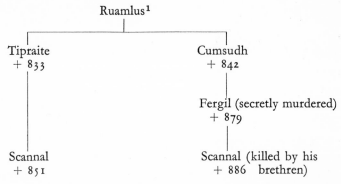

Ruamlus[1]

| Tipraite | Cumsudh |
| + 833 | + 842 |

Fergil (secretly murdered)
+ 879

| Scannal | Scannal (killed by his |
| + 851 | + 886   brethren) |

At Kilmoone abbot Máel-fothardaig son of Flann died in 809, and was succeeded by Feidlimid, anchorite and scribe (died 814), while Feidlimid's successor, who lived only a year, has a religious-sounding name, Céle-Isu (gillie of Jesus). As far as we know, these two men had no natural heirs, but Robartach son of Máel-fothardaigh was abbot until his death in 846, and his son Eochu succeeded him (died 882). Máel-fothardaig and his grandson Eochu both combined the abbacies of Fennor and Kilmoone.[2] The old method of family inheritance had not been eliminated.

Moreover, rivalry over appointments continued. We have seen that at the turn of the eighth and ninth centuries Armagh had been troubled with rival abbots. Dub-dá-leithe (died 793) and his son Condmach (who 'perished by a sudden death' in 807) had disputed the succession with Cú-dínisc (died 791), Airechtach (died 794), Faendelach (died 795), and Gormgal (died 806), and Éogan Mainistrech in 827 had had to meet a rival claimant. A further

[1] Ruamlus is the father of Tipraite and Cumsudh, but abbot Ruamnus died in 801. Is this a scribal slip? It is an uncommon name.
[2] At Lismore and Emly there is no evidence of sons succeeding fathers, but there may have been family influence. At Lismore: *A.I.* 814 Aedan moccu Raichlich, *A.F.M.* 854 Suibne descendant of Roichlich, anchorite and abbot, *A.F.M.* 878 Martin descendant of Roichligh. At Emly: *A.F.M.* 817 Rechtabra descendant of Mugthigern, *A.F.M.* 870 Cennfáelad descendant of Mugthigern, lord of Cashel. He had been abbot of Emly.

period of uncertainty followed Éogan's death in 834, though now the conflict does not appear to gain support from secular politics. Éogan was succeeded by Diarmait Ua Tigernáin, described in the annals as a learned man, but he was replaced in 835 by Forannán, bishop and anchorite. Diarmait, however, must have retained the most precious insignia of his coarbship, for the next year he went to Connacht *cum lege et vexillis Patricii*, to impose the law (*cáin*) of Patrick and to take the relics on circuit. Meanwhile Forannán was at Kildare with Patrick's household, and was there involved in a battle with Feidlimid king of Cashel, who took the oratory against him, and made him prisoner with his company. Diarmait must have returned to Armagh after a profitable tour of Connacht, whereas Forannán's plight was unfortunate. In 839 Armagh reversed her decision of four years previously, and now accepted Diarmait in place of Forannán. Forannán, however, was not yet eliminated, for the Vikings with a fleet from Limerick took him prisoner in 845 when he was at Cluain-comarda in Munster, seizing his reliquaries (*mind*) and his household. Presumably he must have escaped them, or been ransomed, and returned to Armagh, where he was once more accepted; for in 848 Armagh again reinstated Diarmait in place of Forannán.[1] Their deaths occurred in the same year, 852. The seventeen years covered by their rule are a revealing comment on abbatial office, years in which a 'bishop and scribe' was prepared to hold a disputed position, in which the appointing body changed its decision on several occasions and when abbots and their households could be subjected to violence from native kings as well as from raiding vikings. The abbot's office was important enough to rouse rivalry, and religious revival had not changed human nature or constitutional practice.

Monasteries continued, on occasion, to go to war with each other. In 807 there was a battle between the *familia* of Cork and the *familia* of Clonfert, with a great slaughter of the men of the church and of the noblest of the *familia* of Cork. This entry implies that the monastic officials as well as the *manaig*, the monk-clients, were involved in the fighting. In 817 Cathal son of Dúnlang, king of Uí Chenselaig (South Leinster), together with the house of

---

[1] It is possible that this entry is a duplicate of 839, but not very likely.

Taghmon fought against the house of Ferns, and 'four hundred persons were slain'. Both these monasteries were in South Leinster, and when Cathal died in 819 it was as King of Uí Chenselaig and *secnap* of Ferns.[1] The community of Kildare plundered Tallaght in 824, and in 828 the monastery of Cork took the initiative in stirring up a major battle: 'The community of Cork again collected the Uí Echach and Corcu Laígde and Ciarraige Cuirche to Múscraige, and they left two hundred (dead) with them again.' Such action would have been deprecated by the reformers, but they had not been able to put a stop to the evil practice.

There were other occasions when the church was subjected to violence from the laity. In 833 Cellach son of Bran, king of Leinster, defeated the church of Kildare in a battle 'where many were slain'. This may have been a battle for which the church must bear some responsibility, but the majority of occasions cited in the Annals on which violence was offered to the church relate to violation of sanctuary. In 818 the erenagh[2] of Cell-mor-Enir was profaned, and the *secnap* was wounded while under the abbot's protection; in 839 Máel-Sechnaill I of Meath killed the *economus* of Durrow. But on such like occasions the church often tried and succeeded in exacting compensation for its injuries. Tallaght prevented the celebration of the Fair of Tailltiu on one Saturday in 811 'because of the violation of the *termon* of Tallaght by the Uí Néill'; the action was directed mainly against king Aed, who afterwards 'offered many gifts'. This same king Aed was solemnly cursed at Tara in 817 by the family of Columcille, who regarded him as responsible for the slaying of the abbot of Rathboth. When in 834 the lord of Uí Maine (one of the kingdoms of Connacht) violated Clonmacnois by throwing its *secnap* (from a Munster sept) into the Shannon, where he was drowned, 'the rights of seven churches were given to Ciarán with great service'. There was still a strong feeling that ecclesiastical property and lives were sacrosanct, and that legal compensation was required for their violation, not to mention supernatural vengeance.

In 804 the church succeeded in securing a further extension of the practice of protection. The Annals say that Aed (king of the

---

[1] For the *secnap* see *infra*, p. 211.   [2] See *infra*, p. 223.

Northern Uí Néill and over-king of the Northern Half of Ireland) then exempted the clergy from their attendance at expeditions and hostings, and that this was 'according to the judgement of Fothad of the Canon'.[1] The clergy, in particular the clergy of Armagh, had been urging their need of exemption:[2] the prefaces to the Martyrology of Oengus mention the 'Song of the Complaint' and the 'Song of the Canon', both of which Fothad showed to Oengus when they met on king Aed's hosting. This suggests that Fothad, who formulated the *cáin*, and Oengus the Culdee were in agreement on this policy. The ascetic revival may have given fresh support to those of the old-established churches who were attempting to separate the church from secular violence. The new law seems to have been effective for a time in the north, for our records of pitched battles in which churches took a major part in the years following 804 relate to the south of Ireland; but as the Viking terror gained force in the 830s and 840s it ceased to be effective.

Feidlimid king of Cashel (i.e. Munster) was responsible during his reign (820–47) for more violence towards the church than any other Irishman.[3] As we have already seen, it is he who heads one list of ascetics, and he is described in his obituary notice as *optimus Scotorum, scriba et ancorita*. He must have patronized the anchorites, but the annals provide a long sequence of profanations. In 823 he burned Gallen, 'with its entire habitation and its oratory', and Fore was burned by him in 830. In 833 he killed the family of Clonmacnois and burned its *termon* to the door of the church: 'in the same manner did he treat the family of Durrow to the door of its church'. 836 saw his attack on the oratory of Kildare and his imprisonment of Forannán and his company, 'with great insult towards them'. The Annals of Ulster, in the same year, record that the abbot of Cork died without communion in Cashel, while the Annals of Inisfallen give 'the entry of Feidlimid into the abbacy of Cork'. In 838 he 'occupied the abbot's chair at Clonfert'. But Ciarán got him in the end, for when Feidlimid once more plundered the *termon* of Clonmacnois in 844 the saint pursued him, thrust at him with his crozier, and gave him an internal wound, from which he later died.

[1] *A.U.* 804.   [2] *A.F.M.* 799.   [3] See *infra*, p. 200.

Feidlimid clearly represents the weaknesses of the religious reform. It left the constitution of the church precisely as it had been, so that each autonomous house was a prey to unscrupulous power. Worst of all, there was no authority within the church to control the quarrels of churchmen: as the English Council of Celcyth remarked in 816, the Irish church had no metropolitan.[1] Feidlimid's religious sympathies seem, in fact, to have made him feel more free to interfere violently with the churches. A revival of religion, however grand, can hardly continue for long or permeate a whole institution unless it is supported by administrative machinery. So the old practices went on, and while one anchorite dwelt alone in his hermit's cell, renouncing this wretched world,[2] another, who held a kingdom, assumed abbacies, burned churches beyond his own borders, and slew their inhabitants.

[1] Haddan and Stubbs, *Councils*, iii, 581.
[2] Murphy, *Lyrics*, pp. 18, 22.

IV. ADVERSITY AND RECOVERY

CHAPTER 18

The church and the Viking terror

Acts of violence by laymen against the church did not become frequent or widespread until the decades after 830. It is remarkable that before this period the disputes involving churchmen in which there was most damage and loss of life were either pitched battles between monasteries or battles between secular rulers which were initiated by churchmen, or in which churchmen were leading figures.[1] There are a few instances of battles between secular powers in which abbots were among the slain, occasions when we do not know whether or not the church was willingly participating,[2] and one record of a 'conflict' at Clonard (776) between king Donnchad and the monastic family, for which we cannot assign responsibility. But it is certainly true to say that normally when laymen committed acts of violence against the church before 830 they were actions directed against individuals, usually the killing or wounding of monastic officials,[3] and that kings sometimes intervened to avenge the violation. Monasteries could and did claim compensation for violation of their sanctuary, while the *cána* protected the property of churches and the persons of non-combatant clerics. The church could also invoke supernatural vengeance, and men insulted the saints' relics at their peril. Although churches were sometimes burned, this may often

[1] E.g. *A.Tig.* 759, the battle at Emain Macha between the Ulstermen and the Southern Uí Néill at the persuasion of Airechtach priest of Armagh through disagreement with abbot Fer-dá-crích, or *A.U.* 793, when Gormgal attacked his rival Faendelach at Armagh and the Uí Cremthainn plundered the city.

[2] *A.U.* 776 a battle between the Uí Néill and the Munstermen involving Durrow, 780 a battle among the Airthera, when the abbot of Daire-Eithnig was among the dead.

[3] *A.U.* 746 (the profanation of Domnach Pátraic, *vi cimmidi cruciati*) should be considered as one of these acts of violation directed against individuals rather than as an indiscriminate plundering raid. The *cimbid* was a person whose life was forfeit to another, and who might be imprisoned or slain at will. It looks as if these six *cimbidi* had sought sanctuary in the church, were pursued there, and put to death by torture.

well have been by accident. Feidlimid was the first Irish king to
make a practice of plundering churches.

His reign coincided with the worst shock of the Viking terror.
The Norse had already reached the coasts of Great Britain before
the end of the eighth century, and coming via the Northern and
Western Isles of Scotland, made their first appearance in Ireland
in 798. Their object was plunder, not settlement, they wanted
portable objects of value and did not care what they destroyed or
whom they killed in the process; but they did not stay, and they
came in small groups, not in large armies. They confined themselves mainly to the coasts, and seem for twenty years or more to
have been regarded as an occasional annoyance rather than the
permanent horror which they were soon to become. Some of the
island monasteries learned early of the Viking terror: Iona was
burned in 802, and four years later sixty-eight of its community
were slain, Inishmurray off the north-west coast was burned in
807. But Irish kings brought out their little armies and defeated
the Gentile forces on several occasions. In the 820s the raids became more serious, as more and more adventurers in Scandinavia
learned that Ireland was a rich storehouse of treasures. In this
decade a number of mainland houses were sacked, and prisoners
were taken. Bangor was plundered, and the relics of Comgall
shaken from their shrine, an appalling desecration, for which Irish
law demanded heavy penalties; but the Vikings cared nothing for
this. Downpatrick and Moville (825), Lann Leire and Clonmore
(in Co. Louth, 828) were burned and plundered, and some of the
community of Armagh carried off (828), though not from the
monastery itself. The Vikings were not only on the eastern mainland: the formidable rocks of Skellig off the Kerry coast did not
protect Etgal (824), who died of hunger and thirst as their prisoner, while Blathmac of Iona, refusing to reveal the place where
the shrine of Columcille had been hidden, was martyred with those
monks who had not already fled (825). Kings and churches made
counter-attacks when they could. In 828 the Gentiles were defeated by the combined forces of the king of Uí Chenselaig
(south Leinster) and the community of Taghmon,[1] while the

---

[1] A combination which had been used in 817 against the monastery of
Ferns, see above, p. 190.

king of Dál Araide (in Ulster) won a victory in the same
year.

The real terror began in 832. From that time on Ireland was
never without the Vikings, they came in ever-increasing numbers,
they struck in many different areas, they took large numbers of
prisoners for the Norse slave-markets, they sacked and plundered
on an unprecedented scale. In 832 Armagh was attacked for the
first time, three times in one month, and the areas to the west,
south, and south-east of Armagh were all plundered. If the Viking
fleet was centred on Dundalk Bay, as seems likely, all these areas
would have been easily accessible. The same areas were raided in
the following year, though the Irish gained a victory at Derry,
which seems to have been the farthest limit of the Viking attack.
But after this their scale of operations widened. In 834 they were
in Co. Limerick and in North Leinster (plundering Glendalough)
as well as in the east, and in 835 Limerick and south Leinster were
attacked. Ships harboured at Wicklow sacked Kildare in 836,
burning half the church (presumably the 'new' church which
Cogitosus had so proudly described in the seventh century[1]),
Vikings took their 'first prey' from southern Brega (the area to
the north of Dublin), killing many and taking captives, conducted
'a most cruel devastation of all the territories of Connacht', and
inflicted 'a battle-slaughter upon the northern Déisi'. In 837 they
put large fleets[2] on the Boyne and the Liffey, from whence they
plundered westwards as far as the Shannon. In 838 they were
defeated in Connacht, but in 839 they were on Lough Neagh,
from thence destroying 'all the territories and churches of northern
Ireland', taking captive bishops, priests, and men of learning (the
men with the highest honour-price) and putting others to death.
In the 840s they began to build their fortresses. They had come to
stay.

The effect of the Viking terror on the churches was physically
and mentally devastating. The Irishman's prayer on the cover of
the Reichenau Bede asks for deliverance from 'a flood of foreigners
and foes and pagans and tribulations'.[3] Respect and veneration

---

[1] *Supra*, p. 85.
[2] Each of sixty ships, so there might be about 2,000 men in each fleet.
Native armies were small.   [3] *Thes. Pal.* ii. 256.

had been accorded to the church for so long that the Viking treatment left men bewildered. It is true that pre-Viking Irish society had provided no one strong king to direct the church, but at the same time kings had been too weak to do her much damage. It looks as if, in the eighth century, monasteries could put armies into the field as big as those of a petty king, so that, even had kings not been deterred by legal and spiritual penalties, alliance with churches was usually more profitable to lay princes than hostilities would have been. But against the Vikings the church was defenceless. The wrath of the saint meant nothing to them: they were prepared to shake Comgall's bones from their reliquary, scratch a Viking woman's ownership on a saint's stolen shrine ('Ranvaig owns this casket'), kill bishops and churchmen, burn not only the *termon* but the church itself, excavate the holy ground to look for valuables. What can have been the effect on the Irish when they saw these desecrations occur, not once but many times, with no supernatural vengeance? God and his saints provided no physical protection: of what use was it to ask the Vikings for legal compensation?

The political organization of Irish society, with its numerous petty kings, had allowed endless opportunities for minor battles. It was not uncommon for such kings to take advantage of a neighbour's difficulties to conduct a cattle-raid. At first the Viking raids merely seemed like another embarrassment, to be met by each area as best it could. There was no idea of a common defence, and in the years when the Viking terror ravaged Ireland, Irish kings continued the usual course of their own battles against each other. It may be, moreover, that the successful depredations of the Gentiles on church property, uncompensated and unavenged, in some cases broke down Irish inhibitions against desecration. The attacks of king Feidlimid coincided with the years of early Viking pressure. He was before the Vikings at Fore, Clonmacnois, Durrow, and Birr, but the Vikings were first at Kildare. Did such a man merely recognize that he could now attack monasteries with impunity, or did he tell himself that he, as Irish king, a scribe and anchorite in addition, had more right to the church's flocks and herds than the advancing Vikings?

Irish monks had no adequate defence. In the years before the

Viking settlement they could only pray for storms to keep the raiders at bay.

> Bitter is the wind tonight,
> It tosses the ocean's white hair:
> Tonight I fear not the fierce warriors of Norway
> Coursing on the Irish Sea.[1]

Sometimes they hid their treasures (at Iona they buried them in a barrow), sometimes they took their most precious relics away from the areas of greatest danger to other monasteries. Some houses were deserted. Some men of learning departed, with their books, for the Carolingian schools. Very occasionally they fought back; but after centuries of protection they were singularly ill-equipped to deal with the savagery of the Viking raiders.

The Viking terror was a shock to security. It meant also extensive damage to property. By the 830s many churches had enshrined their relics. The original wooden shrines had been covered with precious metal, set with stones and enamel. At Kildare in Cogitosus' day votive crowns hung above the tombs of Brigit and bishop Conlaed, and in 800 a new shrine was made for Conlaed's relics. When the Vikings arrived they found the little churches rich in precious ornaments. The numbers of such objects found in Viking graves deposited on the Norwegian coast in the ninth century indicates the magnitude of the material loss of Irish wealth.

Such objects had been produced in a world of wealth and leisure, by skilled craftsmen after long training. The Viking raids meant not only the seizure of materials needed for such work but a desolating loss of life. Successors to such craftsmen could not be made in a day, and when the church tried subsequently to replace its treasures the new objects often have a rather mass-produced look, as if the new generation of metal-workers had neither the skill nor the heart to concentrate upon them.

The 830s provided a dreadful contrast with all that had gone before. The seventh-century disturbances in the church had been concerned with conflicting ideas: bishops, abbots, and *sapientes* had met in synods to talk over their differences, and the most

---

[1] *Thes. Pal.* II. 290. Translation by K. Meyer, *Selections*, p. 101.

violent action recorded was merely the ejection of a non-conforming abbot. In the eighth century rivalry had led to occasional battles, but the *cána* had protected clerics, church property, women, and children from the violence of laymen, kings had paid compensation for violation of sanctuary, and society had recognized supernatural immunities. Now men were bewildered, accepted standards proved worthless, society was in anarchy, and the church had no protectors. How was she to survive the Viking settlement?

CHAPTER 19

The ecclesiastical order and the early Viking settlement

From the time when the Vikings built their first permanent fortresses throughout the rest of the century they devastated Ireland; towards the end of the century with diminished intensity, as their warriors were diverted to expeditions in Scotland or England, but never for long ceasing their attacks. The monastic cities, with their concentrated population, wealth of stock, and portable valuables, bore the brunt of their assault. In the same period Scandinavians were travelling into Russia, or through the Straits of Gibraltar into Africa:[1] to men of such a breed it was nothing to cross half Ireland, from Annagassan to the Shannon, to ravage a monastery.[2] Their fleets on the great lakes brought them within striking distance of the whole of Ireland. Occasionally the saint had his ultimate revenge, as in 881 when 'the oratory of Cianán (Duleek) was plundered' by the Gaill (the term often used for the Vikings) and its full of people were taken out of it, and Barith, a great tyrant of the Norsemen, was afterwards killed by Cianán; but more often there was no adequate resistance. Armagh was plundered for at least the eighth time in 895, when the Dublin Gaill 'carried away seven hundred and ten persons into captivity', and the historian adds:

> Pity, O holy Patrick, that your prayers did not stay
> The Gaill with their axes when striking your oratory.

The Viking settlement, moreover, altered the scale of native political disputes. Kings had formerly been accustomed to make war on each other, sometimes joined by their fellow-kings, but all knew the rules of war, and, on the whole, most kings followed them.[3] Now they were able to summon Viking allies against each

---

[1] Third Fragment, p. 162, says they brought back Moorish prisoners, long known in Ireland as *na fir ghorma*, the black or swarthy men.

[2] As in 842 *A.U.*

[3] See Binchy, 'The passing of the old order', *Congress* 1959, p. 128.

other, well-armed hardened fighters, eager for plunder, men who knew and cared nothing for Irish military traditions.

An Irish saga put together in the twelfth century and known as *The War of the Gael with the Gaill*[1] has depicted the history of Ireland in the Viking age as a struggle of the native kings against the Foreigners. Most subsequent historians have followed this interpretation of events, but the contemporary annals show that, for the ninth century, it is far from the truth. The Vikings themselves were disunited, each group operating in its own interests, with major battles in 849 and in 851-2, when a new fleet of Foreigners, probably Danes, arrived to dispute mastery with those, probably Norsemen, who had already settled. Irish kings were similarly divided among themselves. The Northern Uí Néill kings (with their centre of power in Ailech) and the Southern Uí Néill kings (based on Meath) were the two great powers of the Northern Half of Ireland, alternately holding the overlordship of Leth Cuinn (the Northern Half), but constant rivals for power. The great province of Munster with its capital at Cashel dominated the Southern Half of Ireland, but had to face a powerful native rival in Cerball of Osraige, whose kingdom lay on the eastern border of Munster.[2] Cerball plundered in Leinster, and may have tried to secure recognition of his overlordship there, in a province which by tradition gave its hostages to the king of Tara. The Vikings were a new element in an already complex situation: the native kings sometimes aided each other against the Vikings, but sometimes used Viking allies against each other.

The annals show this to be an indisputable fact. In 850 Cináed,

---

[1] Ed. J. H. Todd. See also Goedheer, *Irish and Norse Traditions*, pp. 1-45, and Ryan, *I.H.S.*, ii, 93-7.

[2] The activities of this king are recorded in some detail in a text known as the Third Fragment, and edited by J. O'Donovan, *Three Fragments of Irish Annals*, Dublin, 1860. It is not a laconic, year-by-year record, but the material for a saga, cast in the form of Annals. It may be based on sources kept at Clonfertmulloe, a monastery in Osraige, for the annals say that its abbot, Oengus, led the learned of Ireland in composing praise-poems in honour of Cerball 'in which they commemorated every victory which he gained'. This record is not contemporary, but I think it may be earlier than *The War of the Gael and the Gaill*. In *A.U.* and *A.F.M.* Cerball is called 'son of Dúngal', in the Third Fragment he is 'son of Dúnlang'. He died in 888, after a reign of over forty years.

king of Ciannachta, the kingdom on the central eastern sea-board, which was particularly vulnerable to Viking raids from Annagassan or Dublin, joined the Foreigners in a successful attack on Meath, in which the royal fort of Lagore was destroyed and the monastic city of Trevet burned with considerable loss of life. Cináed was killed by the Irish the following year, and his brother Flann succeeded him. This same Flann later joined Aed son of Niall, king of the Northern Uí Néill, in battle against the king of Meath.[1] Aed and his successor Domnall were prepared to accept help from the Foreigners in their attacks on Meath[2] and Flann King of Meath used Foreign allies in battle against the king of the Northern Uí Néill.[3] Cerball of Osraige was joined by a con-tingent of Danes, whom he assisted against their Norse enemies, and whom he used as his own allies. The speech put into his mouth by the story-teller on one occasion shows him aware that he is surrounded by potential enemies: by the Norse, against whom he is fighting, but also by the Danes and the Munstermen, at this time his allies.[4] In 859 Cerball joined Olaf and Ivar, leaders of the Gaill, in an attack on Meath, but the following year he seems to have been with the king of Meath in his hosting against the Northern Uí Néill.[5] In the later 850s a company of Gall-Gael were fighting now with the Gaill, now with the Gael.[6] They were Irish foster-children of the Norse, presumably those orphaned by the ravagings of the thirties and forties, and, if anything, even more violent than the Vikings by whom they had been reared.[7] As the saga writer truly proclaimed: 'The Irish suffer evils, not only from the Norse, but they also suffer many injuries from each other.'[8]

Ireland was submerged by confusion and anarchy. It was as if a shoal of sharks had got into a paddling pool. Inevitably the changed political situation caused partial disintegration of the old legal stability. The security of the pre-Viking system had

---

[1] *A.U.* 860. *Third Frag.*, p. 140. Also *A.U.* 862, when they were joined by the Gaill. But in 868 Flann was killed, with a great number of Foreigners, fighting against Aed.

[2] *A.U.* 861, 862, 889.   [3] *A.U.* 882.

[4] *Third Frag.*, pp. 130 ff.   [5] *A.U.* 859–860; *Third Frag.*, pp. 146 ff.

[6] *A.U.* 856 with the king of Meath against the Gaill, against the king of the Northern Uí Néill in 856, with the Gaill in Munster 857.

[7] *Third Frag.*, pp. 128, 138.   [8] Ibid., p. 194.

depended on its balance, for though there was no strong executive authority each grade of society had been kept in control by those above it. Now the law of status was completely undermined. Without warning, and through no fault of his own, a man could be bereft of all the material adjuncts which marked his position, without hope of compensation. Small wonder that the Irish law tracts now 'atrophy', and the theory of Irish law becomes ever more widely divorced from its practice.

The disintegrating effects of the Viking settlement can be seen in the sphere of ecclesiastical law. Between 697 and 842 the annals contain a long series of entries recording the promulgation of *cána*, those ecclesiastical 'laws' originally aimed at protection, by which the churches concerned gained profits of jurisdiction. After 842 these records end. It seems most likely that their cessation is due to the disturbances caused by the Viking settlement. Under such circumstances, when clerics were being killed, church property destroyed, and women carried off to the slave markets of Norway, neither abbots nor princes could have had much heart for the promulgation of the *cána*.

Nevertheless, the church continued to make efforts for the preservation of law and order, trying to exact compensation wherever opportunity offered. In 851 (*A.U.*) the abbot of Armagh supported the kings of Meath and Lagore in their vengeance on Cináed of Ciannachta, who had devastated their lands along with the Gaill. Cináed was drowned 'with the approval of the good men of Ireland, and particularly of the coarb of Patrick'. According to the account in the Third Fragment of Annals, Slógedach abbot of Leighlin ('who was a deacon at this time, but afterwards a bishop and coarb of Ciarán of Seir') made peace in 870 between Cerball of Osraige and the Leinstermen who had provoked him to battle.[1] In 889 the coarb of Patrick stopped a battle at Armagh between two princes, one of the Cenél Eógain, the other of the Ulaid, which they and their armies were fighting: he obtained compensation for the violation of Armagh and sureties for its payment.[2] But only the most important abbots

---

[1] *Third Frag.*, p. 176. Slógedach died *A.F.M.* 885.

[2] *A.F.M.* The coarb, Máel-Brigte was of the Clann Conaill. *A.U.* does not give this entry, but records the death of his predecessor the year before.

seem to have had the authority to enforce peace and obtain their rights.

Throughout the century the church suffered heavily from the attacks of the Gaill, and sometimes also from Irish princes.[1] Churchmen seem to have been present at some of the battles. In 888 (*A.U.*) when the Gaill attacked Flann son of Máel-Sechnaill king of Meath and overlord of Leth Cuinn two important churchmen were among the slain, the bishop of Kildare and the abbot of Kildalkey. The saga-writer whose account is incorporated into the Third Fragment tells how, in battle with the Leinstermen, Cerball of Osraige ordered two of his men to stand beside him and keep watch for him. One was killed by a javelin-throw, and he was Folachtach vice-abbot of Kildare.[2] On one occasion the bishop of Tulen urged two Meath tribes to war against a third people, though his motive was to defend his church.[3] There is not, however, a single instance in the annals between 840 and 900 of a major battle between two churches, no example of churches going to war from motives of pure aggression and aggrandisement. In this respect the church during the early years of the Viking settlement has a much better record than the church of the pre-Viking age. When churches fought now, they fought for existence.

Some churches were more successful in this fight than others. It is noticeable that, in the later ninth century, some of the churches decline, while other more distinguished ones remain in positions of comparative power. If the entries in the annals may be taken as a guide a number of houses seem to have maintained *scriptoria* in the later eighth and the first half of the ninth century, for whom scribes and men of learning are not mentioned afterwards, or at least not until very much later.[4] Finglas had a series of four masters of the *scriptorium*, each lasting about a generation, from the later eighth century until 867, the last one probably appointed in 838; Kildalkey had a *scriptorium* in the ninth century, until 868. Both these houses must have been exposed to the

---

[1] Irish forces were involved in the burning, plundering, or profanation of churches on the following occasions: *A.U.* 850, 851, 854, 870, 874, 891, 896.

[2] *Third Frag.*, p. 190. On the vice-abbot, see *infra*, p. 211.

[3] *C.S.* 872.   [4] Hughes, 'Irish *scriptoria*', p. 250.

Vikings of Dublin, and it probably became impossible to maintain the monastic school. All the same, houses such as Armagh, Clonmacnois, and Clonard, though frequently plundered, succeeded in maintaining their *scriptoria*. It looks as if the effect of the Viking raids was to depress the smaller monastic houses. Those with greater resources, though attacked with equal savagery, were able to recuperate more readily, and emerged in the tenth century to positions of even greater power in comparison with the rest. The indirect effect of the Viking settlement was to emphasize the material disparities already existing between monastic houses, a tendency which becomes more apparent in the tenth century.

It is possible also, as Professor MacCana points out, that the early Viking attacks were particularly damaging in their impact on the *scriptoria* of the eastern coastal monasteries.[1] The Ulster Cycle seems to have been first written down during the late seventh and eighth centuries by scribes of the north-east, whereas its later textual history is to be associated with the Shannon region. The prosperity of Bangor and its intellectual activity seems to have sharply declined in the ninth century, whereas Clonmacnois had energy enough to promote minor cycles of tales about King Guaire and Diarmait mac Cerrbeoil. Though Clonmacnois suffered from Viking attacks, it seems likely that the first shock struck the eastern houses with especial severity, and that their men of learning migrated elsewhere.

Armagh seems to have been successful, during this period, in maintaining her connexion with the dominant Uí Néill kings of the North and in asserting ecclesiastical leadership in the areas under their overlordship. The monastery was the centre of an assembly in 851 attended by two kings, Máel-Sechnaill king of Meath and overlord of the Northern Half and Matudán king of Ulster, together with the nobles of each province, by Suairlech abbot of Clonard with the clerics of Meath and by the community of Patrick headed by Diarmait coarb of Patrick and Fethgna bishop (and later abbot) of Armagh. We do not know what took place at this meeting, but eight years later some important political decisions were made at another royal assembly

---

[1] 'The Influence of the Vikings on Celtic Literature', *Congress* 1959, pp. 103–8.

held at Ráith-Aedo (probably Rahugh), where Fethgna, now coarb of Patrick, played a leading part. The kings who attended were Máel-Sechnaill, Máel-guaile King of Munster, and Cerball of Osraige, who had in that same year made a hosting into Meath with the Viking chiefs Olaf and Ivar as his allies. At the assembly of Ráith-Aedo 'Cerball king of Osraige made complete submission to the community of Patrick and his coarb, and thereat Osraige was permanently alienated to Leth Cuinn, and Máel-guaile king of Munster gave sureties for this alienation.'[1] The temporal overlordship of Máel-Sechnaill here seems to go hand in hand with the recognition of Armagh's ecclesiastical authority.

Armagh was probably also more successful than other houses in her attempts to recover and extend her hold on revenues, which she needed, like so many other houses, to recoup her appalling losses. In the pre-Viking period she may have been already one of the richest of all the Irish churches.[2] Early in the ninth century, before the Vikings settled, Armagh had a steward (*maer*)[3] to collect her income from Brega, the plain between the Liffey and the Boyne. Feidlimid, abbot of Kilmoone, 'steward of Brega on the part of Patrick' died in 814. Thus, Armagh had already evolved some administrative machinery for the collection of her revenues in this area. No other steward is mentioned in the Annals until 888, when Máel-Pátraic, abbot of Trevet (about five miles south-west of Kilmoone), held a similar position as 'steward of Patrick's household south of the mountain'. Máel-Pátraic's successor as steward of Patric 'south of the mountain' died in 894. The mountain here mentioned may be Sliabh Fuait (the Fews), the range of hills which divides Armagh from the land to the south. In 922 the steward of Armagh, who was abbot of Lann Léire (possibly Dunleer), seems to have collected revenue from the area north of the Boyne: 'from Belach-dúin to the sea, and from the Boyne to Cossan'. It is clear from the annals that by the end of the century

[1] *A.U.* 859. I am indebted to Professor Binchy for the translation of this passage.

[2] The Annals record Patrick's 'law' as promulgated more frequently than that of any other saint between 800 and 840.

[3] See *Contributions to a Dictionary*, M, cols. 22–3. Later this comes to be the title given to the heredity keepers of certain relics, e.g. *A.F.M.* 1425: 'O'Mellan, keeper (*maer*) of the Bell of St Patrick's Will.'

Armagh was once more attempting to control some of her sources of income, though there is no mention of the promulgation of Patrick's 'law'.

It may have been the shortage of monastic income which led to a marked increase in the practice of holding office in more than one city, though this development may also have been affected by a shortage of candidates. As we have already seen, the recorded numbers of men holding in plurality rise in the 830s and 840s[1] and mount very sharply in the sixties,[2] falling off a little in the rest of the century.[3] Abbots who died in the sixties would probably have been appointed at the height of the Viking disturbances which followed the settlements, and it seems likely that the troubles caused an increase in this practice.

Family influence on appointments continued, but seems to have shown little, if any, increase. At Domnach-Sechnaill (Dunshaug-lin) the custom of family inheritance, begun in the pre-Viking period, continued until 886.[4] Glen-Uissen in Leinster (Killeshin) shows a somewhat similar system of inheritance during the second

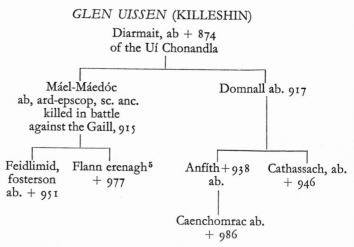

GLEN UISSEN (KILLESHIN)

Diarmait, ab + 874
of the Uí Chonandla

Máel-Máedóc
ab, ard-epscop, sc. anc.
killed in battle
against the Gaill, 915

Domnall ab. 917

Feidlimid,
fosterson
ab. + 951

Flann erenagh[5]
+ 977

Anfíth + 938
ab.

Cathassach, ab.
+ 946

Caenchomrac ab.
+ 986

[1] Six cases between 800 and 830, eight between 833 and 849.
[2] Ten cases between 863 and 869.
[3] Sixteen cases.   [4] See *supra*, p. 189.
[5] If Flann was the son of this Máel-Máedóc he must have been born to a fairly old father, who had probably taken episcopal orders; and he must himself have been old at his death. All the entries on this table are from *A.F.M.*

half of the ninth and much of the tenth century: the family connexion can best be appreciated in the table on the previous page.

At Kilmoone an abbot of the pre-Viking age (Máel-fothardaig,
died 809) was succeeded after two intervening reigns by his son
(*obit A.F.M.* 846) and grandson (*obit A.F.M.* 882). Lann Léire,
which in the eighth century had appointed a man and his two
grandsons, in the ninth had two brothers, one of whom, an
anchorite, officiated as bishop (died 845) and the other as abbot
(died 850), while the abbot's son succeeded him (died 869). At
Clondalkin, where family influence had existed in the eighth
century,[1] a father and son seem to have succeeded each other in the
ninth (died *A.F.M.* 879, 885): the first of these, the father, was a
bishop as well as abbot. At Lusk,[2] Emly,[3] Monasterboice,[4] and
Cell Delga (Kildalkey)[5] it would seem that fathers and sons
reigned as abbots, though not directly succeeding each other,
while more distant family connexions can be discerned at Lismore[6] and Seir.[7] It would appear that family influence over
appointments merely maintained the hold over the monastic constitution in the second half of the ninth century which it had
already exercised in the pre-Viking age.

One development in the practice of appointments does, however, appear: it becomes not uncommon for a reigning prince to
hold a monastic office, usually that of abbot or vice-abbot, a
custom already known before the period of the Viking settlements. Both these offices were important, for while the abbot was
the monastic head, the *tánaise abbad* or *secndap* or *secundus abbas*,
terms usually translated as 'vice-abbot', acted as prior of the
monastery and seems to have been the abbot designate.[8] This

---

[1] See *supra*, p. 164.

[2] Ruaidrí, *A.F.M.* 848; Óenacán s. Ruaidrí, *A.U.* 881; Tuathal s. Óenacán,
A.U. 929.

[3] Cenn-fáelad grandson of Mugthigern, *A.I.* 872 (a family already represented at Emly, *A.F.M.* 817); Eogan s. Cenn-faelad, *A.F.M.* 886.

[4] Cuana, *A.F.M.* 800; Flann s. Cuanach, *A.F.M.* 847.

[5] Fedach, *A.F.M.* 836; Congal s. Fedach, *A.U.* 868.

[6] Áedán moccu Raichlich, *A.I.* 814; Suibne descendant of Roichlich, *A.U.*
856, Martin descendant of Roichlich, *A.F.M.* 878.

[7] Slógedach descendant of Raithnén, *A.F.M.* 885; Aed descendant of
Raithnén, *A.I.* 923.

[8] Binchy, *Celtica*, iii (1956), 222–4.

practice may have appeared in Munster before the end of the eighth century, for Ólchobar son of Flann is described in the Munster Annals of Inisfallen as 'abbot of Inis Cathaig' and by the Four Masters as 'son of Flann son of Erc, scribe, bishop and anchorite', but the Annals of Ulster give him the title 'king of Munster'. He was of the Uí Fidgeinte, a Munster people in Limerick, where his brother had reigned as king; he seems not to have been universally recognized as king of Munster, for he appears in none of the Munster king lists, and must have been replaced by Artrí in 793.[1] It appears certain that Ólchobar was an ecclesiastic, and he may also have been a king; but it is impossible to say whether he held the abbacy concurrently with the kingship, or only after his deposition. The next case is clearer: Cathal son of Dúnlang died in 819 as king of Uí Chenselaig and vice-abbot of Ferns, one of the most important cities in his kingdom. Were the monastic family of Ferns forced into his appointment? It may be significant that Cathal made war on Ferns in 817, with the help of Taghmon, a neighbouring monastery.[2] In 836 the Munster Annals of Inisfallen record the 'entry of Feidlimid into the abbacy of Cork'. This seems to be Feidlimid king of Cashel, and the entry of the Annals of Ulster in the same year, when juxtaposed with Feidlimid's appointment, has a somewhat sinister ring: 'Dúnlang son of Cathassach, abbot of Cork, died without communion in Cashel of the Kings.' How was Feidlimid's appointment secured, and how was his predecessor disposed of?[3] Ólchobar abbot of Emly, another of the great Munster monasteries, in 848 became King of Cashel, and in the same year gained a great victory over the Gaill. When he died in 851 the Munster Annals enter him as 'abbot of Emly and king of Cashel'. Here a monastery had already appointed a first-rate war-leader and a man who was the material of a king. A generation later (*A.I.* 872) Cenn-fáelad grandson of

---

[1] *A.U. Ordinatio Artroigh mic Cathail in regnum Mumen.* See L. O'Buachalla, *Jrnl. of the Cork Hist. Soc.*, lvi (1951), 71, 76. Mr O'Buachalla accepts Ólchobar's reign as genuine. Another Ólchobar (son of Cináed) reigned as king of Cashel half a century later.

[2] *Supra*, p. 190.

[3] On Feidlimid see *supra*, p. 192. In 838 (*A.I.*), at the assembly held at Clonfert, he 'occupied the abbot's chair', but he is not named as one of the abbots of Clonfert.

Mugthigern also died as abbot of Emly and king of Cashel.[1]
The Annals of Ulster record both Ólchobar and Cenn-fáelad as
kings, but ignore their abbatial office: but the Annals of Inisfallen,
which provide the ecclesiastical information, are particularly detailed in their entries on Emly's affairs in the ninth century, and
they are likely to be correct.[2] In any case these Munster kings,
though the greatest, were not the only princes to hold monastic
office during the ninth century. In 863 Muiredach son of Máeldúin, king of Airthir and vice-abbot of Armagh, was slain by
Domnall king of the Northern Uí Néill. Airthir was the petty
kingdom in which Armagh was situated, and it probably did not
suit Domnall, its overlord, who was himself concerned with the
affairs of Armagh as the greatest monastery in his lordship, that
the interests of Airthir and Armagh should be so closely united.
The Four Masters in 881 mention a man who was vice-abbot of
Terryglass and Clonfert, and one of the lords of Loch Riach
(Loughrea, about twenty-five miles west of Clonfert and twenty
miles north-west of Terryglass), a combination of appointments
all in the same locality, probably made for purposes of better
defence, which monasteries near the Shannon must urgently have
needed against the Gaill. This may also have been the purpose
behind the combination of the abbacy of Lathrach-bruin and the
lordship of Fotharta-Airthir-Liphe, about fifteen miles to the
south of the church. We should not be too ready to assume that
such lords appropriated the abbacies concerned: it may be that
the monastic families wanted as abbot some lord in the vicinity
with forces of his own to protect them. Muiredach son of Bran,
king of Leinster and abbot of Kildare (died *A.U.* 885), had a
great reputation as a warrior, 'a hero of whom many deeds are
told, king of all Leinster, even to the sea of ships'.[3] A Leinster king
who was reputed to be able to control his coastal areas must have
been a most desirable abbot. When, before the serious Viking
troubles had begun, king Cathal held the vice-abbacy of Ferns in
819, or king Feidlimid in 836 took the abbacy of Cork, these may
have been genuine appropriations of monastic office by lords who

---

[1] It seems to be this man's son who held the abbacy of Emly somewhat
later (died *A.I.* 890).

[2] S. MacAirt's edition, p. xxiv. [3] *A.F.M.* 882.

P

wanted to use the monastery's revenues. But the circumstances of the Viking age suggest that the monastic *familiae* may have been quite as anxious to secure a local lord as abbot as the lord was to secure the abbacy. Such combinations of royal and ecclesiastical office are always personal: an abbacy never becomes permanently appropriated to a royal office, and church property continued to belong to the 'tribe of the church'.

The Viking settlements seem to have encouraged the practice of combining ecclesiastical appointments in more than one church, and of combining ecclesiastical and secular office. During the period following 840 the church was obviously pre-occupied with the need for defence: nevertheless, claims that the church became more 'secularized' or more dominated by worldly ambitions than it had been in the preceding period need to be carefully analysed. The disturbance and anarchy of these years, while it dislocated some of the monastic *scriptoria*, damaged the craftsman's art of metal-work, and brought the regular sequence of *cána* to an end, does not seem to have destroyed personal religion. On the contrary. This is the century of monastic rules with their devotion and discipline, and of religious lyrics with their lively piety. The Christian's refuge must be in God. 'God be with me against all trouble,' prays the poet, 'against violence or sudden death, against all brigands' plunderings. . . . May I be at every need beneath the protection of God's hand.'[1] The Viking terror did not kill spiritual desire.[2] The records of those princes who end their lives *in clericatu* suggest no diminution in men's awareness of God. Above all, the cessation of inter-monastic wars which had marred the church in the preceding period removed by far the worst of the ecclesiastical abuses of the pre-Viking age.

[1] Murphy, *Lyrics*, pp. 22–7.

[2] The poem on Jesus coming as an infant to be nursed by S. Íte (*Lyrics*, pp. 26–9) is to be dated *c.* 900.

CHAPTER 20

The world in the church

The period 902–1014 began and ended with great battles. It saw
the growth of Irish political power, and the lessening of Scandinavian aggression. Cerball king of Leinster inflicted a heavy
defeat on the Dublin Gaill in 902, which brought freedom from
serious foreign attacks for a dozen years. From 914 onwards
Viking fleets were once more coming to Ireland in large numbers,
to Dublin, Waterford, and Limerick, but throughout the first half
of the century considerable Viking energy was diverted to war in
Northern England. Irish kings took advantage of Viking weakness to attack Dublin in 944, carrying off 'a great spoil', while
later in the century the Battle of Tara (980) struck a decisive blow
at Viking pretensions. From 952, when Olaf Cuaran abandoned
his claims to rule at York and returned to Ireland, the Dublin
Gaill were living under fairly stable government, wanting peace
rather than plunder. Dublin was known as a great trading centre:
English and continental coins had already begun to enter the
Hiberno-Norse settlements in the ninth century, throughout the
tenth English and some Kufic coins were in use, and at the very
end of the century the first Hiberno-Norse coins were minted at
Dublin.[1] Norse and Irish art-styles met and mingled, the nobility
of both peoples intermarried, the Norse accepted Christianity.
When the Battle of Clontarf was fought in 1014 the Viking settlements, especially Dublin, were already becoming Hiberno-Norse.[2]

The Viking troubles of the ninth century had shown Irish kings
their need of power: the lessened Viking pressure of the late ninth
and tenth centuries gave them opportunity to develop it.
Throughout the century wars between the Irish kings continued,
becoming fiercer as the kings of Munster and the Uí Néill tried to
strengthen and extend their overlordships. In 908 (*A.U.*) Cormac
king of Cashel fought the combined forces of Flann king of the

---

[1] About 995. See Dolley and Ingold, *Anglo-Saxon Coins*, pp. 241–65.
[2] Cf. MacCana, *Congress* 1959, pp. 102–3.

Uí Néill, Cerball king of Leinster and Cathal king of Connacht at Belach Mugna, where he was defeated. Only the Third Fragment gives the reason for this battle, which it maintains was initiated by Munster's attempt to collect hostages from Leinster and Osraige, and encouraged by the pride and bellicosity of Flaithbertach abbot of Inis Cathaig (later king of Cashel). The demand for hostages is probably correct, for the Annals of Inisfallen tell how, in the preceding year, Cormac and Flaithbertach had taken the hostages of the Uí Néill and of Connacht, and how Cormac had spent Christmas with his troops at Clonmacnois. Thus, the demand for the hostages of Leinster and Osraige would be a continuation of Cormac's attempt to secure recognition for his overlordship. The attempt failed, and with the exception of Cellachán (died 954) Munster had no more outstanding kings until the emergence of the Dál Cais house with Mathgamain and Brian. Meanwhile, from 927 to 938 there was rivalry between the Northern and Southern Uí Néill, between Donnchad king of Tara and the Northern Uí Néill, led by Muirchertach, 'the Hector of the Western World'[1]; but in 938 at 'a challenge of battle' between the two princes 'God made peace between them', and from this time on, they acted as allies until their deaths in 943 and 944. In the last decades of the tenth century Irish politics became simplified. Brian son of Cennétig, securely established in Munster, and Máel-Sechnaill II overlord of all the north were the two great rivals for the supreme kingship of all Ireland, a power which Brian secured early in the eleventh century.

As the power of the great Irish overlords increased, a sense of nationality (for want of a better word) seems to have grown with it. In the ninth century the Foreigners had been enemies or allies of the Irish, as the situation demanded. In the tenth century some Irish kings occasionally allied with them, but nearly always the less important kings. For example, in 918 the king of Cnogba tried to treat with them in order to defend the north of Brega with their aid, 'which availed him nothing'. The kings of Ulster and of Leinster and some kings of Munster occasionally allied with them, but the kings of the Northern and Southern Uí Néill were their almost consistent opponents, while late in the century the

[1] His obituary notice, A.U. 943.

Dál Cais kings of Cashel became the native champions against them. Strong combinations of provincial Irish forces were sometimes raised against them, as in 917 when the Northern and Southern Uí Néill and their Leinster allies came to the help of Munster against the Foreigners. The nationalist feeling which finds its fullest expression in *The War of the Gael with the Gaill* seems to have grown up in the tenth century. The annals of Tigernach record that when, in 979, Máel-Sechnaill II, overlord of the North, made a hosting with the king of Ulster against the Foreigners of Dublin he proclaimed: 'Let every one of the Gaels who is in the foreigners' province come forth to his own country for peace and comfort.' As the authority of the great native overlords increased, they could, for the first time, afford to regard the Gaill with consistent hostility, and not as their potential allies against each other.

During the ninth and tenth centuries the church became increasingly involved with secular interests. This is the true period of 'secularization' in the Irish church, when the effects of the ascetic revival are passing away and the consequences of violence are still felt. The churches, like the overlords, needed to possess power themselves, since society no longer adequately protected them. The most effective means to power, and one forced on them by events, was alliance with the secular lords. It was not a new policy, for long before the tenth century abbots of great houses such as Armagh and Kildare had been closely connected with their provincial kings. But in the eighth century the pursuit of power had gone hand in hand with religious revival and social security, whereas in the tenth it was stripped of these modifying features. The effects of the Viking settlements in the ninth century had already been to depress the poorer houses, and to widen the gap between those which had sufficient resources to make a good recovery and those which had not. In the tenth century royal patronage had a potent effect on the fortunes of the great houses of Armagh, Clonard, and Clonmacnois, and perhaps a corresponding effect on the fortunes of their rivals.

We have already noted the way in which Armagh and the Uí Néill kings were working together in the ninth century. In 946 the Cenél Eógain, the leading people of the Northern Uí Néill, made a generous grant of silver to Armagh in return for 'the blessing of Patrick and his coarb'.[1] Towards the end of the century the coarb of Patrick went on a visitation of Tír Eógain, 'where he conferred the degree of king on Aed son of Domnall in the presence of Patrick's congregation'. After Aed had thus been recognized by Armagh as king of the Northern Uí Néill, Patrick's coarb 'made a full visitation of the north of Ireland'. About 985 Armagh had an opportunity to insist on a circuit of Meath. Máel-Sechnaill II, king of Meath and overlord of Leth Cuinn, had abducted the shrine of Patrick from Ardee (in modern Co. Louth) to Assey, near Tara.[2] Afterwards 'Máel-Sechnaill submitted to the award of the coarb of Patrick', by which the coarb gained fines, feasts, and the right to make a circuit. The Tripartite Life of Patrick, written between 895 and 900, claims that 'no one is king of Cashel until Patrick's successor installs him, and confers orders (*grád*) on him'.[3] But the close connexion between Munster and Armagh is more reliably attested by the annal entry of 972, when Dub-dá-leithe, coarb of Patrick, made a circuit of Munster 'and obtained his demand'[4] though he and the coarb of the Munster patron, Ailbe of Emly, had 'quarrelled about the levy'.[5] The rights to tribute exercised by Armagh over the provincial kingdoms may have been only irregular, but her relations with the Northern Uí Néill kings seem to have been close and friendly, while her coarbs made visitations, on occasion, of Meath and Munster. When Brian, as *imperator scotorum*, made his visit to Armagh in 1005 he recognized on behalf of future kings of Cashel the rights of Patrick's coarb, and a record to this effect was entered, in his presence, into the Book of Armagh.[6]

Armagh, as far as we know, was the only church which received such wide support from provincial kings, but Clonard and Clon-

---

[1] *A.U.* 946, *A.F.M.* 945.

[2] *C.S.* 984 (*recte* 986) and *A.F.M.* 985. This was 'in consequence of the rebellion of Mac Cairellán.' *A.U.* does not mention this, but speaks of a great battle in Armagh.

[3] *Tr. Life*, i, 196, Mulchrone, 2302–3.   [4] *A.U.* 973.

[5] *A.I.* 973. At the end of the *Tr. Life* of Patrick a note has been added listing 'twenty four persons' in the 'unity' of Joseph (presumably the coarb of Patrick, *A.U.* 936) and saying that this number is to be at the king of Cashel's table from the time of king Feidlimid.

[6] *Arm.* 16 b 2.

macnois both maintained their positions as major Leth Cuinn monasteries.[1] In the eighth and early ninth centuries the 'law' of Ciarán had been promulgated by the kings of Connacht over their province, but later the spirit of Máel-Sechnaill I, king of Meath and overlord of Leth Cuinn, appeared to Cairbre Crom, bishop of Clonmacnois (died 904). It was the prayers of a bishop and twelve priests of Clonmacnois which rescued Máel-Sechnaill and his soulfriend from the pains of hell.[2] This is a later legend, though mentioned in the *Chronicon Scottorum*,[3] but there is convincing evidence that Máel-Sechnaill's son Flann built the great church at Clonmacnois, with the help of abbot Colmán.[4] It seems to be this Flann in whose honour the early-tenth-century Cross of the Scriptures was raised by abbot Colmán.[5] Colmán was abbot of both Clonmacnois and Clonard, and so also was Célechair, who died in 953. During his abbacy Congalach, king of Meath and overlord of Leth Cuinn, granted a privilege to Clonard; her freedom (*sáire*) 'without coigny (*coindem*) of king or prince': Clonard was not to contribute hospitality for the king's troops. In the tale of the Battle of Carn Conaill the king of Meath grants to Clonmacnois exemption from providing hospitality for the king and his company, a privilege which is supposed to have been granted in the seventh century but is much better suited to the tenth.[6] Both Clonmacnois and Clonard were receiving support from Meath kings in that period.

But if some churches were supported by Irish kings, others were attacked. Early in the century Brega was under the partial control of the Dublin Vikings. Its churches were attacked by Flann, king of Meath and overlord of the Northern Half in 913,

---

[1] For the emergence of Clonard as a primarily Leth Cuinn monastery, see Hughes, *I.H.S.*, ix (1954), 1–27.

[2] Ed. W. Stokes, *Revue Celtique*, xxvi (1905), 362–9, with translations; G. Dottin, *Manuel d'irlandais moyen*, ii, 119–23, without translation.

[3] *sub anno* 904.   [4] *C.S.* 908.

[5] Henry, *La sculpture irlandaise*, Paris, 1933, pp. 17–18. L. and M. de Paor, *Early Christian Ireland*, p. 146, state that the man named on the cross is 'Flann, king of Munster, who died in 904'. But since Flann son of Máel-Sechnaill had already helped in the building programme of Clonmacnois, and Colmán was abbot not only of Clonmacnois but of Clonard as well, the other identification seems more likely.

[6] Ed. W. Stokes, *Z.C.P.*, iii (1901), 206–7.

by his successor Donnchad in 938 and 939, and by Domnall, king
of Ailech and overlord of the Northern Half in 969, on the last
occasion at least with heavy loss of life.[1] The same king Domnall
plundered the churches of Meath in 970.[2] There seems no longer
to have been any feeling that churches should be immune from
violence. The ecclesiastical cities were defensive positions, and if
occupied by a rival power it was almost inevitable that they would
be attacked. When a king 'spoiled all the churches and forts' of
an enemy area, he may have regarded it as merely part of his
campaign. Donnchad seems to have been occupying Kells in 903,
when his father king Flann attacked him, 'and a great many
people were beheaded round the oratory'. In 972 the Viking chief
Ivar seems to have made his headquarters at Inis Cathaig and was
under the protection of its patron Senán, for when another Viking
leader from the Hebrides attacked Inis Cathaig and carried him off,
the annalist noted 'the violation of Senán thereby'. Brian son of
Cennétig again profaned the holy island in 975 when he slew the
chief Ivar and his two sons there. If a monastic city was occupied
by one party, by now it was no longer secure from attack by the
enemy. When Brian conducted his hosting across south Munster
in 987 (*A.I.*), to establish his position as king, he found it necessary to take hostages from the three great monasteries of Lismore,
Cork, and Emly, 'as a guarantee of the banishment of robbers and
lawless people therefrom'. He did not intend those monasteries
(all of which had on some occasion in the past been united with
the kingship) to harbour his political enemies.

Occasionally during this century churches may be seen deliberately joining kings as allies to fight their battles. The abbot
of Cork and the abbot of Cenn Eitig were both killed fighting for
king Cormac of Cashel at the Battle of Belach Mugna. Neither of
these monasteries lay anywhere near the battle-ground, and there
can be no doubt that the abbots were deliberately present to
support their lord in his aggression against Leinster. The later
saga incorporated into the Third Fragment of Annals puts the
major responsibility for the battle on the abbot of Inis Cathaig:

---

[1] *A.F.M.* 968: 400 wounded and burned at Lann Léire in the refectory,
'both men and women'.

[2] *A.F.M.* Clonard, Fore, Llynally, Dísert Tola.

it was he who taunted Cormac into refusing the peace-offers of the Leinstermen, who led part of the troops in the battle and was taken captive by the king of Leinster. According to the same account, the abbot of Emly, with his clerics, remained at Leighlin with the servants and provisions, and took no part in the fighting. But this is not a contemporary annalistic entry, and its record is open to suspicion. In any case, accounts of churches raising troops to take part in major battles are rare in the tenth century.[1] It is much more common to see churches occupied by secular lords pursuing their own wars, with monastic *termon* violated, though in a few cases monasteries were influential enough to secure exemption.

In the tenth century the Irish church seems to be less separate from the world than ever before in its history. In the south of Ireland on a number of occasions kingship was held not only by ecclesiastical officials but by churchmen in major orders. Cormac son of Cuilennán king of Munster, killed at Belach Mugna in 908, was already a bishop when he 'took the kingship of Cashel'.[2] The Tripartite Life, probably written just before Cormac's reign, as we have already noted, claims that the abbot of Armagh installed and conferred *grád* on the king of Munster.[3] The most common meaning of this word is 'ecclesiastical orders', and this seems to be the meaning here, for the Life goes on to say that twenty-seven kings had ruled in Cashel 'under a crozier' until the time of Cenn Gégáin, who, according to the Annals of Inisfallen, was king from 896 to 902. Nevertheless, though kings who were abbots are attested for the ninth century, Cormac son of Cuillennán is our first certain instance of a king-bishop.[4] In 920 another Cormac, this time son of Mothla, king of the Déisi, died:[5] the

---

[1] Possibly an instance occurs at 970, when the king of Brega and the lord of Dublin fought Domnall of the Cenél Eógain at Cell-mónai. Among the slain were the king of Ulster and 'Donnacán, son of Máel-Maire, erenagh'.

[2] *A.I.* 901.   [3] *Tr. Life*, i, 196. Mulchrone, 2302–9.

[4] A quatrain in the margin of one of the MSS. of *A.U.* refers to the *bachall* ('staff' or 'crozier') of Feidlimid, but this word does not necessarily indicate a bishop. Had Feidlimid really held episcopal orders, the fact is likely to have been recorded in one of the obituary notices.

[5] *C.S.* 918 (*recte* 919) and *A.F.M.* 915, 917 record him as 'son of Mothla', and he would seem to be the Cormac Mothla who took the kingship of the Déisi in 897 *A.I.*

Annals of Inisfallen, by a confusion, enter him as 'Cormac son of Cuilennán, bishop and *secnap* of Lismore, abbot of Cell Mo-Laise'. It seems likely that the ecclesiastical titles accorded to this man (in the Annals of Inisfallen only) in fact refer to the great Cormac son of Cuilennán, king-bishop of Cashel. Cell Mo-Laise and Lismore were both within the kingdom of Déisi, and great monasteries of Munster. Whether the ecclesiastical offices belong to Cormac son of Cuilennán king of Cashel, who died in 908, or Cormac Mothla, lord of Déisi, who died in 920, they show the close association existing between the king and the great abbeys. According to the Third Fragment of Annals,[1] Flaithbertach son of Inmainen, the comrade-in-arms of Cormac, who took the kingship of Cashel in 914, had previously been abbot of Inis Cathaig,[2] but the statement is unsupported by the other annalists, and of doubtful value.[3] Rebachán, who died in 934, seems to have been both king of Dál Cais and abbot of Tomgraney, one of the churches in his territory, while the abbot of Kildare who died in 905 was a royal heir of Leinster. Máel-suthain Ua Cerbaill (*obit* 1009) was not only lord of the Eóghanacht of Loch Léin (Killarney) but also 'chief doctor of the western world in his time' and one of the community of Inisfallen, a monastery on the Lower Lake of Killarney. Thus, it would appear that, in the Southern Half of Ireland, the same man might hold administrative office in both church and kingdom; that he might, moreover, be in major ecclesiastical orders and still be king. When this happened it must have been almost impossible to separate spiritual and secular interests.

The community of interests between church and state during this period is seen not only in the appointments. It was not merely that kings might be bishops or abbots, or that family interest might control the abbatial successions in certain monasteries.[4] Much more important an influence in the secularization of the churches was the fact that they were no longer generally regarded as inviolable by Irish princes. They did not now choose to make

---

[1] For this source, *supra*, p. 204.   [2] *Third Frag.*, pp. 200–16.

[3] The entry in *A.U.* 944 seems to be incomplete.

[4] There are examples of this in the tenth century at Achad Bó, Slane, Lismore, Killeshin, Ferns, and other houses, but I doubt if it increased much.

war; they were occupied, over-run, plundered, and prophecies of disaster to those who pillaged them seem to have had little effect. The interests of the churches *had* to be the interests of a powerful lord if they were to survive with success. The Vikings had broken the legal balance of the old order: now the Irish kings were contending for sovereignty, mobilizing their resources as never before. The churches, already materially weakened by Viking depredations, could not withstand the pressure of secular interests.

The change in the terminology used to describe the abbot's office during this period may indicate a shift in emphasis on the abbot's function. Though the old words continue, *princeps* becomes more frequent in the Annals of Ulster and the *Chronicon Scottorum*, and *comarba* is now more generally used.[1] Both these terms emphasize the abbot's powers of jurisdiction, whereas *abbas* had more especially described his religious office. Moreover, in the later ninth century, and more commonly in the tenth, another title comes into more frequent use, that of *aircinnech*, anglicized 'erenagh', an old term, known to the Laws, but rarely occurring before this time in the annals. Cormac's Glossary glosses it as 'noble head'.[2] The erenagh exercises the same powers as the abbot had done—indeed, he is the abbot—but he is often spoken of in the tenth century and more especially later as a man with worldly interests. Much of a tenth-century abbot's energy must have been spent on trying to collect revenue and keep his church inviolate from physical harm.

Some of the developments we have described may be discerned in the Saints' Lives written during this period. It is the nature of hagiographical literature to glorify the patron, to show him able to protect his followers and destroy his adversaries. It is also true that income must always be important to the church as an institution, and that churches with an active spiritual and intellectual life may still be deeply concerned to protect their property rights. Nevertheless, the emphasis which writers of the late ninth and

[1] A. Gwynn, 'Some Irish ecclesiastical titles in the tenth and eleventh centuries', *Bull. of Ir. Ctee of Hist. Sciences*, No. 17, February 1942; J. Barry, 'The erenagh in the monastic Irish church', *I.E.R.*, lxxxix (1958), 424–32.

[2] Ed. W. Stokes, p. 10.

tenth centuries put upon the material success and prosperity of their patrons can be extremely crude. The Tripartite Life of Patrick was composed as a homily in three parts for the saint's festival. No doubt a good preacher would 'get up' his sermons from the material supplied by the hagiographer, who, in his turn, had used earlier Patrician sources. The Life would be attractive material for the preacher, for it offers entertainment, elements of poetry and moral teaching; above all, it would popularize Patrick's shrine and attract gifts to it. Patrick unconquerable, heroic, triumphant is the theme. Calamities overwhelm those who oppose him, like the man who was 'peeled like an onion' by his enemies every seventh year:[1] long life, distinguished progeny, and prosperity are the reward of those who endow generously.

Earlier sources had recorded the boons which Patrick had obtained of God,[2] but the Tripartite Life is the first to include among them a demand for 'nine companions' load of gold and silver to be given to the Gael for believing'.[3] Patrick is now prepared to press his claims and bargain with God. Tírechán had described how Patrick, remaining forty days and forty nights on Crúach Pátraic, was permitted to see the fruit of his labours.[4] The Tripartite Life now gives a long account of a contest on the mountain between the saint and an angel:

> The angel came to converse with [Patrick], and said to him: 'God gives thee not what thou demandest, because it seems to him excessive and obstinate, and great are the requests.' 'Is that his pleasure?' says Patrick. 'It is,' says the angel. 'Then this is my pleasure; I will not go from this Rick till I am dead, or till all the requests are granted to me.' Then Patrick abode in Cruachán in evil mind.

This is only the beginning of the story. The angel tries to cajole Patrick with offers of spiritual privileges, and Patrick makes higher demands, refusing to go away until they are satisfied. In the end all his demands are met, and full honours lie with Patrick, God saying wryly, 'There hath not come and there will not come after the apostles a man more admirable, were it not for thy hard-

---

[1] *Tr. Life*, i, 208.
[2] Muirchú, *Arm.* 8 a 1, Tírechán, *Arm.* 15 b 1. Cf. *Coll.* LXVI. 5.
[3] *Tr. Life*, i, 30; Mulchrone, p. 19. Cf. Confession, cc. 52–3.
[4] *Arm.* 13 a 2–13 b 1.

ness.'[1] The outrageous impudence of this bargaining is not the only example of the kind in the Tripartite Life. On another occasion Patrick urges a young woman on the point of marriage to become a nun, and her father agrees to it 'if heaven were given to him in exchange, and if he himself were not compelled to be baptized'. Patrick, we read, 'promised those two things, although it was difficult for him.' The hagiographer obviously felt uneasy about the theological implications of the tale, and adds a postscript describing how Patrick resurrected the man after his death and baptized him.[2] The hagiographer's object is to prove Patrick's power, and if God is belittled in the process, or Christian doctrine made ridiculous, it does not seem to matter.

The Life of Senán is in some respects reminiscent of the Tripartite Life, and probably goes back to a tenth-century text.[3] Like other saints' Lives, it stresses the spiritual advantages which accrue from burial in the saint's cemetery,[4] and burial, as we have seen, brought substantial fees to the monastery. Material advantages are prophesied for those who do the saint's will, 'the vengeance of God, here and beyond' on those who deny him.[5] Senán successfully resisted the king's demand for tribute from his monastery, saying that 'he would not be under tribute (*fo chís*) or service (*na fa fhoghnam*) to an earthly king'.[6] Here Senán seems to be claiming a privilege similar to that which Clonard had been granted by king Congalach.[7]

The material well-being of the monastery had often been present in the minds of earlier hagiographers, and earlier writers had allowed their patrons occasionally to indulge in some crude manifestations of authority, but those tendencies become even more pronounced after the end of the ninth century. Moreover,

---

[1] *Tr. Life*, i, 112 ff.; Mulchrone, pp. 70 ff.

[2] *Tr. Life*, i, 178–80; Mulchrone, pp. 108–10.

[3] Kenney says it depends directly on a Life written at Inis Cathaig, not later than the tenth century. It can hardly be earlier. The introduction echoes the introduction of Part III of Patrick's Life, and the conclusion has similarities with the conclusion of Part I and Part III of *Tr. Life*. The story of Senán's contest with the king's druid (*Lis.* 2277 ff.) seems to be influenced by the account of Patrick's contests with king Lóegaire's druid.

[4] *Lis.* 2242–3.   [5] *Lis.* 2371–2.

[6] *Lis.* 2115.

[7] *C.S.* 950 (*recte* 951), *supra*, p. 219.

early saints' Lives had usually been written for the clerics themselves, whereas Lives like the Tripartite Life or the Life of Senán
seem to have been composed for a predominantly lay audience.
The writer put in what was likely to entertain his audience, and he
seems to have enjoyed doing it. The description, for instance, of
the monster which Senán expelled from Inis Cathaig is full of
rhetorical alliteration:

> When the monster heard [Senán and the angels,] singing their praises
> to God it shook its head, and its hair stood up upon it, and its rough
> bristles; and it looked at them, hatingly and wrathfully. Not gentle,
> friendly, mild was the look it bestowed upon them, for it marvelled
> that anyone else should come to visit it in its island. So it went to
> them strongly and swiftly, insomuch that the earth trembled under
> its feet. Hideous, uncouth, ruthless, awful was the beast that arose
> there. . . . A horse's mane on it, an eye gleaming flamingly in its
> head, and it keen, savage, froward, angry, edged, crimson, bloody,
> cruel, bounding . . . and so on.

The saints' Lives of the period show a close community of interest
between the church and secular society. By the tenth century
the world has not only come inside the monastic enclosure; its
standards now dominate the ideas of many of the leading ecclesiastics.

CHAPTER 21

Spiritual, intellectual, and artistic life

By the end of the tenth century, the ascetic revival had spent its impetus, and the original ideals of the movement had been partially eclipsed: the church's administrators had accepted many of the values of secular society, and its propagandists were appealing to popular taste in their search for wealth and power. Yet this is not to say that spiritual life was completely dead or that the anchorites had disappeared.

One of the most delightful of the tenth-century religious poems, ascribed to Manchán of Lemanaghan, pictures an idyllic life for a group of thirteen religious.[1] They have a little settlement in the desert, with church and house to live in, situated beside a stream and facing south to the sun; near by is a wood, filled with birds. Their diet is to be leeks, hens, salmon, and honey. Not only does every prospect please, but the monks themselves are to be 'young men of sense'. The ideal is contemplative, not a life of hard manual work, but of prayer, 'to be sitting awhile, praying to God'. Such is the anchorite's lot in the poet's imagination.

Anchorites lived, in fact, in or near a number of tenth-century churches,[2] but they are mentioned much less frequently than in the preceding century. Some of these men were in major orders, since the annals specifically refer to them as bishops or priests; one either was or had been a king: 'Finnechta son of Lóegaire, chief anchorite of Ireland, king of Kerry and chief counsellor of Munster'.[3] In the eleventh century Conn, an anchorite of Clonmacnois, himself the son of a confessor (who was presumably therefore a priest) there, had sons who became important members of the ecclesiastical *fine*, one of whom contributed two causeways through the city.[4] His grandson Máel-Maire was a learned cleric,

---

[1] Murphy, *Lyrics*, pp. 28–31.
[2] Including Armagh, Clonfert, Bangor, Terryglass, Dísert-Diarmata, Leighlin, Glendalough, Fore.
[3] *A.I.* 929.   [4] *A.F.M.* 1070.

one of the scribes of *Lebor na Huidre*, a manuscript compiled at Clonmacnois.[1] 'Conn of the Poor, head of the culdees and anchorite of Clonmacnois' was not celibate, but he was a benefactor who endowed a settlement for the poor of Clonmacnois.[2] Such men were not leading a life isolated from public affairs, and they had lapsed from the original ascetic ideals of the anchorites and culdees, but we have no reason to condemn them as degenerate or irreligious. Since the reformers of the late eighth and ninth centuries had created no new administrative machinery to enforce discipline, their successors were almost bound to slip into the accepted practices of the church as time went on and the first enthusiasm weakened.

The outlook of administrators engaged in public affairs was not purely materialistic, and some clerics were well aware of the moral dangers which the church suffered in her pursuit of wealth and power. The Vision of Adamnán, probably composed in the tenth century, describes the pains suffered in the afterlife by merciless erenaghs who misuse ecclesiastical property for their own purposes,[3] and by ordained men who have violated their orders.[4] Many men of affairs were well aware that their active lives had been no fit preparation for the life to come, and resigned kingship or abbacy to end their lives in pilgrimage. Kings 'took the pilgrim's staff', though the annalists do not tell of any who went to the Continent: the Irish shrines, such as Armagh or Iona, seem to have been the limit of their journeys.[5] But ecclesiastics occasionally made their way to Rome, like Céledabhaill, abbot of Bangor, who set out in 928 when he was fifty-nine years old. For him it was

> Time to talk of the last day, to separate from familiar faces,
> Time to dread the terrors of the tumults of the day of judgement,
> Time to defy the clayey body, to reduce it to religious rule,
> Time to barter the transitory things for the country of the king of heaven.

[1] *Lebor na Huidre*, ed. Best and Bergin, pp. x–xiii, xv.
[2] *A.F.M.* 1031.
[3] Ed. E. Windisch, *Irische Texte*, p. 186.   [4] Ibid., 188.
[5] It is of interest that Olaf (Cuaran) son of Sitric, king of the Dublin Gaill, went to Iona in 979 (*A.F.M. recte* 980) and died there. The Hiberno-Norse by this time were, at least partially, Christianized.

Time to defy the ease of the little earthly world of a hundred
pleasures,
Time to work at prayer, in adoration of the high king of angels.

He died at Rome in the September, either of the same or the
following year.[1] In the same year another Irish abbot, Fergil of
Terryglass, died in Rome on pilgrimage. Maybe the two had been
travelling companions. After a busy life of administration, of the
journeyings, and justice and attempts to collect revenue which
contribute so much to the abbot's activity, these two had undertaken a final act of religious devotion.

A tenth-century religious poet knew the need for discipline,
the danger of straying thoughts, though in his verse he pursues
their wanton beckoning 'through eager assemblies, through companies of foolish women, through woods, through cities, swifter
than wind . . . slippery as an eel's tail sliding out of my grasp'.
This is a poem of delightful humour and honesty, ending with a
prayer of devotion: 'May I attain perfect companionship with
thee, O Christ: may we be together; thou art neither fickle nor
inconstant, not as I am.'[2] Another poet, of the tenth or eleventh
century, prays: 'Be thou my vision, beloved Lord . . . my medita-
tion . . . my speech . . . my understanding . . . my battle-shield
. . . my shelter . . . be thou alone my heart's special love, let there
be none other save the high-king of heaven.'[3] These and other
poems do not come from a spiritual life which was moribund.
Some men, at least, were rejecting the profit-making motive for
the life of the spirit. The poem attributed to the abbess Íte, in
which Jesus comes to her as a babe for fostering, is instinct with
aristocratic pride, which declares itself uninterested in all favours
other than Christ's.[4] 'The nursing done by me in my house is no

---

[1] The annals enter his departure in *A.U.* 928, *A.F.M.* 926. *A.F.M.* gives
a poem said to have been composed by him at his departure, giving his age
as fifty-nine. Both sets of annals record his death in the following year, giving
the September date, 'in the fifty-ninth year of his age'. It is possible that the
news took a year to travel home, and that he died probably soon after he
reached Rome, in the same year as he set out. On the other hand, the poem
giving his age on departure as fifty-nine may have been composed not by
him, but by a monk of Bangor after the news of his death had been received.
Or the knowledge of his age may have been only approximate.

[2] Murphy, *Lyrics*, pp. 38–42.
[3] Ibid., pp. 42–5.   [4] Murphy, *Lyrics*, pp. 26–9.

Q

nursing of a base churl: Jesus with Heaven's inhabitants is against my heart every night. . . . It is noble angelic Jesus and no common cleric who is nursed by me in my little hermitage.' And this heavenly prince has a prince's quality, generosity: 'He never fails to give.' His gifts are superior to the material gifts which may be expected from the great ones of the earth. 'Though princes' sons and kings' sons come into my countryside, it is not from them I expect profit: I love little Jesus better'; 'though a cleric have great wealth, it is all deceitful except little Jesus.'

Such poems provide the reverse side of the image of the church shown in some of the saints' lives. Both pictures are true. Lack of rigidity and uniformity was a strength as well as a weakness to the Irish church. Secular life and secular standards had established a firm lodging in the monasteries, and the church was out to attract wealthy men to its shrines. It might be supposed that this would lower the general level of spiritual life. But the Irish church was so decentralized that it is not really accurate to speak of a general level: while one cleric might be advertising a shrine another might be directly building up the life of the spirit. And if the world was in the church, the church was also in the world, for the openness of the monasteries to the laity meant that lay society was permeated by Christian concepts and imagery. When the Viking settlements in Ireland began, the invaders were heathen whose terrifyingly savage behaviour might have been expected to earn them lasting hatred from their victims, but less than a hundred and fifty years later a Viking chief was ending his life in pilgrimage on Iona. As far as we know, Christianity was not imposed on any Norse-Irish prince at the sword's point, or as part of a political agreement: it must have percolated through from Irish society to Norse society. This is surely a witness to the vitality of religion throughout the country.

The literature of the tenth and eleventh centuries shows a much closer combination of interest between the lay world and the clerics than did the ecclesiastical literature of the pre-Viking age. Much more is now written in the vernacular. Earlier scribes had written mainly in Latin for the monastic community, now the church's men of learning are frequently writing in Irish, for a wider public. Earlier scholars had taken their learning from the

Bible and the Fathers, from Isidore of Seville and from classical authors still available to them; now the Irishman's own imagination, invention, and fantasy have much freer rein.

These qualities can be clearly seen in a text known as The Evernew Tongue, written in Irish in the tenth or eleventh century, probably on the basis of a Latin original.[1] The ancestry of the text is apparent. It is a homily, cast in the form of a vision: seventh-century Irish writers had been masters of the homily, and it was the Vision of Fursey the Irishman which launched the vision literature on medieval Europe. The Evernew Tongue employs the old schoolman's technique of question and answer, allows the demonstration of the schoolman's traditional knowledge, as well as a display of Hebrew learning (though this, 'the language spoken in Heaven', has degenerated into incomprehensible gibberish). But what distinguishes the work from earlier homilies is the prominence given to apocryphal and poetic elements. It is full of fantastic and haunting allusions: there are the four hundred and seventy melodies sung by the waves of the sea which encircles the earth, the colours put on the diverse seas which wash the shores of the world, the qualities of the various trees planted by God at the creation, the strange beast washed up on the eve of Christ's nativity, or the great bird found in the lands of India, to mention only a few.

The vision of the creation, of hell and heaven, revealed in the Evernew Tongue mingles the scholar's lore, apocryphal legend, and poetic invention. The man who composed or adapted it had skill enough to charm the minds of religious and laymen with curiosities, with wonders, with images evoking worship and love. He strays a long way from the canonical scriptures, yet he offers spiritual teaching. His image of the terror of God's might is juxtaposed with the picture 'of the infant sleeping between the Virgin's arms, while the elements, and even the angels, trembled, and the heavens and earth with its inhabitants, and the monsters in the seas and the dwellers in hell'. Yet 'such are the beauty and effulgence of his face that if all the souls in Hell were to look on the splendour of his countenance, they would not perceive

[1] Ed. Stokes, *Ériu*, ii (1905), 96–162. Discussed in Hughes, 'Irish Monks and Learning', pp. 22–4.

trouble, nor pain, nor punishment in hell'.[1] In the Evernew Tongue the religious contemplative speaks to the common man. We are in a Christian society, but one in which fantasy is as important as literal truth.

Fís Adamnáin is one of the earliest and finest of all the Visions.[2] It provides a splendid vision of heaven, with the Lord indescribably glorious: 'For none shall tell his ardour and energy, his glow and gleam, his dignity and beauty, his constancy and firmness.'[3] The horrors of hell are recounted in detail, but certain persons easily escape them: the ascetics, those who have performed penance and those who have suffered red martyrdom (like so many victims of the Viking terror).[4] Even men who have lived carelessly in sin yet have practised charity are saved from the fires of hell by being marooned on islands.[5] In the tenth century the call to repentance was still heard, made with a wealth of symbolism, allegory, and imagery.

The *Saltair na Rann*, composed in 987 or 988,[6] gives its account of sacred history in Irish metrics. The first part of one of its sections (no. xi on the Penance of Adam and Eve) follows the apocryphal story of the *Vita Adae et Evae*,[7] but with elaborations of its own: it well expresses the pity of man's fall, the sadness of loss and repentance, the love between Adam and Eve, the conscienceless guile of the devil. It is Eve who wins our sympathy: Eve begging Adam to kill her to turn the wrath of God, bewailing the lost physical comforts of Paradise, standing for penance up to her neck in the waters of the Tigris with her hair floating on the stream, betrayed again by Lucifer into forsaking her penance, overcome by the grief of Adam (who had meantime been pardoned by God, after all the creatures of the Jordan, in which Adam stood, had joined with him to fast upon God). The author

---

[1] Ed. Stokes, *Ériu*, ii (1905), pp. 140–2.

[2] Possibly on the basis of an earlier original. For discussion and translation, C. S. Boswell, *An Irish Precursor of Dante*, London, 1908. Cf. Dillon, *Early Irish Literature*, p. 133.

[3] c. 9.   [4] c. 23.   [5] c. 27.

[6] Ed. W. Stokes, Oxford, 1883. Cf. Dillon, *Early Irish Literarure*, p. 150; the date has recently been discussed by G. S. MacEoin, *Z.C.P.*, xxviii (1960–1), 51–67.

[7] Seymour, 'The Book of Adam and Eve in Ireland', *P.R.I.A.*, xxvi, c. 121.

of this poem did not trouble to distinguish between canonical and apocryphal authorities, but he understood both what truths he wished to convey and the art of expressing them.

The mingling of myth and magic, poetry and religious teaching is nowhere more successful than in the voyage tales. Their sources are classical tradition, Christian legend, historical memory,[1] and pure invention, cast in the form of the saga. Christian hermits had sought their deserts sometimes among the islands of the ocean, and the search for the *terra repromisionis* (which was also the land of the *semper viventes*, the 'land of the immortals') was the object of the voyage, the search fraught with terrors and delights. Already by about 800 a number of saints were reputed to have made voyages,[2] while legends of Brendan's voyage were known in the ninth century to the Breton compiler of the Life of Malo.[3] The *Navigatio Brendani* was written, in Latin, in the tenth century, by an Irishman, but perhaps on the Continent, since the early manuscripts have a Lotharingian–Rhenish provenance.[4] He has an exciting story to tell, and does it with an excellent command of narrative. His *mirabilia*, such as the column of crystal (presumably an iceberg)[5] or the smoking mountain,[6] entice the curious. The senses are satisfied, sight, sound, smell, and taste.[7] There are humorous situations to amuse, as when the monks anchor on a bare island to spend Easter, light their fire, and find themselves in the middle of an earthquake: they have landed on a sleeping sea-monster.[8] Even the twentieth-century reader of the *Navigatio* feels the lure of the islands of the blest, where no cold or heat overcomes the inhabitants, where old age and fatigue do not trouble them,[9]

[1] E.g. Adamnán's account of Cormac's voyages in search of a desert in the ocean, *Life of Columba*, II. 42.

[2] Traditions of the *immrama* (voyages) type seem to have centred on Brendan, the Uí Chorra, Ailbe and Ibar by this date. See Hughes, 'On an Irish Litany of Pilgrim Saints compiled *c.* 800', p. 316 and notes. The Voyage of Máeldúin (in Irish) may be of the ninth century, the Voyage of Snedgus (also in Irish) of the ninth or tenth.

[3] C. Selmer, *Catholic Hist. Rev.*, xxix (1943), 169.

[4] C. Selmer, *Navigatio Sancti Brendani Abbatis*, pp. xxvii ff.

[5] Selmer, *Navigatio*, pp. 58–9.

[6] Ibid., pp. 64–5.

[7] E.g. the smell of the island like ripe apples (p. 54), the songs and wings of the birds (p. 43); conversely, the din and stench of hell (pp. 61–3).

[8] Ibid., pp. 20–1.   [9] Ibid., p. 32.

where there is no sickness of the spirit,[1] where Christ is the light:[2]
how much more compelling must these tales have been to people
prepared to believe in the physical existence of these islands, who
knew Brendan's port of embarkation,[3] who believed that a man
might return from the Land of Promise with its sand warm in his
shoes?[4]

The *Navigatio* shows us the Irish religious ideal in various forms.
The island of Ailbe, visited by Brendan on his travels, held a
community of twenty-four. There was a square church with a
central altar, flanked by two other altars; before the central altar
three candles, two candles before each of the other two altars.
Twenty-four seats were arranged around the church, the abbot's
between 'the two choirs'. The brethren ate together in the
refectory, but lived separately, each in their own cells, receiving
guests into their cells.[5] On the flat, treeless Island of the Three
Companies were three groups of people, boys clad in white, young
men in blue, seniors in purple dalmatics, maintaining a round of
psalmody.[6] But it is the hermit, Paul, alone on his island 'like a
bird on this rock, naked except for my hairs',[7] who reaches the
heights of asceticism. Paul leads the angelic life, sustained by the
direct intervention of God. The ascetic ideal still had power to
command veneration, however far the churches had in fact
departed from it. In the eighth century the ascetic life had been
practised by a few reformers, emaciated hermits had lived in the
deserts, often on meagre rations, giving up their lives to prayer:
in the tenth century and after, the voyages were popularizing the
ascetic ideal as never before, lifting it out of the hard discipline
of fact into a world of adventure and enchantment.

The first century of Viking occupation struck a heavy blow at
the craftsmen of metal-work and manuscript illumination; for the
smiths and scribes, both venerable and highly respected groups,
could not withstand undamaged the shock of the Viking on-
slaught. The Book of Kells, written and illuminated before the
scriptoria felt the full effects of Viking depredations, is the master-

---

[1] Selmer, *Navigatio*, p. 36.   [2] Ibid., p. 80.
[3] Ibid., pp. 10–12.
[4] Life of Munnu, *Acta SS. de Cod. Sal.*, cols. 411–12.
[5] *Navigatio*, pp. 33–5.   [6] Ibid., pp. 50–2.
[7] Ibid., p. 73.

piece of Irish book production, showing a dramatic power and delight in fantasy, which qualities are ordered with consummate technical skill. The early-tenth-century artist of the Psalter B.M. Cotton Vitellius F. xi[1] retains the delight in drama and fantasy, but without his predecessor's mastery: his full-page illustration of David and Goliath is powerful, whereas the earlier artist's picture of Christ's Temptation or Arrest had been beautiful.[2] The small number of surviving tenth-century illuminated books witnesses to either the loss of manuscripts or the decline in the production of luxury books, probably to both. Metal-work also lost some of its intricate command of colour and texture: the ornaments of the late ninth and tenth centuries are on the whole simpler and cruder than the metal-work of the eighth, though vigorous and useful in design.[3] Tenth-century work on the croziers of Kells and of S. Dymphna and S. Mel shows, however, that the smiths were busy in a style which was lively, if less delicate than before.[4]

But whereas the illuminators and smiths, among the most privileged craftsmen of the old régime, were hard hit by the new conditions, the masons seem to have been positively encouraged by the Viking settlements. Perhaps monastic patrons felt that it was safer to spend income on great stone crosses which could be neither looted nor destroyed than on manuscripts and metal-work, the first things to disappear in any disturbance. The free-standing, wheel-headed cross, already evolved in the eighth century, in the ninth developed a complex iconography, which continued to mature in the tenth. The Cross of the Scriptures at Clonmacnois and Muiredach's Cross at Monasterboice are examples of the mature style, the former probably commissioned between 916 and 926,[5] the latter associated with Muiredach,

[1] Henry, *P.R.I.A.* lxi (1960), C 23–4; *L'art irlandais*, ii, 157 ff.

[2] See Plates VIII and IX.

[3] Henry, *L'art irlandais*, ii, 162 ff.

[4] MacDermott, *Archaeologia*, xcvi (1955), 59–113, *P.R.I.A.*, lviii (1957), C 167–95.

[5] See arguments above, p. 219, and Plate XI, below. Flann died in 916, Colman in 926 (*A.U.*). Dr Bieler's *Ireland* illustrates the Cross of the Scriptures, erected for Flann, opposite p. 34 (right-hand side). The illustration on the left side of the same page, which is labelled 'Flan's Cross', is in fact the southern cross of Clonmacnois. The illustrations are excellent, but the labelling may cause confusion, since the south cross belongs to the type of

abbot of Monasterboice, *secnap* of Armagh, and high-steward of the southern Uí Néill, who died in 924.[1] Both these crosses carry, on the crossing of the west face, a crucifixion, in which Christ hangs naked on the cross attended by two soldiers (and in Muiredach's Cross by two angels). Beneath are three panels of New Testament scenes, each depicting three figures: on the east face of each is a Last Judgement, with further panels beneath. Both crosses are dramatic and spirited presentations, part of the series of figured crosses which Dr Henry has described as 'a magnificent preface to mediaeval sculpture'. The Christian church was now displaying its iconography on stone to the many, rather than on vellum to the few.

The impetus towards rebuilding in stone which seems to be felt in the ninth and more particularly in the tenth century may have been encouraged by disturbed conditions. The round towers, a feature of Irish monastic sites, seem to have been constructed first in this period. Stone churches with chancels appear in the tenth century.[2] Some monastic cities, originally constructed in wood, must at about this period have taken on an appearance recognizable at the present day: at Glendalough S. Cóemgen's church was probably built in the ninth century, followed by the Round Tower, while S. Mary's Church, built just outside the city (probably for nuns), was designed as a single-chambered structure, with a fine west door. Trinity Church to the east of the city and Reefert on the upper lake were both built with their existing chancels in the tenth century, and the tiny church of S. Ciarán with its miniature chancel may belong to the same period. It is

---

cross with mainly geometrical ornament, though a crucifixion is shown in a panel on the west face, directly beneath the central wheel. Henry, *La sculpture irlandaise*, Plates 56 and 78, makes the separate identity of the crosses perfectly clear, also *L'art irlandais*, i, Plates 84–5; ii, Plates 90–95, 110, 112.

[1] Muiredach's Cross is superbly illustrated in Bieler's *Ireland*, opposite p. 131. For details see L. and M. de Paor, Plates 56 and 57, and pp. 148–9, and Henry, *L'art irlandais*, ii, Plates 76–85. On these and other crosses of the period see *L'art irlandais*, ii, 194 ff.

[2] Mr Leask suggests (*Irish Churches and Monastic Buildings*, i, 76) that this may have been partly due to increased numbers of the laity attending church services, necessitating the separation of the people from the sanctuary. Some such separation had occurred at Kildare in the seventh century. More emphasis on the liturgy might also form a reason for constructing chancels.

uncertain whether the great cathedral in the main city at Glenda-lough originally had a chancel, but it probably dates also from the tenth century. Glendalough was within striking distance of the Dublin Vikings, and the scale of its ninth- and tenth-century reconstruction is a lively testimony to the church's powers of recovery, and probably to its attraction for pilgrims.

By the tenth century the church had adapted itself to the con-ditions brought by the Viking swords,[1] and had achieved a material recovery. Her men of learning were in touch with Eng-land[2] and the Continent, while Scandinavian civilization was influencing her men of art. The illuminators and smiths had lost some of their finesse, but the sculptors and masons had extended their activity. And while the stone crosses displayed the Old and New Testament iconography, the monastic story-tellers recounted their dialogues, visions, and voyages in prose and verse, for the delight of the crowds.

[1] They appear on the crosses; see L. and M. de Paor, *Early Christian Ire-land*, p. 148.

[2] See, for example, J. Armitage Robinson, *The Times of Saint Dunstan*, Oxford, 1923, pp. 55–9, 69–70, for contacts between Irish scholars and the court of Athelstan.

CHAPTER 22

Restoration

Brian Boru had established the high-kingship of Ireland as a fact. Where other provincial kings had striven for overlordship with only partial success, he, 'a stranger in sovereignty', had seized the mastery.[1] But his overlordship was personal, and after the Battle of Clontarf leadership was resumed by Máel-Sechnaill II of Meath until his death in 1022. In Munster, Donnchad son of Brian ruled until 1063 (*A.I.*), but failed to hold the position which his father had won in the Southern Half and was defeated by his nephew Toirdelbach (Turlough) Ua Briain, who became the most powerful king in Ireland, securing the submission not only of Munster but of Connacht, Meath, and Breifne, and appointing his son Muirchertach as king of Dublin. Toirdelbach's death in 1086 was followed by a period when leadership was disputed between his son Muirchertach king of Munster and Domnall Mac Lochlainn king of Ailech. When these two died in 1119 and 1121, the rising star was the king of Connacht, Toirdelbach Ua Conchobair.

During the eleventh century, therefore, the church was still to some extent at the mercy of warring princes. But the establishment of an effective overlordship by Brian and the protection extended to the church had its effects. Already in the tenth century the church had been regaining much of the power which she had lost in the devastations of the early Viking age; in the eleventh her recovery continued, and her power was once more exercised in political affairs. During the worst years of Viking pressure the Irish clergy had cried in vain for help to their patrons, for the saints had not saved them from the Viking swords, but by the eleventh century the prowess of the saints seems to be fully restored. The annals, in all versions, show them taking vengeance on their enemies:[2] the Annals of Tigernach and the Annals of

---

[1] Binchy, 'The Passing of the Old Order', *Congress*, 1959, pp. 130–1.

[2] *A.Tig.* 1026, 1030, 1041, 1043, 1045, 1046, 1060, 1065, 1066, 1076, 1089. *A.U.* 1015, 1035, 1066, 1070. *A.I.* 1045, 1059. *A.F.M.* 1005, 1018, 1034,

the Four Masters are particularly well informed about the supernatural influence exercised by Ciarán of Clonmacnois, but other
saints are mentioned in the annals of the period: Patrick, Columcille, Sechnall, Tola, Mo-Chuta, Féichíne, Fintan Mo-Chuta,
Colmán, Rónán, Mochta, and Do-Beoc all prove their powers.
The saints could no longer be insulted without dread of reprisals.

Several of the vindications described in the annals are reprisals
for murder by the kin of the victim, when the murdered man had
been under the protection of the saints.[1] Sometimes the killing
had violated sanctuary, as when a grandson of Brecc, royal heir
of the Déisi, was killed in the stone church of Lismore by a kinsman's son. The murderer surrendered himself to S. Mo-Chuta in
retribution, but eight years later we read that Máel-Sechnaill
grandson of Brecc, King of the Déisi, was killed by Mo-Chuta. It
is possible that these two events are connected.[2] Occasionally the
annalist conveys the skeleton of some exciting raid and rescue. In
1060 Clonmacnois was razed by two Munster tribes from thirty
miles or so to the south: they took prisoners from the Cross of the
Scriptures and killed a student and a layman. But 'God and Ciarán
incited the Delbna[3] and their lord . . . to go in pursuit of them'.
They caught up with the marauders and returned in the early
morning 'bringing the prisoners to the place from which they had
been taken'.[4] Occasionally a king seized the opportunity to conduct a great raid in revenge for the profanation of a holy relic.[5]
On another occasion 'God and Ciarán wreaked vengeance' on a
raiding tribe by sending an unknown plague upon them, so that
they hastened to pay the compensation adjudged by the clergy of
Clonmacnois, in this case the personal service (*manchuine*) of
thirteen young nobles, besides a payment from every fort of the

---

1043, 1044, 1045, 1060, 1065, 1069, 1073, 1076, 1080, 1081. *C.S.* 1028, 1041,
1042, 1043, 1044, 1050, 1058 (for correct dates add two years), 1062, 1066
(for correct dates add three years).

[1] *A.F.M.* 1005, 1073, 1076.

[2] *A.I.* 1051, 1059. See also *A.F.M.* 1034.

[3] Probably the Delbna Nuadat in the barony of Athlone, and thus the
neighbours of Clonmacnois.

[4] *A.Tig., A.F.M.* 1060.

[5] *A.F.M.* 1044. See also *A.U.* 1066, where the king of Uí Briúin died
immediately after rifling the shrine of Patrick, *A.Tig.* 1030.

raiders.[1] When there was no prince at hand to exact reprisals on the clergy's behalf they could still pray for vengeance. In 1043 [2] the clergy of Ciarán fasted 'at Telach Garbha against Aed lord of Tethba. The *bearnán Ciaráin* was rung against him with the Staff of Jesus.[3] And in the place where Aed turned his back on the clergy, in that place was he beheaded before the end of the month, by Muirchertach Ua Máeleachlainn.' Two years later the king of Calraige 'died of an unknown disease before the end of three days' after he had forced the monastery to billet his troops in defiance of its immunity.[4] Donnchad, king of Munster in 1044, knew better than to anger the saint. When his men in his absence had plundered Clonmacnois he granted the church the award which she claimed in compensation. By the eleventh century the saints' power is completely rehabilitated, probably as effective as it had been before the Vikings arrived. Secular princes are once more able and willing to act as ecclesiastical champions.

The close connexion of the churches with the secular princes continued to bring the same disadvantage as in the preceding century. One tribe might plunder a church in the territory of a rival prince, who replied by sacking a church of his enemy. When the king of Dublin plundered Ardbraccan the king of Meath sacked Swords 'in revenge for it';[5] when the king of Leinster and his ally the king of Munster burned Ferns, the Uí Chenselaig sacked Killeshin as reprisal.[6] Churches might still be destroyed in wars between princes, as in 1073, when Conchobar king of Meath was murdered by his nephew when he was under the protection of the Staff of Jesus. His nephew and his son then went to war, and 'Clonard and Kells with their churches (*co na templaibh*) were all burned in one month'.[7] But though such disasters continued, the churches seem to have been much more successful at securing compensation or revenge than they had been in the previous two centuries. At the end of the century the saints (except for Patrick)

---

[1] *A.F.M.* 1044. See also 1045. *A.I.* 1051.

[2] *A.Tig.*, *A.F.M.* 1043, *C.S.* 1041 (*recte* 1043).

[3] Irish bells were tongueless and were struck to ring them. The Staff of Jesus was a crozier said to have been granted to Patrick.

[4] *A.Tig.* 1045. This means that Clonmacnois had 'freedom' like that granted to Clonard in 951. See *supra*, p. 219.

[5] *A.U.* 1035.   [6] *A.Tig.* 1041.   [7] *A.F.M.* 1073.

were said to be entreating God to send a mortality to avenge the destruction of churches brought about by 'monastic clients and lords and erenaghs',[1] and measures were taken to improve the situation. On the whole, the church gained materially more than she lost by secular interest.

The eleventh century saw a marked extension of a movement begun earlier, by which churches were freed from their economic obligations to secular lords. All Irish churches in the pre-Viking period had not enjoyed equal status: some had enjoyed the privileges of 'freedom' or 'nobility' (*saíre*), others had been *sub censu*, owing obligations to a secular lord.[2] King Aed had freed 'the clergy of Ireland from expeditions and hostings' in 804,[3] but other obligations remained, and the liabilities of the churches may have increased during the Viking troubles. Tenth-century churches had sometimes tried to assert their freedom, and the King of Meath had recognized the freedom (*saíre*) of Clonard in 951, no king or prince having claims of free billeting for his troops upon it. Brian Boru, on his hosting into Mag Muirtheimne in 1011 (*A.U.*), gave full freedom (*ógshaíre*) to Patrick's churches. One of the charters in the Book of Kells records a grant made between the years 1033 and 1049 by Conchobar Ua Máel-Sech-lainn, king of Meath, by which Kildalkey with its territory and lands was given to the community of Kells 'without rent or tribute, or expedition or hosting or free billeting of king or chief on it'.[4] The Poem of Prophesies from the Book of Hy Many attributed to Bec mac Dé, which used two documents of the early eleventh century and seems to have been composed in its present form before about 1150, speaks of the billeting of troops (*coind-med*) which had been imposed on Munster as an 'oppression' and disapproves of abbots being in company with soldiery.[5] In 1096 when Irishmen were struck with an extraordinary fear that plague which had been prophesied would overwhelm them, the clergy proclaimed fast days and kings 'gave freedom (*saíre*) to many

[1] Second Vision of Adamnán, ed. W. Stokes, R.C., xii (1891), 424–7.
[2] *Coll.* XXIX. 6. [3] *M.O.*, pp. 4–5, *A.U.* 804, *supra*, pp. 191–2.
[4] *cen cis cen chobach cen fecht cen luaged cen choinnim rig na toisig.* 'Irish Charters in the Book of Kells' ed. J. O'Donovan, *Misc. of the Irish Arch. Soc.*, i (1846), 138–9.
[5] Ed. K. Knott, *Ériu*, xviii (1958), pp. 60–1, 72–3.

churches which were in difficulty'.[1] The conscience of Irish princes had awakened, and the churches were gradually being freed from the obligations of tribute and service to secular lords.

The growth of the church's power during the eleventh century was occasionally attended by faction fights to secure authority. For the whole period the abbot's office at Armagh was dominated by the Clann Sinaich, but in 1060 another claimant, Cummascach Ua Eradhain fought Dub-dá-leithe, its holder, for his position: 'a great war in Armagh . . . respecting the abbacy' say the Annals of Ulster. He seems to have had no permanent success, for Dub-dá-leithe was succeeded on his death in 1064 by another of the Clann Sinaich, and Cummascach's obituary notice years later describes him as 'head of the poor of Ireland'.[2] There was a quarrel in 1076 over the succession at Clondalkin.[3] After a show of force this was settled by compromise, for the abbot in power retained his office,[4] while the claimant obtained two hundred and forty cows as compensation and 'a church with its land at Clondalkin was given to the culdees for ever'.[5] It is hard to tell whether the violence reported in the annals over this incident was occasioned by a struggle for the succession, or whether it arose from a personal feud. The latter seems to be the case at Armagh in 1038 (*A.U.*), when the king of Uí Echach, a distant kinsman of the Clann Sinaich abbots, was killed by the Clann Sinaich at Armagh as vengeance for having slain Eochaid son of the abbot and so violated Armagh. In the middle years of the century the Ua Cellacháin family perpetrated some acts of violence there. Cellachán had been king of Airthir, the sub-kingdom in which Armagh lay, and his son Trénfer had been *secnap* of Armagh. In 1037 Árchú, great grandson of Cellachán, king of the Uí Bresail sept, was slain by his brother Matudán. The slain man's son killed the

[1] *C.S.* sub anno 1092 (*recte* 1096).

[2] *A.U.* and *A.F.M.* 1074. *A.F.M.* 1075 describes him as abbot of Armagh, but this seems to be a mistake.

[3] *A.F.M.* 1076. 'An army was led by the clergy of Leth-Mogha with the son of Máel-dalua to Clondalkin, to expel Ua Rónáin from Clondalkin after he had assumed the abbacy in violation of the son of Máel-dalua.'

[4] Ua Rónáin died as erenagh of Clondalkin in 1086 *A.F.M.*, *A.U.*

[5] Mac Máel-dalua died as 'senior, confessor of all Ireland', in 1095 *A.U.*, *A.F.M.*

reigning *secnap* in 1052, but himself died in battle (as king of Uí Bresail) two years later. Matudán, killer of Árchú, appears as *secnap* of Armagh in 1063. The causes of this quarrel are not apparent, but it is clear that family feuds sometimes arose within a monastic city. At Emly there was violence in 1032, when the monastic household (*muinter*) killed a royal heir of Munster.[1] Twenty years later 'MacCarthach took the abbacy of Emly by force and expelled Ua Lígdae the lector from the abbot's seat';[2] but when Ua Lígdae died in battle in 1058, it was as abbot.[3] The abbot of Cork was slain by his own community in 1057 'when coming from nocturns',[4] while in 1070 the abbot of Iona was killed by the son of a former abbot Ua Máel-doraid, 'coarb of Columcille in Ireland and Scotland', who had died in 1062.[5] Monastic office was attractive to an ambitious man, and consequently it sometimes bred violent quarrels. On one occasion, in 1056, there was a pitched battle between Dub-dá-leithe coarb of Patrick and a Meath abbot at Martry in Meath:[6] 'the victory was gained by the coarb of Patrick and the Staff of Jesus, and many fell there'. Such battles between rival church forces were, however, uncommon in the eleventh century. It is, indeed, unlikely that this was a battle between monasteries in the manner of the eighth- and ninth-century contests. Most probably the retinues of the two abbots on visitation met and quarrelled, possibly over rights of hospitality or taxation. Monasteries were no longer putting armies into the field as they had once done, and were protesting when kings tried to billet their troops on the church; but increasing prosperity had brought a competitive rivalry into important monastic appointments, much as there had been in the eighth century. The domestic peace of the early Viking age had passed.

During the eleventh century the church was resuming the part she had once played as a powerful mediator in secular society, exercising her influence to secure peace and stability. In 1050 a great assembly of the clergy and laity of Munster was held at Killaloe under the presidency of the king of Munster, where they

[1] *A.Tig.*   [2] *A.I.* 1052.

[3] *A.Tig.* coarb, *A.I.* erenagh.   [4] *A.Tig.* 1057.

[5] *A.U.* 1070. See Reeves, *Columba*, p. 401, note b.

[6] *A.U., A.Tig.* 1055. The other abbot was 'coarb of Finnén (Clonard) and Columcille' (Kells), two great Meath houses.

'enacted a law (*cáin*) and a restraint (*cosc*) upon every injustice'. The church was joining in legislation for public order. The occasion of the assembly was the anarchy arising from famine, with the breakdown of normal restraints, the disregard of oaths and compacts or of the protection extended to churches and forts. It is significant as an attempt at civil government in which church and secular power combine. The chiefs of the great churches frequently acted as peace-makers between warring princes, and the saints' relics were used to bind agreements of peace on the participating peoples. In 1093 the kings of Ulster and Ailech swore friendship with each other and common cause against Munster, 'with many relics including the Staff of Jesus as pledges', and in the same year the two Munster princes Diarmait and Muirchertach 'made peace and a covenant in Cashel and in Lismore, with the relics of Ireland, including the Staff of Jesus, as pledges, and in the presence of Ua hÉnna (bishop of Munster) and the nobles of Munster'.[1] The great relic of Armagh, the Staff of Jesus, was in wide demand. In 1101 it was used with other relics in an agreement between Ailech and Ulster, when a ceremony took place in the *damliag* of Armagh.[2] The abbot of Armagh made peace on several occasions between the kings of the north and south. 'God and the coarb of Patrick made peace between them' in 1097, 1099, 1102, and 1105, the coarb on the last occasion (in Dublin) catching the sickness from which he died. The tenth century had seen the re-establishment of the church's prosperity: the eleventh saw her increasing activity in affairs of government.

The ecclesiastical overlordship of Armagh already acknowledged by Brian, *imperator Scotorum*, seems, in this century, to become more than ever clearly recognized. The coarb of Patrick was present on important state occasions, not only among the Uí Néill but farther afield. When in 1026 Donnchad son of Brian Boru spent Easter at Cenn Corad, he was accompanied by the abbot of Armagh and his 'venerable clerics'.[3] This was the year in which Donnchad took hostages from Meath, Brega, Dublin, Leinster, and Osraige, bringing the king of Osraige to Cenn

[1] *A.I.* 1093.
[2] *A.F.M.* 1101. *Damliag* = stone house, stone church.
[3] *A.I.* 1026.

Corad with him. When later in the century Toirdelbach Ua Briain led his army to Dublin and received the submission of Máel-Sechnaill king of Meath, the coarb of Patrick was present, with the Staff of Jesus.[1] The coarbs of Patrick, Columcille, Ciarán, 'and most of the seniors of Ireland' were at the death-bed of King Máel-Sechnaill II, but it was the coarb of Patrick who gave him the last rites.[2] Armagh was the burial place of the great Brian: the coarb of Patrick 'with the seniors' brought his body and that of his son Murchad, with the heads of Brian's nephew and the king of the Déisi from Swords, where they had been carried after the Battle of Clontarf, and buried them at Armagh in a new tomb.

Each of the abbots of Armagh, after his appointment, seems to have gone on circuit. Amalgaid was instituted in 1020, and in 1021 'went into Munster for the first time' and made a visitation, bringing away a tax. His successor Dub-dá-leithe, appointed in 1049, visited Cenél Eógain (the Northern Uí Néill homeland) the following year, returning with three hundred cows. Máel-Ísu, the next abbot, appointed in 1064, did not make his circuit of Munster until 1068, but he then 'obtained a full visitation tribute'. Domnall visited the Cenél Eógain in 1092, the year after his installation, and his first visitation of Munster came in 1094. The position of the coarb of Patrick was modelled on that of the high-king, who made his circuit and collected his tribute after his institution to office. It was the Irish means of recognizing superior authority.

The coarb of Patrick had no equal in ecclesiastical importance. Yet his position was very unlike that of Lanfranc or Anselm. From 966 onwards the abbacy of Armagh had been held by members of the Clann Sinaich, each succeeded by his nephew, brother, or son, none of them in major orders.[3] The first of the series, Dub-dá-leithe, died in 998. His brother Eochaid had been erenagh of Lis-oigedh (the 'guest house') and of Clonfeakle (a church of the Patrician *paruchia*), and Eochaid's son Máel-Maire succeeded to the abbacy of Armagh and ruled for twenty-two years. Two of Máel-Maire's sons, Amalgaid and Dub-dá-leithe,

---

[1] *C.S.* 1076 (*recte* 1079); *A.F.M.* 1080.

[2] *A.F.M.* 1022.

[3] See the family tree by T. Ó Fiaich, *Seanchas Ardmhacha*, 1961–2, opposite p. 96, or Lawlor, *Malachy*, p. 164.

R

succeeded him in turn, to be followed by the two sons of Amalgaid, Máel-Ísu and Domnall. Dub-dá-leithe also had a son, Aed,
whom the Annals of Ulster describe as 'material of a coarb', but
he never succeeded.[1] The hereditary succession did not end with
Domnall's death in 1105, but his successor Cellach, 'instituted . . .
in the succession of Patrick, by choice of the men of Ireland', was
immediately ordained,[2] and so ended the series of abbots without
orders.[3] Family influence may be seen in the succession of other
Irish monasteries beside Armagh.[4] The Irish saw no disgrace in
the spectacle of a married layman as the saint's heir, nor of a
married woman either, for the coarb of Moninne of Killeevy, who
died in 1077, was not only the daughter of an abbot but wife of
the king of Airthir.[5] Marriage for the coarb had become a
respectable and recognized convention.

The prosperity of the eleventh-century church can be seen in
the metal-work of the period. Irish smiths had been at work in
the tenth century, enshrining relics: in the eleventh century their
activity increased. Additions were made to the Kells Crozier

[1] The term means that he was eligible for the succession. *A.U.* 1108.
Flannacán, son of Máel-Ísu, *obit.* 1113, is also so described.

[2] *A.U.* Domnall had died in August. Cellach was ordained on the feast of
Adamnán, 23 September.

[3]

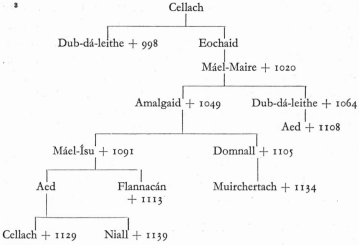

[4] See the Ua Rebacháin family at Lismore, or the Ua Selbaig at Cork.
[5] See *A.U.* 1077.

about the middle of the century. Between 1062 and 1098 the abbot of Kells had the *Cathach* enshrined, and the shrine of the *Misach* has a similar provenance.[1] Related in style to these two book-shrines is the crozier shrine of the abbots of Clonmacnois. A smith of the family of Clonmacnois (*do muintir Cluana*) made a shrine for the Stowe Missal between 1023 and 1052. Bells were enshrined, the most famous being the bell of S. Patrick. Many of the shrines show the influence of Scandinavian styles, while the smith who made the shrine of the *Cathach* himself has a Norse name, Sitric. It looks as if some descendant of the Viking plunderers was now employed in creating shrines for the church.

Two of the contemporary shrines are of particular interest, since they may illustrate characteristic churchmen. The shrine of the *Soiscél Molaise*, probably executed in the first quarter of the century, has one panel showing a cleric in a long tunic covered by a cloak. He appears to be tonsured in the Roman manner – at least, his hair is very short – but he has a big beard carefully trimmed into a fork. In his left hand he carries a book; in his right hand, supported on his left arm, is an object which looks like a whetstone or sceptre. This might well be the early-eleventh-century idea of a saint, with his *insignia*. Of the eleven figures which survive on the *Breac Maodhóg*, which is later in date,[2] three are women, who stand with hands clasped in an attitude of piety. Their hair is arranged in long ringlets which hang down to their waists. The eight men wear their hair shoulder-length, some straight, some wavy, some arranged in ringlets: two seem to be either shaven or bald in front, but none has a Roman tonsure. Seven have beards, four in the forked style. Two of the men carry books; one, beardless (but long-haired), bears a cross in his left hand; another has a sword. Did a 'family of the church' in the eleventh century look anything like this?

Certainly a book might be regarded as one of the symbols of the eleventh-century church. Even S. Bernard, who condemns the hereditary abbots of Armagh as 'an evil and adulterous

---

[1] See L. and M. de Paor, *Early Christian Ireland*, p. 166; F. Henry, *The Effects of the Viking Invasions on Irish Art*, pp. 67–8; *L'art irlandais*, iii, 143 f.

[2] For a description see Henry, *L'art irlandais*, iii, 162–3. Reproduced, Plate XIV.

generation', admits that, in spite of this, they were men of letters.[1] Several monasteries had historians and chroniclers of high reputation, and occasionally a monastic official won distinction in secular learning or law.[2] At Monasterboice some, if not all, of the monastic library was kept in the bell-tower, which was burned in 1097. Sulien the Wise, bishop of St. David's, born into the family of the church at Llanbadarn Fawr in Wales and educated in the schools there, came to Ireland for further education,[3] and the revival of Welsh hagiographical writing which began in the eleventh century seems to have been partly inspired by Irish models.

Monastic scribes were busy making collections of texts. Two volumes of hymns and other devotional compositions survive, both written by accomplished scribes,[4] and in the second half of the eleventh century a series of Passions and Homilies was composed mainly in Irish on the basis of Latin originals.[5] About the year 1092 a scholar wrote down the first part of the Annals of Inisfallen using documents belonging to the monastery of Emly.[6] Antiquarian activity, which reached its height in the twelfth century, was already well under way.

The conditions of the eleventh century might well have led to comfortable relaxation within the church and to neglect of the spiritual welfare of those outside it. There are, however, some indications that public conscience was re-awakening, for during the eleventh century religious observances once more became a matter of public legislation. In 1040 the *Cáin Domnaig* (The Law of Sunday) was re-enacted, 'such as was not enacted since Patrick's time', says the Munster annalist inaccurately, though it is true that there had been a long hiatus since this law was previously promulgated.[7] Laws of abstinence and almsgiving, lasting for a year, were enforced in 1096.[8] Prophecies stress the

---

[1] *Life of Malachy*, c. 4 (19). Translated Lawlor, p. 45.

[2] K. Hughes, 'Irish *Scriptoria*', pp. 265–9.

[3] Haddan and Stubbs, *Councils*, i, 665.

[4] Kenney, *Sources*, pp. 716–18. See Plate XVI.

[5] For dating see Ó Máille, *Ériu*, vi (1911), 1. Kenney, pp. 739–40.

[6] S. MacAirt, *A.I.*, p. vii.   [7] *A.I.* 1040. *Supra*, p. 179.

[8] *C.S.* 1092 (*recte* 1096). The Second Vision of Adamnán (ed. Stokes, *R.C.* xii (1891), 420–43), which is probably to be connected with the troubles of

evils which arise from a broken monastic rule, uncelebrated hours, lying priests, an inhospitable church.[1] Such a degree of concern for the religion of the country as a whole may appear very lukewarm when compared with the efforts of reforming churchmen on the Continent, but it seems to be an improvement on the preceding period.

The 'secularized' monastic family was not hostile to a personal religion, which reveals itself in litany, invocation, and lyric. The poems of Máel Ísu Ua Brolchán of Armagh (who died in 1086 as a master of both Irish and Latin learning) embody a lively and genuine piety.[2] But perhaps the best epitome of the Irish religious ideal is the anonymous eleventh-century poem beginning:

> It were my mind's desire to behold the face of God. It were my mind's desire to live eternally with Him.
> It were my mind's desire to read books studiously. It were my mind's desire to live under a clear rule.[3]

God's presence must be felt in scholarship, religion, and asceticism, so that all may be infused with light and love. 'It were my mind's desire to be cheerful towards all. . . . It were my mind's desire to be for ever in company with the King.' Under the Irish ecclesiastical system the same monastic city might contain the married cleric and the ascetic, neither denying the place of the other. To concentrate on one aspect of the church to the exclusion of the other is inevitably to draw a false picture.

1096, insists on fasting, the presence of two ordained men in every church to minister, that boys be set to study and that Sunday be strictly observed.

[1] *Ériu*, xviii. 60–1, 64–5, 70–1.

[2] See Murphy, *Lyrics*, nos. 22–5.   [3] Ibid., no. 26.

V. TRANSMUTATION

CHAPTER 23

Influences from abroad

During the later tenth and the eleventh centuries the church in Ireland once more came closely into contact with the church on the Continent. There the reform of Benedictine monasticism was infusing new vitality into religious life; the papacy, restored to spiritual authority under the Ottonian emperors, and later freed from imperial control over papal elections, concerned itself more effectually than ever before in the affairs of western Christendom. Improved administration brought distant churches within the active surveillance of the popes, and the evils resulting from non-celibate clergy, the purchase of benefices, and secular control over ecclesiastical appointments were widely canvassed. From 1070 to 1109 England had two archbishops, Lanfranc and Anselm, who were both deeply concerned at the state of the church in Ireland. The result was that Irish churchmen became much more conscious than they had been earlier of the differences between their own church and that of western Europe.

Such awareness probably had its roots in the tenth century. From the second half of that century, Germany was the best governed and most intellectually lively state in Europe. The monastic reform led by Gerard of Brogne and John of Gorze had established itself firmly in Lotharingia, and already in the tenth century Irish religious had found a spiritual home at Metz, Toul, Verdun, Cologne, and elsewhere.[1] At Waulsort near Dinant Otto I granted a charter in favour of 'certain servants of God coming from Scotia by grace of pilgrimage, and wishing to live under the rule of S. Benedict'.[2] Gerard bishop of Toul (963–94) supported a number of the Irish at his own expense and allowed them to assemble daily in his chapel with the Greeks, whom he also patronized, but at different altars, worshipping 'in the manner of

---

[1] See especially Kenney, *Sources*, pp. 608–19; Binchy, *Studies*, xviii (1929), 194–210; Gwynn, *Studies*, xxix (1940), 409–30.
[2] *M.G.H. Dip. Regum et Imp. Germ.*, i, 160.

their own land'.[1] Adalbero bishop of Metz (984–1005) was a friend of the Irishman Fíngen, who was abbot of the two monasteries of S. Clement and S. Symphorian at Metz and of S. Vannes in Verdun. The abbey of S. Martin's at Cologne was assigned to the Irish in 975, and early in the eleventh century this church and another (S. Pantaleon) were under the rule of an Irish bishop named Elias.

Later in the eleventh century two famous Irishmen, each named Marianus in the Latin documents, came to Germany. The historian Marianus Scottus (Máel-Brigte) from Moville came to Cologne in 1056, proceeded to Fulda, was ordained as a priest at Würzburg in the cathedral of the seventh-century Irish martyr Kilian, spent the next ten years as an *inclusus* at Fulda (1059–69), and lived for the remainder of his life as an *inclusus* at Mainz. Here for part of the time he had the services of an Irish scribe, a penitent, who noted characteristically in the margin of the Chronicle which he was writing for Marianus:

> Pleasant it is for us today, O enclosed Máel-Brigte, in the cell of the *inclusus* in Mainz, on the Thursday before the feast of Peter, in the first year of my sentence, that is, in the year of the killing of Diarmait king of Leinster;[2] and this is the first year I came from Scotland in my pilgrimage. And I have written this book for love of you and of all the Scots, that is the Irish, because I am myself an Irishman.[3]

Máel-Brigte, the Irish ascetic walled up in his cell, seems to have been less cut off from news of current events than one would suppose. The other Marianus (Muiredach mac Robartaig) set out from Ireland for Rome in 1067 with two companions, but after a year at Bamberg remained at Ratisbon, where he became head of the Irish priory of Weih Sankt Peter. The monastery of S. James of Ratisbon, consecrated in 1111, established daughter-houses during the twelfth century, and in 1215 was recognized as the head of the Irish Benedictine Congregation in Germany.[4]

Irishmen who came to the Continent in the eleventh century were not undertaking a new venture. In the pre-Viking period they had come as pilgrims; in the ninth century many came as scholars, to enjoy the patronage of princes and bishops of the

---

[1] *AA.SS.*, April, iii, p. 213, § 25.   [2] *A.U.* 1072.
[3] Kenney, p. 615, note.   [4] Binchy, *Studies*, xviii (1929), 197 ff.

Carolingian renaissance. In the tenth century they learned the ways of the Benedictine reformers: Professor Gwynn has suggested that there may sometimes have been friction between the Irish and Benedictine observance,[1] but Irish houses adopted the Benedictine Rule. The house at Waulsort had been founded under it, while the Scotsman Cadroe (who had been educated at Armagh) and his companion Malcalan both sought Benedictine houses for instruction when they first came to the Continent.

The records of the Irish emigration of the eleventh century differ from those of the preceding period in an important particular. The men at home were now taking a much livelier interest in their brethren abroad than they had done earlier. Not only was foreign news brought home (this must have happened in preceding centuries) but Irish scribes found it sufficiently interesting to record in their annals. The reigns and even battles of German emperors are occasionally given,[2] with the *obits* of some Irishmen who died in the Irish communities at Cologne and Würzburg.[3] Irishmen at home now seem to be more in touch with their fellow-countrymen abroad than they had been for centuries. This tendency developed still further in the twelfth century, when abbot Domnus of Ratisbon sent monks to Ireland, who returned with gifts from the king of Munster, while his successor Gilla-Christ MacCarthaig himself visited Ireland, possibly seeking recruits. Information about the Benedictine reform must have been reaching Ireland in the eleventh century, though with no apparent effect on the structure of Irish monasticism.

Irish pilgrimages to Rome seem to have had a more substantial effect on the church at home. Irish churchmen had found their way to Rome in the tenth century, and continued to travel there in the eleventh, but the eleventh century was chiefly remarkable for the number of Irish princes who went to Rome on pilgrimage. Professor Gwynn points out that the pilgrim route to Rome was freed in 1027 through the mediation of the Emperor Conrad II and Cnut.[4] In 1026 the king of Cenél Conaill had set off on a pilgrimage to Clonfert; from thence he proceeded to Iona, and

---

[1] *Studies*, xxix (1940), 426–8, at Vannes and Cologne.
[2] E.g. *A.Tig.* 1023, 1038. [3] *A.F.M.* 1027, 1042, 1085.
[4] *I.H.S.*, viii (1953), 197; *I.E.R.*, lvii (1941), 103–7.

then went on to Rome.[1] Thus, the older fashion of royal pilgrimage to local shrines gave way to the new. In 1028 Sitric king of Dublin and his neighbour Flannacán king of Brega set off for Rome together. It may have been on this occasion that plans for the new diocese of Dublin were discussed.[2] Their journey was followed by other royal pilgrimages: Flaithbertach Ua Néill king of Ailech went in 1030, and returned the following year.[3] Olaf Sitricsson's journey in 1034 was cut short by his violent death.[4] Ua Domnaill set out in 1042 (*A.I.*), the king of Gailenga and his wife went together in 1051 (*A.U.*), and Donnchad king of Munster, after his deposition, retired to Rome in 1064 and died there in the monastery of S. Stephen. In 1080 the king of the Déisi (in Munster) went to Jerusalem, and possibly finished his life in Rome.[5] Five Jews had come from oversea the previous year with gifts for the king of Munster: perhaps they had told the Irish princes of the eastern Mediterranean. The royal pilgrimages must have brought Irish courts into contact with Rome, where the reforms of Leo IX and his successors were active from 1048 onwards.

In the early twelfth century the Pope was represented by his own legate in Ireland. According to S. Bernard, writing shortly after S. Malachy's death in 1148, Gilbert (or Gilla-espuig), appointed bishop of Limerick early in the twelfth century, was 'said to have been the first to exercise the office of legate of the Apostolic See throughout the whole of Ireland'. But it is possible that Bernard is incorrect, and that Máel-Maire Ua Dúnáin, bishop of Meath, was his predecessor as papal legate.[6] In the account of the Synod of Cashel contained in the *Senchas Síl Briain*,[7] Ua Dúnáin is the only cleric mentioned by name, and is termed *áirdlegaid, áirdepscop agus áird senóir innse Eirenn* 'by authority

---

[1] *A.I.* 1026.

[2] This is Professor Gwynn's view, *I.E.R.*, lvii (1941), 106–7.

[3] *A.U.* 1030. *A.I.* 1029 records a pilgrimage to Armagh.

[4] *A.U.* 1034, he 'was killed by Saxons on his way to Rome'.

[5] A note, 'he finished his life in Rome', is written along the upper margin of the folio on which the annal for 1080 is entered, but without any mark in the text to indicate where it belongs. *A.I.* f. 28ʳ.

[6] See Gwynn, *I.E.R.*, lxiii (1944), 361–70.

[7] Ed. S. H. O'Grady, *I.T.S.*, xxvi (1928), 175, trsl. xxvii. 185–6.

of the pope himself'. The element *ard* means 'eminent', 'high', 'chief', and the whole title is a clear statement of legatine authority. This is, unfortunately, the only account of the Synod, and the manuscript from which it is edited is of the eighteenth century. The evidence of the annalists neither supports nor contradicts it, for they mention neither Ua Dúnáin's legatine position nor Gilbert's. The titles which they give to Ua Dúnáin may be regarded as titles of dignity,[1] though their unanimity on his importance is, if anything, in favour of his papal authority. An element of doubt is raised by the very moderate character of the reforming programme of the Synod of Cashel, a reform less fundamental in at least two respects than might have been anticipated from a papal legate.[2] If Ua Dúnáin was Ireland's first papal legate he was replaced by Gilbert, who was prepared to advocate more sweeping measures. Gilbert himself resigned his charge in favour of Malachy in 1140.

Though the Hiberno-Norse see of Dublin may have been founded after the pilgrimage of king Sitric to Rome, the dominant influence upon the development of the Hiberno-Norse sees came from England. The Dubliners were trading with England, and their eleventh-century coinage followed English patterns; their type of settlement, centred on the town, was English rather than Irish in style, better suited to the English diocesan see than the Irish monastic *paruchia*. Dúnán the first bishop, who died in 1074, ruled his diocese as bishop, not as abbot. He was an Irishman, but we do not know where he was trained, or where and by whom he was consecrated.[3] There is, however, contemporary evidence to show that during the reigns of his successors the archbishops of Canterbury were making determined efforts to include the new Hiberno-Norse sees within their own primacy. The successors of Dúnán at Dublin, Patrick (died 1084), Dúngus or Donatus (died 1095), and Samuel (died 1121) were all consecrated by archbishops

---

[1] 'Head of the clergy of Ireland' (*A.U.*, *A.F.M.*), 'eminent bishop of Ireland' (*A.I.*, *A.Tig.*, *C.S.*), 'noble senior of Ireland' (*A.U.*, *A.F.M.*, *A.L.C.*), 'eminent bishop of Munster' (*A.Tig.*, *A.F.M.*). Writing to Anselm in 1096, Ua Dúnáin calls himself 'bishop of Meath'.

[2] *Infra*, pp. 263 ff.

[3] Professor Gwynn thinks it likely that he was consecrated at Canterbury but took no oath of obedience. *I.E.R.*, lvii (1941), 107–12.

of Canterbury and took oaths of obedience to them, though on Samuel's death the archbishop of Armagh seems to have disputed Canterbury's claim to primacy.[1] Malchus was chosen as first bishop of Waterford in 1096, and Anselm was asked to consecrate him. Gilbert, the first bishop of Limerick, was a friend and correspondent of Anselm, though he seems not to have been consecrated by him,[2] but his successor Patrick was consecrated by archbishop Theobald, to whom he made profession of obedience.[3] When the Synod of Ráith Bresail was held in 1111 Dublin was not included among the Irish sees. Its position of obedience to Canterbury was recognized by the omission, though Limerick under the papal legate Gilbert was included as a bishopric within the province of Cashel. The position of the Hiberno-Norse settlements at Waterford and Wexford seems to have been still uncertain in 1111. The Synod named all the proposed sees, but in some cases with alternative titles: among these are Lismore or Port Láirge (i.e. Waterford) in the province of Cashel, Ferns or Loch Garmon (i.e. Wexford) in the province of Leinster. Malchus (Máel-Ísu Ua hAinmire), though appointed as first bishop of Waterford, is described by Bernard[4] as bishop of Lismore:[5] the Annals of Tigernach describe him as bishop of Waterford, and so do the Four Masters, though they say he died at Lismore.[6] The death of a bishop of Ferns is given under the year 1117 (*A.U.*). Ultimately the Hiberno-Norse settlements at Waterford and Wexford were both included in the larger Irish see, and at the Synod of Kells in 1152 Dublin was made an archbishopric under the primacy of Armagh. Thus the archbishops of Canterbury failed to secure any permanent control over the jurisdiction of the Irish church.

Nevertheless, in the period between 1074 and 1111 English influence was probably more effective than any other element from abroad in shaping ecclesiastical opinion in Ireland. Most of

---

[1] *Infra*, p. 268.

[2] Lawlor, *Malachy*, p. 47, note 3.   [3] Ibid., p. 73, note 1.

[4] *Life of Malachy*, ed. *AA.SS.*, 11 November, Part i (1894), pp. 143–66. I have given references to the paragraphs of this edition.

[5] *Life of Malachy*, c. 1, § 5, transl. Lawlor, p. 19. He signed the Synod of Ráith Bresail as archbishop of Cashel: Keating, *I.T.S.*, ix, 306.

[6] 1135.

the Hiberno-Norse bishops were English trained. Patrick, second
bishop of Dublin, was a Benedictine monk trained at Worcester,[1]
his successor Donatus, another Benedictine, was trained at Christ
Church, Canterbury; and Samuel the fourth bishop was trained at
St Albans. Malchus, first bishop of Waterford, had been a monk
at Winchester before his appointment, and Gilbert of Limerick,
earlier in his life, had been a companion of Anselm. These men
were Irishmen, and generally on good terms with their fellow-
ecclesiastics in Irish sees. Malachy, educated at Armagh and
ordained priest there, went to bishop Malchus for further training
in liturgical matters, with the blessing of Imar, the hermit of
Armagh who had been his teacher, and the full approval of
Cellach, coarb of Patrick.[2] Máel-Maire Ua Dúnáin, bishop of
Meath, and Domnall Ua hÉnna, bishop of Munster, were
associates of the English trained bishops of the Hiberno-Norse
sees of Dublin and Waterford. Domnall had written to Lanfranc
asking for information on the rite of baptism and the communion
of children, and putting other *quaestiones saecularium literarum*.[3]
When Anselm wrote to the Irish bishops encouraging them to
consult him, he addressed himself to Domnall and Donatus of
Dublin by name, while three Irish bishops, Domnall, Ua Dúnáin
and 'Ferdomnach bishop of Leinster', as well as Samuel of
Dublin, signed the letter recommending Malchus for consecration
as bishop of Waterford.[4] The influence of the Hiberno-Norse
bishops seems to have spread outside the Norse settlements among
some of the Irish bishops, and possibly also among the princes,
for Muirchertach Ua Briain, king of Munster, and his brother
Diarmait also signed the letter about Malchus. It was not by
chance that the first of the reforming synods, that of 1101, was
held at Cashel in Munster.

For a whole generation before the Synod of Cashel the correspondence of Lanfranc and Anselm must have forced the church
in Ireland to recognize some of its peculiarities, and no doubt

[1] Gwynn, *The Writings of Bishop Patrick*, Dublin, 1955, p. 6.
[2] *Life of Malachy*, c. 1, § 5, transl. Lawlor, pp. 18–20.
[3] Lanfranc's reply, Ussher, *Works*, iv, 495–7. See Kenney, *Sources*, pp.
759–60.
[4] Ussher, *Works*, iv, 518–19. Kenney, p. 760.

Irish contacts with the English-trained bishops who were subject to Canterbury quickened their understanding of the issues. Lanfranc and Anselm both protested against the Irish customs of marriage and divorce.[1] In Ireland marriage was permitted within the seven degrees prohibited by the papacy. So it had been from at least as early as the seventh century, when Irish church legislators noted that their compatriots recognized only four prohibited degrees.[2] As the practice of the church everywhere became increasingly uniform, so marked an anomaly was bound to be severely criticized. Divorce and remarriage for a variety of reasons were also permitted by native custom, which Lanfranc stigmatizes as a 'law of fornication' rather than a law of marriage. Some early Irish canonists had taught that the marriage contract was indissoluble and was not terminated by the unfaithfulness of either party,[3] while others thought that adultery provided the only ground for divorce and remarriage;[4] but the native law had triumphed over the stricter provisions of the church, to the disgust of the Anglo-Norman prelates, who were used to very different customs.

Another cause for complaint in the letters of both Lanfranc and Anselm concerns the Irish method of episcopal consecration. A bishop might be consecrated in the Irish rite by one bishop alone instead of by the minimum of three normally required by Roman practice. The Celtic and Roman churches of the seventh century had disagreed on this issue, and Theodore had set himself to correct the Celtic usage.[5] The Roman system obviously provided better safeguards for securing suitable candidates for consecration, and in any case, by the twelfth century, uniformity had become necessary for its own sake. Anselm, writing to king

[1] Lanfranc to Toirdelbach king of Munster, Ussher, *Works*, iv, 492–3. Lanfranc to Godred king of Dublin (1074), ibid., pp. 490–1. Anselm to Muirchertach king of Munster (1096), ibid., p. 521; and (probably 1101/2), p. 523. For a statement of Irish marriage law see Gwynn, *I.E.R.*, lxvii (1946), 109–22.

[2] *Pa.* II. 29. Cf. Haddan and Stubbs, *Councils*, iii, 201, and *H.E.* I. 27, Plummer's notes.

[3] *Vi.* 42–3 (S), *Coll.* XIV. 14, 17, 19, 29.

[4] *Pa.* II. 28.

[5] *H.E.* IV. 2. Gregory's teaching to Augustine on this issue is set out in *H.E.* I. 27 (questio VI).

Muirchertach in 1096, also protests that bishops are consecrated 'in places where they ought not to be ordained'.[1] Anselm was accustomed to a diocesan episcopate and a Roman-type hierarchy, and in objecting to bishops without see or jurisdiction he echoed the disapproval of earlier English administrators.

Lanfranc's statement that holy orders were given by the bishops for money[2] is a charge of simony very common in the church at this period. How far this criticism is applicable to the Irish church it is difficult to say. The ninth-century Rule of the Céli Dé had cursed those who bought or sold the church of God out of greed and envy, but the men who committed this sin were erenaghs and kings.[3] Bec mac Dé prophesies disaster to those 'who barter the church of God', but again they are kings.[4] Whereas control of a church with its flocks and herds, land, service, and jurisdiction must have been a tempting prize, holy orders gave no such administrative superiority, and there is reason to think that the church had to encourage men to take up major orders.[5] In Irish tradition, although the bishop's position carried high honour, it also demanded greater self-denial than that of the lay abbot. If a man wanted material power and comfort in the eleventh century he might bid for a church, but it is hard to believe that there was fierce competition for bishops' orders. Is it possible that Lanfranc, by a natural confusion, spoke of the purchase of orders when he meant the traffic in administrative office in the church, or even that, accustomed to the sin of simony, he may have misunderstood or exaggerated his information?[6]

By the beginning of the twelfth century the king of Munster and many of the clergy of Ireland were aware of the discrepancies between current Irish practice and the rulings of the 'coarb of Peter' as they thought of the Pope. The letters of Lanfranc and

---

[1] Ussher, *Works*, iv, 521. See also *Life of Malachy*, c. 4, § 13; Lawlor, p. 46.
[2] *Quod sacri ordines per pecuniam ab episcopis dantur*. Ussher, *Works*, iv, 493.
[3] § 65.
[4] Ed. Knott, *Ériu*, xviii, 66–7.
[5] *O. Ir. Pen.* II. 10, Rule of the Céli Dé, § 63.
[6] Bernard's *Life of Malachy* has nothing about simony. Where major offices went by family inheritance it is hard to see how simony in its cruder forms was practised. It must also be remembered that Ireland (outside the Hiberno-Norse areas) still had no currency and that the purchase of orders would have to be made by some other form of exchange.

Anselm, the contacts made by bishops trained in English Benedictine houses, possibly the direct influence of a papal legate had
convinced the Irish church of the need for reform. The pestilence
of 1096 may have added a sense of urgency. The Council of Cashel
in 1101 began the process which streamlined the cumbrous body
of the Irish church into the conventional form of Roman
Christendom.

CHAPTER 24

Reformation and revolution

The metamorphosis of the Irish church began with the Synod of Cashel in 1101. This was in truth a reforming synod, whereas the later synods of Ráith Bresail, Uisneach, and Kells brought about a revolution. The first of the synods was, according to the Annals of the Four Masters, a meeting of the Southern Half, led by King Muirchertach Ua Briain with the chiefs of the laity, and Ua Dúnáin with the chiefs of the clergy: both these men had been in correspondence with Anselm. They were concerned to free the church from secular tribute, to protect its rights of sanctuary from abuse, to tighten the native law of marriage, and, above all, to regulate ecclesiastical appointments. Some of these measures, as we shall see, were a continuation of earlier Irish legislation, and all were consistent with a reform of the traditional system, while the canon on marriage fell short of the requirements of Rome, and there was no attempt, as far as we know, to introduce a Roman ecclesiastical hierarchy.

Of all the measures of the synod, what most impressed the annalists was Muirchertach's grant of Cashel, free of all claims, to the religious of Ireland.[1] This act of generosity probably had political as well as religious motives, for the Dál Cais dynasty may have been glad to turn over the old Eoganacht capital to ecclesiastical uses. Irish princes had, however, for years past been granting certain churches their freedom (*saíre*) from secular obligations,[2] and the legislators at Cashel attempted to make these measures universal: 'without tribute or tax to king or to chief from the church in Ireland until doom'.[3] A few years after the synod the community of Ciarán of Clonmacnois was trying to obtain the same privilege from the king of Meath for the church

[1] *A.Tig., C.S.* 1097 (*recte* 1101), *A.F.M.* 1101.
[2] *Supra*, pp. 219, 225, 241.
[3] Clause 2. O'Grady, *I.T.S.*, xxvi, 175; xxvii, 185. For a discussion see A. Gwynn, *I.E.R.*, lxvi (1945), 81–92; lxvii (1946), 109–22.

of Cell-mór-maige-Enir,[1] and one of the charters in the Book of Kells describes an agreement made between 1157 and 1166, by which the king of Ailech and the king of Meath persuaded the king of Uí Lóegaire to sell his right to billet troops on Ardbraccan. The charter proclaims that Ardbraccan is now exempt both on account of the general freedom of all churches (a freedom granted in 1101) and on account of this purchase.[2] It had been a long struggle to free churches from their economic subjection to secular lords; churchmen had been actively engaged in it well before the synod met in 1101, and the contest was not ended even then.

Similarly, the rights of ecclesiastical sanctuary had long been debated. In the seventh century church legislators had tried to prevent their abuse, and yet to encourage respect for them, stating that the church was 'not made for the defence of accused persons' but that judges should not use physical violence against those who have fled for sanctuary to the church.[3] Brian Boru had demanded hostages to guarantee the banishment of 'robbers and lawless people' from Lismore, Cork, and Emly in 987.[4] The Synod of Cashel refused sanctuary to anyone who had committed either of the two particularly heinous crimes of treachery or murder within the kindred.[5] Here again the early-twelfth-century reformers were seeking to extend earlier legislation and not to overset it.

The canon on marriage passed in 1101 meant a reform of current practice, though it did not introduce the full requirements of the Roman church. It forbade a man to marry his stepmother or step-grandmother, or his sister or daughter, his brother's wife, or any woman of similarly near kin;[6] but it said nothing of the Irish practices of concubinage and divorce, which

---

[1] *A.Tig.* 1108, = *C.S.* 1104 (*recte* 1108).

[2] Charter VI. O'Donovan, *Misc. Irish Arch. Soc.*, i, pp. 142–7.

[3] *Pa.* II. 9. Cf. *Coll.* XXVIII. 14 d.

[4] *A.I. supra*, p. 220.   [5] *fell ná finghal.*

[6] The Irish reads: *gan ben a athar ná a senathar, ná a siur ná a ingen, do beith ina mnaoi ag fer i nEirinn, ná ben a derbráthar, ná ben ar bith chom fogus sin i ngaol.* I have given O'Grady's interpretation, which, in Professor Binchy's opinion, is to be preferred, since if, in this context, *a* really meant 'her' (referring to *ben*) the Irish would have added *-side*: *na a siur-side*, etc. Professor Gwynn (*I.E.R.*, lxvii, 110) suggests 'either his father's wife or his grandfather's, or *her* sister or *her* daughter' etc.

were opposed to Roman practice. The legislation of 1101 was a first step in the overthrow of the native marriage law, and one very difficult to impose. For Pope Alexander III was later informed that the Irish practised customs similar to those that the legislators of 1101 had condemned: that they 'marry their stepmothers and are not ashamed to have children by them; that a man may live with his brother's wife while the brother is still alive; that one man may live in concubinage with two sisters; and that many of them, putting away the mother, will marry the daughters'.[1]

Four of the canons of the Synod of Cashel attempt to control ecclesiastical appointments. By this time many of the abbots (or erenaghs as they were now often called) were married laymen: the Synod laid down that no layman should be an erenagh in Ireland and that no erenagh of a church in Ireland should have a wife. This is perfectly in accordance with the feeling of the stricter churchmen of the seventh century, or with the reformers of the ninth. Moreover, responsibility for a church was not to be divided between two erenaghs, except in special circumstances. The danger of quarrels arising from disputed control was well known, and the reformers wished to avoid it.

Professor Gwynn regards the first canon of the Synod as a decree against simony. It reads: 'Without making traffic of the church of God to an ex-layman or an ex-cleric until doom.'[2] This expressly prohibits the bartering of churches, a practice which had earlier aroused protests. But the decree is directed not only against simony but against making unsuitable appointments. Professor Gwynn explains the *athlaech* or ex-layman as a word suggesting a 'late vocation'; the *athlaech* may even be a man who has taken the tonsure for the sake of clerical immunity. It is worth noting also that the word carries a suggestion of *contemptibilis*. The eighth-century Irish glossator explained the phrase in I Corinthians 6, verse 5, 'those who are of no account in the church' as 'ex-laymen who are at penance in the churches'.[3] The Old Irish Table of Penitential Commutations gives heavier penances to the

---

[1] Sheehy, *Pont. Hib.* i. 21.
[2] *Gan cennach egailse Dé do athlaochaib ná do aithcléirchib go bráth.* For discussion see Gwynn, *I.E.R.*, lxvi (1945), 82–3.
[3] Wb. 9ᶜ 11. *Thes. Pal.* i. 553.

ex-layman or woman than to the cleric or nun, because 'it is unusual for a layman or laywoman not to have some part in manslaughter'.[1] An eighth-century secular law tract grades the three kinds of ex-laymen in a church, and the one of highest rank rates only as high as the celibate clerk.[2] The *athlaech* may thus be a man of late vocation, or an ex-layman who did not rank high in ecclesiastical dignity. He had not received the normal clerical training. The 'ex-cleric' is a less common and even less-respected figure in Irish literature, for he is the man who has lost his former rank for some serious offence. The twelfth-century reformers felt that canonical status was essential for major ecclesiastical appointments. Neither a person of worldly experience who had not undergone the full clerical training nor a man who had been deprived of his orders was a suitable candidate.

The legislation of the Synod of Cashel set out to improve the existing church, not to destroy and remake it. It accepted the Irish monastic system, merely demanding that abbots should be in orders and celibate. Here the action of Cellach, coarb of Patrick, provided an impressive demonstration of the reformers' policy. Cellach succeeded to the abbacy of Armagh in 1105. His grandfather, Mael-Ísa (died 1091), and Mael-Ísa's brother Domnall were his immediate predecessors. Cellach's own father, Aed, had died in 1095, so Cellach was in the direct line of descent. He was twenty-five years old at his institution, and within a few weeks had himself ordained to the priesthood. The following year he went on circuit to collect his tribute, first from the Cenél Eógain, then from Munster, and in Munster, stronghold of the reformers, he 'received the orders of eminent bishop (*uasal epscop*) by direction of the men of Ireland'. This title did not imply primacy in the Roman sense: Cellach was not the only bishop at Armagh, and there were as yet no diocesan sees. His visitations continued on the traditional lines, though they extended beyond Ailech and Munster, the customary circuits, to Connacht (1108) and Meath (1110). Yet his acceptance of episcopal orders prepared the way for much more revolutionary changes.

Such changes were almost certainly already under discussion early in the twelfth century. A treatise *De statu ecclesiae* written by

[1] § 8, ed, Binchy, *Ériu*, xix, 61.   [2] *A.L.I.* iv. 366.

Gilbert of Limerick outlines for 'the bishops and priests of the whole of Ireland' what ought to be the hierarchical structure of the church.[1] Instead of the monastic *paruchiae* and the separation of the powers of order and administration found in the Irish church, Gilbert envisages dioceses of contiguous territory, each ruled by a bishop. Within the episcopal see and under the bishop's jurisdiction are parishes under the charge of priests and their attendant clergy, and monasteries under presbyter abbots. The bishops (at least three and not more than twenty of them) are to be subject to the jurisdiction of an archbishop, and over the archbishop is the primate, subject immediately to the Pope.

Such a design implied the complete overthrow of the traditional system. Bishops could not be multiplied at will; each bishop had a fixed seat and definite powers of jurisdiction. Archbishops and primates were to receive their *pallia* from the Pope, and to travel to Rome for consecration. There was no place for the coarb without holy orders, for administrative authority was now firmly bound to order. Monks were to exercise no cure of souls among the laity and were to subject themselves to the jurisdiction of the diocesan bishop. It is difficult to see how such a scheme could have been implemented without the co-operation of the coarb of Patrick and a majority of the other great Irish abbots. But public opinion had been prepared for some change, and there was an inner ring of convinced and influential reformers; Gilbert himself, Ua Dúnáin of Meath, Malchus of Waterford and probably Cellach. Once sufficient support had been obtained to initiate plans for the creation of episcopal sees, it is not likely that the existing abbots would want to be left out.

Gilbert, as papal legate, Cellach, Ua Dúnáin, and king Muirchertach Ua Briain met in 1111 at Ráith Bresail, the annalists say, with at least fifty bishops, three hundred priests, three thousand clerics, and the nobles of the Southern Half.[2] Keating, writing his account from the lost Book of Clonenagh, says:

It was at this synod that the churches of Ireland were given up entirely to the bishops, free for ever from the authority and rent of

---

[1] See Kenney, pp. 763–4. It was probably written after Anselm's correspondence with Gilbert and before the Synod of Ráith Bresail, between 1107 and 1111. Text in Ussher, *Works*, iv, 500–10.   [2] *A.U.* 1111.

any princes. It was there also were regulated the sees or dioceses of the bishops of Ireland.[1]

This synod went much farther than the Synod of Cashel had done a decade earlier. It seems to have repeated Cashel's enactment on the freedom of the church from secular tribute. But whereas Cashel had required erenaghs to be celibate and in orders, Ráith Bresail laid down a diocesan hierarchy: two provinces were created, of Armagh and Cashel, the northern province containing thirteen sees (including Armagh itself), the southern twelve, all under the primacy of Armagh.[2] Dublin was not included because its bishops were subject to Canterbury.

Another assembly, and possibly a rival one, was held in the same year at Uisneach,[3] with the king of Meath and the clergy of Clonmacnois prominent in its support. This synod attempted no dispute on the principle of a diocesan hierarchy, but it differed from Ráith Bresail in defining the sees of Meath. Ráith Bresail had given Meath two sees of Clonard and Duleek, and had completely omitted Clonmacnois from her list of dioceses. The Synod of Uisneach divided Meath into the dioceses of Clonard and Clonmacnois.

It is possible that Cellach, now primate of Ireland, seized the opportunity provided by the death of Samuel bishop of Dublin in 1121 to try to withdraw the see of Dublin from the obedience of Canterbury into the primacy of Armagh.[4] Cellach then 'took the episcopacy of Dublin by choice of the Gaill and the Gael'. A party of opposition, which seems to have had the support of Toirdelbach Ua Conchobair of Connacht (the leading king in Ireland since the death of Muirchertach Ua Briain in 1119), sent its candidate, Gregory, for consecration to archbishop Ralph of Canterbury, pleading that 'the bishops of Ireland have great jealousy towards us, and especially that bishop who dwells at Armagh, because we do not wish to be obedient to their ordination, but wish to be always under your rule'.[5] Gregory seems at

---

[1] *I.T.S.* ix. 298–9.

[2] Keating also says that there were twenty-four sees, whereas those named, if we include Armagh, number twenty-five.

[3] Recorded in *C.S.* sub anno 1107. See J. Brady, *I.E.R.*, lxxii (1949), 1–13.

[4] See J. MacEarlean, *Arch. Hib.*, iii (1914), 1–33.

[5] Ussher, *Works*, iv. 532.

this time not to have been in major orders, but he was consecrated and took an oath of obedience to Canterbury. In the end Canterbury failed to retain control of any of the Hiberno-Norse sees, for Cardinal John Paparo, who presided as papal legate over the Synod of Kells in 1152, brought *pallia* for four Irish archbishops, of Armagh, Cashel, Dublin, and Tuam, and restated the primacy of Armagh.

The reformers' policy steadily gained ground between 1101 and 1152, but not without opposition. Cellach, coarb of Patrick and heir of the Clann Sinaich at Armagh, had combined two rôles, the traditional one as ecclesiastical administrator and mediator in Irish politics fused with his activities as a reforming bishop. His piety and ability were acknowledged by Irish and Hiberno-Norse, by conservatives and reformers.[1] A disputed succession at Armagh followed his death on 1 April 1129. On 5 April Muirchertach was instituted as heir of Patrick. He was the son of Domnall, Cellach's predecessor in the abbacy, and a suitable Clann Sinaich candidate, though not a bishop. Cellach himself on his deathbed at Ard Pátraic in Munster, wishing to end the system of hereditary succession, nominated the reformer Malachy, son of a former Master of the Schools of Armagh, an ascetic who was already in episcopal orders and a friend of Malchus and Gilbert.[2] For three years Muirchertach seems to have ruled at Armagh without opposition, until the reforming party persuaded Malachy to assume the episcopacy. For the last two years of Muirchertach's life, Malachy lived outside the town and performed his functions of office throughout the province; while Muirchertach continued to act as coarb of Patrick in the manner of his predecessors, going on circuit, collecting his tribute, and imparting his blessing. Muirchertach's death must have been a blow to the conservative party. His successor was Niall, brother of Cellach, another member of 'the damned race', as S. Bernard describes him. But this time Malachy was installed by force, and Niall fled, taking with him the precious *insignia* of the Gospels and the Staff of Jesus which, in the popular view, proved his authority.[3] Malachy, however, made the coarb's circuit of Munster and obtained his tribute

---

[1] See *A.U.* 1129 for his obituary notice.　　[2] *Supra*, p. 267.
[3] Bernard's *Life of Malachy*, §§ 19–30; Lawlor, pp. 43–61.

there, and in 1135 succeeded in buying back the Staff of Jesus, on the death of its Clann Sinaich keeper.[1] There followed a period of uncertainty. Niall seems to have been re-installed at Armagh in 1136 (*A.F.M.*), and Malachy resigned the see; but the following year Gelasius of Derry was appointed to Armagh with the full support of Malachy. With Niall's death in 1139 the future of Armagh became more secure.

Under the new régime a number of the great Irish monasteries became bishops' seats, others became rural deaneries and parish churches. The reformers wished to introduce a more conventional ecclesiastical discipline with the liturgical practices of the Roman Church, and Malachy seems to have recognized that the life of canons regular under the Augustinian Rule was well suited to the needs of many Irish churches. On a journey to the Continent he visited Arrouaise in Flanders, then under its abbot Gervase (1121–47), and found there an energetic order of canons regular which had adopted some of the Cistercian customs. Malachy had the rule and liturgical practices of the order copied down, and encouraged their adoption 'in episcopal sees and in many other places in Ireland'.[2] Sometimes the innovations cut across vested interests and long-accepted traditions, as at Saul, where Malachy introduced the canons regular. Amlaíb, the son of a coarb of Finnian of Moville, became abbot there,[3] but his practices did not meet the reformers' requirements, and he was later deposed. He, with the king and chiefs of Ulster, retaliated by driving out the canons, allowing them to take nothing but the clothes they stood up in.[4] The bishops of Ulster and the abbots of Bangor and Moville gave the king and ex-abbot no support, and the opposition seems to have been roused by a personal issue, the humiliation of Amlaíb. Hostility to the regular canons was, as far as we know, not widespread, but there must have been some strains between the old and the new order.

The ascetic temper of the influential minority in traditional

[1] *A.F.M.* 1135.
[2] This statement is contained in a late-twelfth-century cartulary. See Dunning, *I.H.S.*, iv (1945), 299–300. For text, *M.G.H. Script.*, xv, Pt. ii, pp. 1121–2, § 7.
[3] Presumably in 1156. See *A.F.M.*
[4] *A.U.* 1170.

Irish monasticism turned, under the new régime, to the Cistercian rule. Malachy, friend of S. Bernard, deeply admired the ardour, simplicity, and discipline of Clairvaux. Here was a way of life with the physical austerity, the spiritual devotion, and total commitment of the early Irish ascetics, together with the organization which twelfth-century opinion recognized as necessary. Four of Malachy's company remained at Clairvaux on his return from Rome in 1140, and after two years' training in Cistercian practices the Irishmen came home with other monks to found a community at Mellifont. S. Bernard, in a subsequent letter to Malachy, hints that there may have been irritations between the Irishmen and the rest, for some of the monks returned to Clairvaux.[1] But the order spread rapidly, and though continentals were unwilling to come to Ireland there was no lack of native recruits or of endowments.[2] Malachy himself died at Clairvaux in 1148 on his way to Rome, in the moment of his death commending his monks to God and to the love of his friend, who writes tenderly to the Irish with the news of his death.[3] His own countrymen had possessed him in life, Clairvaux had been privileged to possess him in death; and sharing him as a father, the spiritual kinship of the Irish and continental Cistercians was deepened.

The first half of the twelfth century witnessed the reorganization of the Irish church in dioceses of Roman type, renewed contacts with the papacy, the introduction of the Benedictine Rule as practised at Cîteaux and of the Augustinian Rule as practised by the canons of Arrouaise. Monastic and clerical life were thus drawn into the continental pattern as never before, and liturgical customs were revised. Twelfth-century architecture and sculpture bear the imprint of these fundamental changes. Cormac's Chapel on the Rock of Cashel, consecrated in 1134, has many of the features of continental romanesque building; twin towers in a transeptal position, blind wall-arcading, a rib-vaulted chancel, a high gable over the north porch, decorated capitals and round

[1] Ep. 357. Lawlor, p. 136. 'Perhaps the brothers of your country, whose characters are less disciplined and who have lent a less ready ear to advice in those observances, which were new to them, have been in some measure the reason for their return.'

[2] Bernard to Malachy, Ep. 357. Lawlor, p. 136.

[3] Ep. 374. Lawlor, pp. 137–40.

arches.[1] The steeply pitched roof is reminiscent of earlier Irish building, but the general effect is markedly different from tenth-century Irish cathedrals. In most Hiberno-Romanesque churches the specifically architectural peculiarities of Cormac's Chapel are not repeated, but the Irish masons concentrate on decorative features, the carving of arches, doorways, and capitals.[2] Here the artists had scope for invention in human heads and grotesques and in a variety of elaborate motifs.

Some of the twelfth-century high-crosses graphically portray the changes in the structure of the Irish church by placing a new emphasis on the figure of the bishop. The crossing of the east face of the high-cross at Dysert O'Dea bears a crucifixion, and beneath stands a mitred bishop carrying a crozier of continental type: one side of the 'Doorty' Cross at Kilfenora shows a similar mitred bishop with continental-type crozier, and beneath him two smaller unmitred clerics, one carrying a tau-headed crozier and the other a curved crozier of Irish type.[3] The bishop reappears on the crosses of Cashel, Glendalough, and Roscrea, the shepherd under Christ of his flock.

The transformation which the reformers had brought about in the life of the Irish church did not prevent a conscious effort by Irish scholars to record their traditions; indeed, the sense of their otherness may have further stimulated antiquarian activity. In the twelfth century the *Book of the Taking* (*Lebor Gabála*) systematized the accepted 'history' of early Ireland, probably on the basis of an eighth-century original.[4] The scribes put together a great mass of miscellaneous material in three great manuscript collections: the

[1] See Plate XIII. Cf. Leask, *Irish Churches*, I, 113–20; L. and M. De Paor, *Early Christian Ireland*, pp. 177–80.

[2] There is not complete unanimity on the dating of Irish romanesque churches. In Leask's opinion some of the more simple ornamentation was introduced in the later decades of the eleventh century, the more developed style (Leask's Phase II) lasted from *c.* 1120–*c.* 1165, passing into a phase of over-elaboration: Cormac's Chapel shows exotic features which were not generally adopted in Irish romanesque architecture. The De Paors, however, regard Cormac's Chapel as the introduction of a style whose architectural features were not generally understood in Ireland.

[3] See Plate XV.

[4] For dating see O'Rahilly, *Early Irish History*, p. 193, and discussion Dillon, *J.R.S.A.I.*, lxxxvi, 62–72. Ed. Macalister, *I.T.S.*, xxxiv, xxxv, xxxix, xl, xliv.

Book of the Dun Cow (*Lebor na Huidre*) transcribed at Clonmacnois, the *Book of Leinster* compiled by Aed abbot of Terryglass, and a manuscript now in the Bodleian Library, Rawl. B.502, the provenance of which is unknown. The masters who determined the compilations did not hesitate to include purely secular material. The *Book of the Taking* defends the arts of *éolas and filidecht* (learning and poetry), for 'though the Faith came, these arts were not put away, for they are good',[1] and Aed included in his volume a version of the *Táin Bo Cúalnge*, part of Ireland's oldest heroic cycle. Aed notes, at the end of the tale, that 'some things in it are the delusions of devils, some things are poetic images, some things are like truth, some not, and some things are for the pleasure of fools',[2] but this did not prevent him from including them.

The literature of pre-reformed Ireland had to meet some criticism. One scholar protested indignantly that the legend of S. Brendan was an insult to the saint.[3] Are we to believe that Brendan, for the sake of a rumour, irresponsibly abandoned the three thousand brethren whom God had committed to his direction; that he wandered for seven years, celebrating Easter on a whale's back, seeking on the seas what is promised in heaven? The whole story is condemned as silly, crazy, and hostile to the faith:

> O what a meagre and miserable hope is that of the Irish,
> By which, after this life, all the rewards of works
> Are bare earth and stones and the blossom of trees.

The writer finishes by advising his brother to throw the fables into the fire and so escape the flames of hell. This satire is meant to be serious, and may be by an Englishman, but the author of the *Vision of MacConglinne* is a mocking caricaturist, an Irishman intimately acquainted with the monastic schools. He parodies the scholar's techniques and blows up the ascetic ideal in a fantastic bubble of laughter; for MacConglinne's vision is not of heaven and hell but of the bliss of good feeding, and his voyage to the isle of the blessed brings him to a fort made of delicious eatables with a well of wine.

---

[1] *I.T.S.*, xli, 164. Cf. p. 240.   [2] *Book of Leinster*, ii, 399.
[3] Ed. Plummer, *V.S.H.*, ii, 295–6.

The existence of such satires indicates a secure tradition. They are aimed in part at some of the practices of the twelfth-century church, rather than at its ideals. Asceticism was still to be pursued, in fact and not in fantasy, as in the newly founded Cistercian houses. Learning was still revered, though MacConglinne makes fun of the pedants.[1] A reputation for hospitality, in which the great monasteries took pride, was still desirable, only the empty show is derided.[2] Men still went to Rome or even Jerusalem on pilgrimage, but there are warnings against the devil in a man's shoes who infects him with the spirit of restlessness.[3] Much of the old spirit remained, though alongside a new concept of organization. By 1152 the transmutation of the Irish church, though not yet complete, was inevitable. A Roman hierarchy, continental religious orders, and legatine commissions were removing the chief anomalies of the traditional system, while new styles in building and sculpture marked the transformation. And at the same time the men of learning were transcribing, compiling, glossing, and composing, in the pride of their unique heritage.

---

[1] E.g. the lore of numbers. MacConglinne finds a practical use for such learning. Meyer, *Vision of MacConglinne*, pp. 48–51.

[2] Ibid., pp. 10–15.   [3] Plummer, *B.N.E.*, i, 310–11.

Liber Angeli

The Book of the Angel has been compiled from a number of different sources: there is the opening passage of narrative and dialogue, which introduces claims to property and jurisdiction, there are short descriptive notes, and important legal statements on privilege. The spelling of the name Armagh varies between the Latin and Old Irish forms (see note 2); and on one issue, the hospitality due to the archbishop, two separate and inconsistent rulings are given.

There has been different opinion on the date of the tract. The date of its transcription into the Book of Armagh provides a *terminus ante quem*. John Gwynn, its editor, gave as his opinion that 'in its present form it can hardly be placed before the last quarter of the eighth century'. Zimmer placed it 'probably about 730', and J. F. Kenney regarded it as a version of the *lex Patricii*, first recorded in the annals under the year 734. More recently T. F. O'Rahilly, Professor James Carney, and Professor Binchy have thought that the *Liber Angeli*, 'or at least the substance of it', was in existence before Tírechán's day, and was used by him.

Tírechán's lists of churches founded by S. Patrick can be most easily explained if we assume that Tírechán assembled his data on the principles stated in the Book of the Angel: thus, the churches which he names in each area are those asserted to be part of the *paruchia Patricii*. Yet Tírechán's claims are sometimes less specific than those of the *Liber Angeli* (see note 7, a case where the book added to Muirchú's Life gives a much closer parallel with the *Liber Angeli*). Moreover, he sometimes uses a different Latin word from the *Liber Angeli* when translating an Irish technical legal term (see note 5): on such an occasion it is not merely the similar sense but the diverse wording of the two texts which is remarkable. It seems to me more likely that Tírechán used some of the sources employed by the compiler of the *Liber Angeli* than that he had seen the text in its present form. This would mean that the main sources on which the *Liber Angeli* is based were at Armagh in the late seventh century, but that the tract did not gain its present form until the eighth.

Armagh historians of the seventh and eighth centuries must have been collecting their information about Patrick and the rights of his successors, adding and reformulating their notices. We have, for instance, several different early versions of the 'Petitions of Patrick', one given by Tírechán (*Arm.* 15 b 1), one in the book added to Muirchú's

Life (*Arm.* 8 a 1), one in the *Collectio Canonum Hibernensis* (LXVI.
5). As we have seen, two different versions of the *receptio archiepiscopi*
were copied into the Book of the Angel. The compiler of the Book of
the Angel put together some, at least, of the available material. His
edition must still have been the *textus receptus* when the Book of Armagh
was copied in the early ninth century. It thus provides a statement of
Armagh's claims in the century following the Easter controversy and
preceding the Viking settlement.

In the following translation I have retained the paragraphing of the
Book of Armagh.

(HERE) BEGINS THE BOOK OF THE ANGEL

20 b 1 Once,[1] therefore, S. Patrick went forth from the city Altum Mache[2]
to baptize, teach, and heal multitudes of both sexes of the human
race beside the spring which is close to the eastern part of the
aforesaid city. And there, before dawn, he waited for many who
were gathering from all parts to the knowledge of the faith.
Suddenly, then, sleep prostrated him, because, for Christ's sake,
he had beforehand been wearied from his night vigils. And
behold, straightway an angel came to him from heaven, and
raised him gently from sleep. And S. Patrick said: 'Here am I.
Have I done anything wrong of late in the sight of the Most
High? If it has happened, I seek pardon from God.' And the
angel replied: 'No. But the Most High Almighty has sent me to
you, that is, for the consolation of your spirit after the conversion
of the Irish through you to Him in the faith; (the Irish) whom
you have won for Him through hardest labour and through
your preaching, enlightening exceedingly through the grace of
the Holy Spirit, fruitful for all people, since you were always
toiling in many seasons, in many perils from the gentiles, in cold
20 b 2 and heat, hungering and thirsting, §§ walking unweariedly from
tribe to tribe every day for the advantage of many tribes.
Therefore the Lord God knows your present place which we
see set upon a nearby hill with a little cell, (a place) narrow and
hemmed in by some inhabitants of the region, and its surrounding territory does not suffice as a refuge for all. So a *terminus
vastissimus*[3] is constituted by God for the city Altum Mache, which
you have loved before all the lands of the Irish: that is, from the
top of Mount Berbix as far as Mount Mis, from Mount Mis to
Bri Erigi, from Bri Erigi to Dorsum Breg. If you wish, it shall
certainly be of this magnitude. And next, the Lord God has
given all the tribes of the Irish by way of *paruchia* to you and to
this city of yours which is called Ardd Machae in the Irish
tongue.' S. Patrick, having bowed down his face in the presence

of the angel, said: 'I give thanks to my God, eternal Lord, who has deigned in his clemency to give such glory to his servant.'

IN LIKE MANNER the saint said: 'My holy Lord, I foresee through the holy spirit that there will be certain elect who will arise in this island through the ineffable goodness of your mercy and through the labour of proclaiming you, dear to me as if they were the issue of my own body, and also serving you devoutly as friends, who seem to need some provision [4] of their own, for the needful maintenance of their households in churches or monasteries after me. So I ought, perfectly and justly, to share in common the gift of abundance indisputably given to me by God §§ with the perfect religious of Ireland, so that both I and they may enjoy in peace the riches of the bounty of God, all this having been given to me by reason of divine charity.'

21 a 1

He also said: 'DOES it not therefore suffice for me whatever Christian men in devotion shall have vowed and wished to give me from their tribal districts (*regionibus*) and offerings through the will of their own freedom?'

ALSO: 'Am I not, assuredly, content to be the apostolic doctor and *dux principalis* for all the Irish peoples, especially since I retain a special tax (*peculiare censum*) rightly to be rendered, even that given to me by the Most High, truly and fittingly owed upon all the free churches of the provinces of this island; and similarly on all the monasteries of cenobites, without any doubt a due (*ius*) will have been decreed to the ruler of Ardd Machae in perpetuity. . . .'

FOR THE RECEPTION of the archbishop, successor in the see of my city, with his company to the number of fifty (not counting pilgrims and those sick with various ills and those deserving to be rejected [5] and so on), there should be worthy and fitting hospitality for each one to the same number, as becomingly by day as likewise by night.

IN THIS SAME city of Altum-Machae Christians of both sexes are seen to live together in religion from the time when the faith first came until the present day; to which aforesaid (city) three orders indeed adhere, (i.e.) virgins and penitents (and those) serving the church in legitimate matrimony.

AND it is permitted to these three orders to hear the word of preaching in the church of the north quarter on Sundays always.

21 a 2

IN the southern church bishops and priests §§ and anchorites of the church and other religious offer well-pleasing praises.

CONCERNING the special reverence belonging to Armagh and the honour of the bishop (*praesul*) of this same city, we may say:

T

NOW this city has been constituted by God supreme (*summa*) and free (*libera*) and has been specially dedicated by the angel of God and by the holy apostolic man bishop Patrick.

By a privilege and by the heavenly authority of the most high bishop, its founder, it precedes all the churches and all the monasteries of all the Irish.

FUTHERMORE, it ought to be venerated for the honour of the great martyrs, Peter and Paul, Stephen, Laurence, and the rest.

BY HOW MUCH MORE, then, should it be greatly venerated and diligently honoured by all.

TO REMIND US of the holy wonder of (God's) unspeakable gift to us there is (at Armagh) by a secret dispensation (a relic of) the most holy blood of Jesus Christ, the Redeemer of the human race, in a sacred linen cloth, together with relics of the saints in the south church, where rest along with Patrick the bodies of holy pilgrims who came from afar, and of other just men from overseas.

WHEREFORE because of his aforesaid authority it is not lawful for any lot (*consortem*) to be cast by any church of the Irish nor by any bishop or abbot against his heir; but he rightly overswears all churches and their bishops if true necessity should demand it.[6]

MOREOVER every free church and (its) city is seen to have been founded by episcopal authority in the whole of the island of the Irish, and every place there which is called *domnach* ought, according to the mercy of Almighty God to the holy doctor and according to the word of the angel, to be in special union
21 b 1 with Bishop Patrick and the heirs §§ in his see of Ardd Machae, because God has given to him the whole island, as we said above.[7]

MOREOVER, we ought to know that any monk of any church, if he returns to Patrick, does not deny his own monastic vow, especially if he has de-vowed it with the consent of his former abbot.

THEREFORE, whoever shall go to his church for love of him must not be blamed or excommunicated, because he will judge all the Irish in the great day of terrible judgement in the presence of Christ.[8]

MOREOVER: Concerning the honour of the bishop of Ardd Machae, the bishop presiding in the seat of the perfect pastor.

If the aforesaid bishop shall come in the evening, in the place in which he shall have been received, the comfort of a worthy refection shall be supplied to him on one occasion and to one hundred of the aforesaid guests, with fodder for their draught-beasts, not counting strangers and the sick, and those who abandon infants on the church[9] and the rest, those who should be rejected and others.

MOREOVER: Whoever shall not receive the aforesaid bishop into the same hospitality and shall close his habitation against him, let him be forced to render seven *ancillae* or similarly seven years' penance.

MOREOVER: whoever shall have despised or violated the consecrated insignia of the same saint, i.e. Patrick, shall pay two-fold. If, however, two *ancillae* shall have been paid for contempt of other insignia, there shall be paid concerning the relics of the great doctor Patrick. . . .[10]

21 b 2 §§ MOREOVER: Similarly, whoever, intentionally or injuriously or wickedly shall do any kind of evil deed against his *familia* or against his *paruchia*, or shall despise his aforesaid insignia, the whole case shall come to the liberty of the judgement of the same archbishop, rightly judging, to the setting aside of other judges.

MOREOVER: Whatever very difficult cause shall arise, one unknown to all the judges of the tribes of the Irish, it shall rightly be referred to the see of the Irish archbishop, i.e. Patrick, and to the examination of that bishop. If, however, there, with his wise men, the case of the aforesaid dispute cannot be easily determined, we decree that it must be sent to the apostolic see, that is to the chair of the apostle Peter, which has authority in the city of Rome.[11] These are they who decreed concerning this, that is Auxilius, Patricius, Secundinus, Benignus.

After the death of Patrick his disciples wrote many books of him.

THE BASIS of the prayer on every Sunday in Altum Machae at the tomb of the martyrs, approaching and returning from it: i.e. *Domine clamavi ad te*, to the end. *Ut quia Deus repulisti* to the end, and *Beati immaculati* to the end of the benediction, and the twelve gradual psalms. Finit.

BETWEEN S. Patrick and Brigit, the pillars of the Irish, such friendship of charity dwelt that they had one heart and one 22 a 1 mind. §§ Christ performed many miracles through him and her.

The holy man therefore said to the Christian virgin: O my Brigit, your *paruchia* in your province will be reckoned unto you for your monarchy; but in the eastern and western part it will be in my domination.

---

[1] Reading *quondam* instead of *quodam*.

[2] I have left the MS. spelling of Armagh, since it varies. The Old Irish form, Ard(d) Mach(a)e and its Latinization are both used. The legal passages of the text use the Irish form. The passage describing the community at

T 2

Armagh and the liturgical ruling at the end use the Latin form: so does the narrative prelude, though this also gives specifically the vernacular form: 'Ardd Machae in the Irish tongue.' The variety of forms emphasizes the diverse origins of the compilation.

³ Binchy, 'Patrick', pp. 60–1: 'The *terminus* (Ir. *termonn*) means the area immediately subject to the abbot of Armagh, that portion of territory over which he exercises direct rule like any *rí tuaithe* or tribal king; the *paruchia* (Ir. *pairche*) is the much wider area over which he exercises indirect suzerainty similar to that enjoyed by a *ruiri* or superior king.'

E. MacNeill, *J.R.S.A.I.*, xviii (1928), 100, defines the territories as follows: 'Benn Muilt (near Cootehill, Co. Cavan) was on the border of Airgialla and Breifne, Sliab Mis on or near the border between Dál Araidhe and Dál Riada, Bri Erigi was in the territory of the Ulaidh and apparently in the Ards peninsula, in the east of Co. Down. Druimne Breg is the ridge of hills south of Ardee and north-west of Drogheda in Co. Lough. . . . Thus the *terminus* which is claimed to be under the special jurisdiction of Armagh extends to the outer bounds of Airgialla, Dál Araidhe and the Ulaidh, and excludes the territories of the Northern and Southern Uí Néill and of Dál Ríada.'

⁴ διοίκησις, 'housekeeping, management, government'.

⁵ *inprobis* here: in the parallel passage of f. 21 b 1 *reprobus*. For the latter, Baxter and Johnson, *Mediaeval Latin Word-List* give usage 680 'those deserving to be rejected'; *c.* 731 'reprobate, wicked'. Perhaps this should be translated here as 'outcasts'. See 1 Cor. 9. 27: 'lest I myself should become a castaway' (*reprobus*).

⁶ Binchy, 'Patrick', p. 62: *supraiurare* translates Ir. *fortach*. Thus the oath of the heir of Patrick is superior in value to that of any other person. *Consors* (as MacNeill pointed out) is glossed in the Milan text of the Psalms with the Irish *co-crand* (see K. Meyer, *Contributions to Irish Lexicography*: Ml. 37 b 13), 'lot-casting'. Tírechán makes a similar claim, *Arm.* 11 a 2: *Sed familiam eius non dilegunt, quod*

1. *non licet iurare contra eum,*
2. *et super eum,*
3. *et de eo,*
4. *et non lignum licet contra eum mitti, quia ipsius sunt omnia primitiuae aeclesiae Hiberniae, sed iuratur a se omne quod iuratur.*

The principle which seems to be employed in the *Collectio* (XXVI. 5) appears to be that lots may be cast between two of the same kind: *Sors aut inter duo dubia aut inter duo aequalia aut inter duo catholica mitti debet.*

⁷ Tírechán reads (*Arm.* 11 a 1): *Cor autem meum cogitat in me de Patricii dilectione, quia uideo dissertores et archiclocos et milites Hiberniae quod odio habent paruchiam Patricii quia subtraxerunt ab eo quod ipsius erat, timentque quoniam, si quaereret heres Patricii paruchiam illius, potest pene totam insolam sibi reddere in paruchiam, quia Deus dedit illi*

1. *totam insolam cum hominibus per anguelum Domini,*
2. *et legem Domini docuit illis,*
3. *et baptismo Dei baptizauit illos*
4. *et crucem Christi indicauit,*
5. *et resurrectionem eius nuntiauit.*

[8] Tírechán, in his statement of the three petitions of Patrick, makes a less specific claim (*Arm.* 15 b 1): *Ut suscipiatur unusquisque nostrum poenitentiam agens, licet in extremo uitae suae, judicii die, ut non claudetur in inferno.* The Addition to Muirchú's Life (known as Book II) gives a different version, with four petitions. The fourth reads (*Arm.* 8 a 1): *ut Hibernenses omnes in die iudicii a te iudicentur, ut [uidelicet] eos quibus apostolus fuisti iudices, sicut dicitur [a Domino] ad apostolos, 'Et vos sedentes [super sedes duodecim] iudicabitis duodecim tribus Israel.'*

[9] On those who abandon infants on the church, the penalties they merit and the church's liability to the child, see *Coll.* XLII. 22, 24.

[10] This sentence appears to be incomplete.

[11] *The Collectio Canonum Hibernensis* quotes similar rulings (XX. 5): *Sinodus Romana: Si in qualibet provincia ortae fuerint quaestiones, et inter clericos dissidentes non conveniat, ad majorem sedem referantur, et si illic facile non discutiantur, ubi fuerit sinodus congregata, judicentur. Patricius: Si quae quaestiones in hac insula oriantur, ad sedem apostolicam referantur.* For discussions of these canons see Binchy, *Patrick*, pp. 49–51, and Hughes, 'The Celtic Church and the Papacy', pp. 19–20.

ABBREVIATIONS

(Any other abbreviations used may be easily identified from the bibliography).

AA.SS.   *Acta Sanctorum*, begun by J. Bollandus, I, 1643. In progress.

A.B.   *Analecta Bollandiana*, Paris, 1882–.

A.F.M.   *Annals of the Kingdom of Ireland by the Four Masters*, ed. J. O'Donovan, 6 vols., Dublin, 1856.

A.I.   The *Annals of Inisfallen*, ed. S. MacAirt, Dublin, 1951.

A.L.I.   *Ancient Laws of Ireland*, 6 vols., Dublin, 1865–1901.

Arm.   *The Book of Armagh*. Edited with introduction and appendices by J. Gwynn, Dublin, London, 1913.

A. Tig.   'Annals of Tigernach', ed. Whitley Stokes, *R.C.*, xvi (1895), 374–419; xvii (1896), 6–33, 116–263, 337–420; xviii (1897), 9–59, 150–303, 374–91.

A.U.   *Annals of Ulster*, ed. W. M. Hennessy and B. Mac-Carthy, 4 vols., Dublin, 1887–1901.

C.G.   *Crith Gablach* ed. D. Binchy, Dublin, 1941.

Co.   Penitential of S. Columbanus, ed. L. Bieler, *The Irish Penitentials*, Dublin, 1963. Also J. Laporte, *Le Penitentiel de Saint Columban*, Tournai, Paris, Rome, New York, 1960.

Coll.   *Collectio Canonum Hibernensis*, ed. H. Wasserschleben, *Die irische Kanonensammlung*, Leipzig, 1885.

Congress 1959   *Proceedings of the International Congress of Celtic Studies, 1959*, on 'The Impact of the Scandinavian Invasions on the Celtic-Speaking Peoples *c*. 800–1100 A.D.', Dublin, 1962.

C.S.   *Chronicon Scotorum*, ed. W. M. Hennessy, London, 1866.

Cu.   Penitential of Cummean, ed. L. Bieler, *The Irish Penitentials*, Dublin, 1963.

Durm.   *Evangeliorum quattuor Codex Durmachensis*, 2 vols, Olten, 1960.

H.B.S.   *Henry Bradshaw Society*, London, 1891–.

Hi.   Canones Hibernenses I–VI, ed. L. Bieler, *The Irish Penitentials*, Dublin, 1963.

I.E.R.   *Irish Ecclesiastical Record*, Dublin, 1863–.

I.H.S.   *Irish Historical Studies*, Dublin, 1938–.

I.T.S.   *Irish Texts Society*, London, 1899–.

J.R.S.   *Journal of Roman Studies*, 1911–.

J.R.S.A.I.   *Journal of the Royal Society of Antiquaries of Ireland*,
              Dublin, 1892–.

J.T.S.   *Journal of Theological Studies*, London, Oxford, 1900–.

Lind.   *Evangeliorum quattuor Codex Lindisfarnensis, Musei
              Britannici Codex Cottonianus Nero D. IV*. . . . pro-
              legomenis auxerunt T. D. Kendrick, T. J. Brown,
              R. L. S. Bruce-Mitford, etc. 2 vols. Olten, 1956–60.

Lis.   See Stokes, *Lives of the Saints from the Book of Lismore*.

M.O.   *Martyrology of Oengus*, ed. Whitley Stokes, *H.B.S.*, xxix,
              London, 1905.

M.T.   *Martyrology of Tallaght*, ed. R. I. Best and H. J. Lawlor,
              H.B.S., lxviii, London, 1931.

P.L.   *Patrologia Latina*, ed. J. P. Migne, 221 vols., Paris,
              1844–64.

P.R.I.A.   *Proceedings of the Royal Irish Academy*, Dublin, 1836–.

R.C.   *Revue celtique*, Paris, 1870–1935.

S.H.R.   *Scottish Historical Review*, Edin., Glasgow, 1904–.

St. Ir. Law   *Studies in Early Irish Law*, Dublin, 1936.

Thes. Pal.   *Thesaurus Palaeohibernicus*, ed. W. Stokes and J. Strachan,
              2 vols, Cambridge, 1901–3. Supplement Halle, 1910.

Third Frag.   See *Annals of Ireland: Three Fragments*.

Tr. Life   *Vita Tripartita Sancti Patricii*, ed. and transl. W. Stokes,
              2 vols., London, 1887.

Wa.   *Canones Wallici*, ed. L. Bieler, *The Irish Penitentials*
              Dublin, 1963.

SELECT BIBLIOGRAPHY

ÄBERG, N. *The Occident and the Orient in the Art of the Seventh Century*, Stockholm, 1943–7.

ADAMNÁN. See ANDERSON, MEEHAN, REEVES.

ALCOCK, L. 'Wales in the Fifth to Seventh Centuries, A.D.', *Prehistoric and Early Wales*, ed. I. Ll. Foster and Glyn Daniel, London, 1965, pp. 177–212.

Ancient List of the Coarbs of Patrick. See LAWLOR and BEST.

ANDERSON, A. O. and M. O. *Adomnan's Life of Columba*, Edinburgh, London, 1961.

Anecdota from Irish Manuscripts, ed. O. J. Bergin, R. I. Best, K. Meyer, and J. G. O'Keeffe, Halle, 1907.

Annals of Clonmacnois, translated into English by Conell Mageoghagan, ed. D. Murphy, Dublin, 1896.

Annals of Ireland: Three Fragments, copied by Dubhaltach mac Firbisigh, ed. J. O'Donovan, Dublin, 1860.

Annals of Loch Cé, W. M. Hennessy, 2 vols., London, 1871.

Antiphonary of Bangor, ed. F. E. Warren, *H.B.S.*, iv, x, London, 1893–5.

BARRY, J. 'The appointment of coarb and erenagh', *I.E.R.*, xciii (1960), 361–5.

BARRY, J. 'The status of coarbs and erenaghs', *I.E.R.*, xciv (1960), 147–53.

BECK, H. G. J. *The Pastoral Care of Souls in South-East France during the Sixth Century. Anelecta Gregoriana*, li, Series Fac. Hist. Eccl., Rome, 1950.

BEDE. *Historia Ecclesiastica Gentis Anglorum*, ed. C. Plummer, 2 vols., Oxford, 1896. A revised edition is now in the press.

BEST, R. I. *A Commentary on the Psalms, Ambrosian Library C.301 inf.*, Dublin, 1936.

BIELER, L. *The Life and Legend of St. Patrick*, Dublin, 1949.

BIELER, L. 'Studies on the text of Muirchu', *P.R.I.A.*, lii (1950), C 179–220.

BIELER, L. *Libri Epistolarum Sancti Patricii Episcopi.* Part I: Introduction and Text. Part II: Commentary. Irish MSS. Commission, Dublin, 1952.

BIELER, L. *The Works of St. Patrick*, London, 1953.

BIELER, L. *The Irish Penitentials. Scriptores Latini Hiberniae*, v, Dublin, 1963. With an appendix by D. A. Binchy.

BIELER, L. *Ireland, Harbinger of the Middle Ages*, London, Oxford, New York, 1963.

BINCHY, D. A. 'The Irish Benedictine Congregation in Mediaeval Germany', *Studies*, xviii (1929), 194–210.

BINCHY, D. A. 'Sick-maintenance in Irish Law', *Ériu*, xii (1938), 78–134.

BINCHY, D. A. *Críth Gablach. Mediaeval and Modern Irish Series*, xi, Dublin, 1941.

BINCHY, D. A. 'The Fair of Tailtiu and the Feast of Tara', *Ériu*, xviii (1958), 113–38.

BINCHY, D. A. 'The passing of the old order', *Congress 1959*, pp. 119–32.

BINCHY, D. A. 'Patrick and his biographers', *Studia Hibernica*, ii (1962), 7–173.

BINCHY, D. A. 'The Old-Irish table of Penitential Commutations', *Ériu*, xix (1962), 47–72.

BISCHOFF, B. 'Wendepunkte in der Geschichte der lateinischen Exegese im Frühmittelalter', *Sacris Erudiri*, vi (1954), 191–281.

BISCHOFF, B. 'Il Monachesimo irlandese nei suoi rapporti col Continente', *Settimane di Studio del Centro Italiano di Studi Sull'Alto Medioevo*, Spoleto, 1957.

Book of Armagh, The Patrician Documents. Facsimiles in Collotype of Irish MSS., Irish MSS. Commission, Dublin, 1937.

Book of Leinster, ed. R. I. Best, O. Bergin, M. A. O'Brien, Dublin, 1954–.

BOSWELL, C. S. *An Irish Precursor of Dante*, London, 1908.

BOWEN, E. G. *Settlements of the Celtic Saints in Wales*, Cardiff, 1954.

BRADSHAW, H. ed. F. J. H. Jenkinson, *The early collection of Canons known as the Hibernensis*, Cambridge, 1893.

BULLOCH, J. B. E. *The Life of the Celtic Church*, Edinburgh, 1963.

BRADY, J. 'The origin and growth of the diocese of Meath', *I.E.R.*, lxxii (1949), 1–13, 166–76.

BURY, J. B. *The Life of St. Patrick*, London, 1905.

CALDER, G. *Auraicept na nÉces*, Edinburgh, 1917.

CARNEY, J. *Studies in Irish Literature and History*, Dublin, 1955.

CARNEY, J. *The Problem of St Patrick*, Dublin, 1961.

CHADWICK, N. K. (ed.) *Studies in the Early British Church*, Cambridge, 1958.

CHADWICK, N. K. *The Age of the Saints in the Early Celtic Church*, Oxford, 1961. Reprinted with corrections 1963.

CHADWICK, N. K. (ed.) *Celt and Saxon*, Cambridge, 1963.

COLUMBANUS. Life of Columbanus, See Jonas.

COLUMBANUS. See WALKER.

Contributions to a Dictionary of the Irish Language, published by the Royal Irish Academy. In progress.

DELIUS, W. *Geschichte der irischen Kirche*, München, Basel, 1954.

DE PAOR, L. 'A survey of Sceilg Mhichíl', *J.R.S.A.I.*, lxxxv (1955), 174–87.

DE PAOR, M. and L. *Early Christian Ireland. Ancient Peoples and Places* viii, 1958.

DILLON, M. (ed.) *Early Irish Society*, Dublin, 1954.

DILLON, M. 'Lebor Gabála Érenn', *J.R.S.A.I.*, lxxxvi (1956), 62–72.

DILLON, M. *Lebor na Cert. The Book of Rights, I.T.S.*, xlvi, 1962.

DOLLEY, R. H. M. and INGOLD, J. 'Viking Age coin-hoards from Ireland and their relevance to Anglo-Saxon studies', *Anglo-Saxon Coins, Studies presented to F. M. Stenton*, ed. R. H. M. Dolley, London, 1961, pp. 241–65.

ESPOSITO, M. 'Conchubrani Vita Sanctae Monennae', *P.R.I.A.*, xii (1910), C 202–51.

ESPOSITO, M. 'Notes on Latin learning and literature in mediaeval Ireland', *Hermathena*, xx (1930), 225–60; xxii (1932), 253–71; xxiii (1933), 221–49; xxiv (1935), 120–65; xxv (1937), 139–83.

FAWTIER, R. *La Vie de S. Samson. Bibl. de l'école des hautes études*, 197, Paris, 1912.

Féil-sgríbhinn Eóin mhic Néill, Essays and studies presented to Professor Eoin MacNeill, ed. J. Ryan, Dublin, 1940.

FLOWER, R. 'The Two Eyes of Ireland. Religion and learning in Ireland in the eighth and ninth centuries', in *The Church of Ireland, 432–1932*, ed. Bell and Emerson, Dublin, 1932, pp. 66–75.

FLOWER, R. *The Irish Tradition*, Oxford, 1947.

FLOWER, R. 'Irish High Crosses', *Jrnl. of the Warburg and Courtauld Institutes*, xvii (1954), 87–97.

FOSTER, I. LL. 'The Emergence of Wales', *Prehistoric and Early Wales*, ed. I.Ll. Foster and Glyn Daniel, London, 1965, pp. 213–35.

FOURNIER, P. 'De l'influence de la collection irlandaise sur la formation des collections canoniques', *Nouvelle rev. hist. de droit français et étranger*, xxiii (1899), 27–78.

GILDAS. *De Excidio Britanniae*, ed. and transl. H. Williams for the Hon. Society of Cymmrodorion, London, 1899–1901, on the basis of Mommsen's edition.

GOEDHEER, A. J. *Irish and Norse Traditions about the Battle of Clontarf, Nederlandsche Bijdragen op het gebied van Germaansche philologie en Linguistiek*, ix, Haarlem, 1938.

GOUGAUD, L. *Christianity in Celtic Lands*, transl. M. Joynt, London, 1932.

GROSJEAN, P. 'Rescherches sur les débuts de la controverse pascale chez les Celtes', *A.B.*, lxiv (1946), 200–44.

GROSJEAN, P. 'Sur quelques exégètes irlandais du VIIe siècle', *Sacris Erudiri*, vii (1955), 67–98.

GROSJEAN, P. 'Edition et commentaire du *Catalogus Sanctorum Hiberniae*', *A.B.*, lxxiii (1955), 197–213, 289–322.

GROSJEAN, P. Bibliography of his works 1924–63, in *A.B.*, lxxxii (1964), 307–18.

GWYNN, A. 'Some Irish ecclesiastical titles in the tenth and eleventh centuries', *Ir. C'tee. Hist. Sc. Bull.*, no. 17, pp. 1–2.

GWYNN, A. 'The Origins of the See of Dublin', *I.E.R.*, lvii (1941), 40–55, 97–112.

GWYNN, A. 'Ireland and Rome in the eleventh century', *I.E.R.*, lvii (1941), 213–32.

GWYNN, A. 'Lanfranc and the Irish Church', *I.E.R.*, lvii (1941), 481–500; lviii (1941), 1–15.

GWYNN, A. 'Pope Gregory VII and the Irish Church', *I.E.R.*, lviii (1941), 97–109.

GWYNN, A. 'St. Anselm and the Irish Church', *I.E.R.*, lix (1942), 1–14.

GWYNN, A. 'The Origins of the Diocese of Waterford', *I.E.R.*, lix (1942), 289–96.

GWYNN, A. 'Bishop Samuel of Dublin', *I.E.R.*, lx (1942), 81–8.

GWYNN, A. 'The First Synod of Cashel', *I.E.R.*, lxvi (1945), 81–92; lxvii (1946), 109–22.

GWYNN, A. 'St. Malachy of Armagh', *I.E.R.*, lxx (1948), 961–78; lxxi (1949), 134–48, 317–31.

GWYNN, A. 'The bishops of Cork in the twelfth century', *I.E.R.*, lxxiv (1950), 17–29, 97–109.

GWYNN, A. 'Ireland and the continent in the eleventh century', *I.H.S.*, viii (1953), 192–216.

GWYNN, A. 'The first bishops of Dublin', *Repertorium Novum*, i (1955), 1–26.

GWYNN, A. *The Writings of Bishop Patrick, 1074–1084. Scriptores Latini Hiberniae*, i, Dublin, 1955.

GWYNN, A. Bibliography of his works, 1918–60, in *Mediaeval Studies presented to Aubrey Gwynn, S. J.*, ed. J. A. Watt, J. B. Morrall, F. X. Martin, Dublin, 1961, pp. 502–9.

GWYNN, A. and GLEESON, D. *A History of the Diocese of Killaloe*, Dublin, 1962.

GWYNN, E. J. 'The Teaching of Máel-ruain', *Hermathena*, 2nd supplemental vol., 1927, pp. 1–63.

GWYNN, E. J. 'Rule of the Céli Dé', *Hermathena*, Second Supplemental Volume, Dublin, 1927, pp. 64–87.

GWYNN, E. J. and PURTON, W. J. 'The Monastery of Tallaght', *P.R.I.A.*, xxix (1911), C 115–79.

HADDAN, A. W. and STUBBS, W. *Councils and Ecclesiastical Documents relating to Gt. Britain and Ireland*, 3 vols., Oxford, 1869–73.

HEFELE, K. J. VON. *Histoire des Conciles*, Nouvelle traduction française. . . . corrigée et augmentée . . ., par H. Leclercq *et. al.*, Paris, 1907–.

HELLMANN, W. *Pseudo–Cyprianus De XII Abusivis Saeculi*, Leipzig, 1909.

HENRY, F. *La sculpture irlandaise pendant les douze premiers siècles de l'ère chrétienne*, Paris, 1932.

HENRY, F. 'Les débuts de la miniature irlandaise', *Gazette des Beaux Arts*, xxxvii (1950), 5–34.

HENRY, F. 'Early Irish monasteries, beehive huts and dry-stone houses in the neighbourhood of Caherciveen and Waterville', *P.R.I.A.*, lviii (1957), C 45–166.

HENRY, F. 'Remarks on the decoration of three Irish Psalters', *P.R.I.A.*, lxi (1960), C 23–40.

HENRY, F. and MARSH-MICHELI, G. 'A century of Irish illumination (1070–1170)', *P.R.I.A.*, lxii (1962), C 101–64.

HENRY, F. 'L'art irlandais', 3 vols., Zodiaque, Yonne, 1963. English translation, vol. 1, London, 1965, vols. 2 and 3 to be published.

HILLGARTH, J. N. 'The Position of Isidorian Studies: a critical review of the literature since 1935', *Isidoriana. Estudios sobre san Isidoro de Sevilla en el XIV centenario de su nacimiento*, Leon, 1961.

HILLGARTH, J. N. 'The East, Visigothic Spain and the Irish', *Studia Patristica*, iv (1961), 442–56.

HILLGARTH, J. N. 'Visigothic Spain and early Christian Ireland', *P.R.I.A.*, lxii (1962), C 167–94.

HOARE, F. R. *The Western Fathers*, London, 1954.

HOGAN, E. *Onomasticon Goedelicum*, Dublin, London, 1910.

HUGHES, K. 'The distribution of Irish *scriptoria* and centres of learning from 730–1111', *Studies in the Early British Church*, ed. Chadwick, pp. 243–72.

HUGHES, K. 'On an Irish Litany of Pilgrim Saints compiled *c.* 800', *A.B.*, lxxvii (1959), 305–31.

HUGHES, K. 'The changing theory and practice of Irish pilgrimage', *Journal of Ecclesiastical History*, xi (1960), 143–51.

HUGHES, K. 'The church and the world in early Christian Ireland', *I.H.S.*, xiii (1962), 99–116.

HUGHES, K. 'Irish Monks and Learning', *Los Monjes y los Estudios, IV Semana de Estudios Monasticos Poblet 1961*, Poblet, 1963.

HUGHES, K. 'The Celtic Church and the Papacy', *The English Church and the Papacy in the Middle Ages*, ed. C. H. Lawrence, London, 1965.

Irish Texts, ed. J. Fraser, P. Grosjean and J. G. O'Keeffe, 5 fasc., London, 1931–4.

JACKSON, K. H. *Early Celtic Nature Poetry*, Cambridge, 1935.

JACKSON, K. H. *Language and history in early Britain*, Edinburgh, 1953.

JACKSON, K. H. 'Angles and Britons in Northumbria and Cumbria', in *Angles and Britons*, O'Donnell Lectures, Cardiff, 1963, pp. 60–84.

JACKSON, K. H. *The Oldest Irish Tradition: a window on the Iron Age*, Cambridge, 1964.

JONAS, Life of St. Columbanus. *Ionae vitae sanctorum Columbani, Vedastis, Iohannis*, ed. B. Krusch, *Script. Rer. Germ. M.G.H.*, 1905.

KEATING, G. *History of Ireland*, ed. and transl. D. Comyn and P. S. Dinneen, *I.T.S.*, iv, viii, ix, xv, London, 1902–14.

KENDRICK, T. D. *A History of the Vikings*, London, 1930.

KENNEY, J. F. *Sources for the Early History of Ireland. I. Ecclesiastical*, New York, 1929.

KNOTT, E. 'A poem of prophesies', *Ériu*, xviii (1958), 55–84.

LAWLOR, H. J. *St. Bernard of Clairvaux's Life of St Malachy of Armagh*, London, 1920.

LAWLOR, H. J. *The Monastery of Saint Mochaoi of Nendrum*, Belfast, 1925.

LAWLOR, H. J. and BEST, R. I. 'The Ancient List of the Coarbs of Patrick', *P.R.I.A.*, xxxv (1919), C 316–62.

Lebor na Huidre. Book of the Dun Cow, ed. R. I. Best and O. Bergin, Dublin, 1929.

Liber Hymnorum. The Irish Liber Hymnorum, ed. J. H. Bernard and R. Atkinson, *H.B.S.* xiii, xiv, London, 1897–8.

LIONARD, P. 'Early Irish grave slabs', *P.R.I.A.*, lxi (1961), C 95–169.

LOWE, E. A. *Codices Latini Antiquiores. A Palaeographical Guide to Latin Manuscripts prior to the ninth century*, 10 parts, Oxford, 1934–63.

MACALISTER, R. A. S. *The Latin and Irish Lives of Ciarán*, London, 1921.

MACALISTER, R. A. S. *Corpus Inscriptionarum Insularum Celticarum*, 2 vols., Dublin, 1945–9.

MAC CANA, P. 'The influence of the Vikings on Celtic Literature', *Congress 1959*, pp. 78–118.

MAC DERMOTT, M. 'The Kells Crosier', *Archaeologia*, xcvi (1955), 59–113.

MAC DERMOTT, M. 'The Croziers of St. Dympna and St Mel and tenth century Irish metal-work', *P.R.I.A.*, lviii (1957), C 167–95.

MCGURK, P. *Latin Gospel-Books from A.D. 400 to A.D. 800*, Brussels, 1961.

MCNALLY, R. E. '*Dies Dominica*: Two Hiberno-Latin Texts', *Mediaeval Studies*, xxii (1960), 355–60.

MAC NEILL, E. 'The authorship and structure of the "Annals of Tigernach" ', *Ériu*, vii (1914), 30–113.

MAC NEILL, E. 'Ancient Irish Law: the law of status or franchise', *P.R.I.A.*, xxxvi (1923), C 265–316.

MAC NEILL, E. See *Féil-sgríbhinn Eóin mhic Néill*.

MAC NEILL, M. *The Festival of Lughnasa*, Oxford, 1962.

Martyrology of Gorman, ed. Whitley Stokes, *H.B.S.*, ix, London, 1895.

MASAI, F. *Essai sur les origines de la miniature dite irlandaise*, Brussels, 1947.

MEEHAN, D. *Adamnan's De Locis Sanctis. Scriptores Latini Hiberniae*, iii, Dublin, 1958.

MEYER, K. *Aislinge Meic Conglinne*, London, 1892.

MEYER, K. *Hibernica Minora: A fragment of an Old-Irish treaty on the Psalter*, Oxford, 1894.

MEYER, K. *The voyage of Bran son of Febal to the Land of the Living*, with an essay by A. Nutt, 2 vols., London, 1895–7.

MEYER, K. *Rawlinson B. 502. A collection of pieces in prose and verse in the Irish language compiled during the eleventh and twelfth centuries*. Now publ. in facs. with introd. and indices, Oxford, 1909.

MEYER, K. *Betha Colmáin maic Lúacháin R.I.A. Todd Lecture Series*, xvii (1911).

MEYER, K. *Selections from Ancient Irish Poetry*, London, 1911, reprinted 1959.

MICHELI, G. L. *'Enluminure du haut moyen age et les influences irlandaises*, Brussels, 1939.

Monastery of Tallaght. See E. J. GWYNN and W. J. PURTON.

MULCHRONE, K. *Bethu Phátraic I. Text and Sources*, Dublin, London, 1939.

MYERS, J. N. L. 'Pelagius and the end of Roman rule in Britain', *Journal of Roman Studies*, L (1960), 21–36.

MYNORS, R. A. B. *Durham Cathedral Manuscripts to the end of the twelfth century*, Oxford, 1939.

NASH-WILLIAMS, V. E. *The Early Christian Monuments of Wales*, Cardiff, 1950.

NORDENFALK, C. 'Before the Book of Durrow', *Acta Archaeologica*, xviii (1947), 141–74.

Ó BRIAIN, F. 'The Hagiography of Leinster', *Féil-sgríbhinn Eóin mhic Néill*, pp. 454–64.

O'CONNOR, F. *Kings, Lords and Commons*, New York, 1959.

O'CONNOR, F. *The Little Monasteries*, Dublin, 1963.

O'KEEFFE, J. G. 'The Rule of Patrick', *Ériu*, i (1904), 216–24.

O'KEEFFE, J. G. (ed.) 'A Poem on the Day of Judgment', *Ériu*, iii (1907), 29–33.

O'RAHILLY, T. F. *Early Irish History and Mythology*, Dublin, 1946.

PATCH, H. P. *The Other World*, Camb., Mass., 1950.

PLUMMER, C. *Vitae Sanctorum Hiberniae*, 2 vols., Oxford, 1910.

PLUMMER, C. *Bethada Náem nÉrenn*, 2 vols., Oxford, 1922.

PLUMMER, C. *Irish Litanies. H.B.S.*, lxii, London, 1925.

PLUMMER, C. See BEDE.

POWER, P. *Lives of Declan and Mochuda. I.T.S.*, xvi, London, 1914.

RALEGH RADFORD, C. A. 'Imported Pottery found at Tintagel, Cornwall', *Dark Age Britain, Studies presented to E. T. Leeds*, ed. D. B. Harden, London, 1956.

REEVES, W. *The Life of St Columba . . . by Adamnan*, Dublin, 1857.

RICHARDS, M. 'The Irish Settlements in South-West Wales', *J.R.S.A.I.* xc (1960), 133–62.

Rule of Ailbe, ed. J. O'Neill, *Ériu*, iii (1907), 92–115.

Rule of St Carthage, ed. Mac Eclaise, *I.E.R.*, 4th ser., xxvii (1910), 495–517.

Rule of the Céli Dé. See E. J. GWYNN.

Rule of Columcille, ed. Haddan and Stubbs, *Councils*, ii, I, pp. 119–21.

Rule of Comgall, ed. J. Strachan, *Ériu*, ii (1905), 191–208.

RYAN, J. *Irish Monasticism, its origins and early development*, London, 1931.

RYAN, J. 'The battle of Clontarf', *J.R.S.A.I.*, lxviii (1938), 1–50.

RYAN, J. 'The abbatial succession at Clonmacnois', *Féil-sgríbhinn Eóin mhic Néill*, pp. 490–507.

RYAN, J. 'The Convention of Druim Ceat, A.U. 575', *J.R.S.A.*, lxxvi (1946), 35–55.

Sanas Chormaic, ed. W. Stokes, Calcutta, 1868.

SELMER, C. *Navigatio S. Brendani*, Indiana, 1959.

SHEEHY, M. P. *Pontificia Hibernica: Mediaeval Papal Chancery Documents concerning Ireland*, 640–1261, Vol I, Dublin, 1962.

SHETELIG, H. *Viking Antiquities in Great Britain and Ireland*, 6 parts, Oslo, 1940–54.

Silva Gadelica ed. S. H. O'Grady, 2 vols., London, 1892.

SJOESTEDT, M-L. *Gods and heroes of the Celts*, trsl. M. Dillon, London, 1949.

STOKES, WHITLEY. *Lives of the Saints from the Book of Lismore*, Oxford, 1890.

STRACHAN, J. 'An Old-Irish Metrical Rule', *Ériu*, i (1904), 191–208.

STRACHAN, J. 'An Old-Irish Homily', *Ériu*, iii (1907), 1–10.

Teaching of Máel-ruain. See E. J. GWYNN.

Testimony of Cóemán, ed. K. MEYER, *Hibernica Minora*, Oxford 1894, pp. 41–2.

THURNEYSEN, R. Die Bürgschaft im Irischen Recht', *Abhandlungen Preussischen Akademie der Wissenschaften*, Berlin, 1928.

THURNEYSEN, R. 'Irisches Recht', *ibid.*, Berlin, 1931.

THURNEYSEN, R. 'Aus dem Irischen Recht I–V', *Z.C.P.*, xiv (1923), 335–94; xv (1924–5), 238–96, 302–76; xvi (1926–7), 167–230; xviii (1929–30), 353–408.

THURNEYSEN, R. *Old Irish Reader*, transl. D. A. Binchy and O. Bergin, Dublin, 1949.

TODD, J. H. *Cogadh Gaedhel re Gallaibh. The War of the Gaedhil with the Gaill*, London, 1867.

TRAUBE, L. 'Perrona Scottorum', *Vorlesungen und Abhandlungen* ed. F. Boll, III (Munich, 1920), pp. 95–119.

WALKER, G. S. M. *Sancti Columbani Opera. Scriptores Latini Hiberniae*, ii, Dublin, 1957.

WALSH, P. 'The dating of the Irish annals', *I.H.S.*, ii (1940–1), 355–74.

WARREN, F. *The Liturgy and Ritual of the Celtic Church*, Oxford, 1881.

WHITELOCK, D. *English Historical Documents c.* 500–1042, London, 1953.

WILMART, A. 'Catécheses celtiques: Reg. Lat. 49', *Studi e testi*, lix (1933), 29–112. Fr McNally is re-editing this text.

NOTES ON PLATES

PLATE 1. Aerial view of Nendrum, situated on S. Mahee's Island in Strangford Lough. The monastery seems to have been built within a fort which occupied the highest ground on this little peninsula: access by water would have been easy. Foundations of buildings may be seen within the outer fortification on the right-hand side of the photograph, while the church and round tower lie within the main enclosure. See H. C. Lawlor, *The Monastery of St Mochaoi of Nendrum*, Belfast, 1925; Henry, *L'art irlandais*, i, 92 f. Photograph by Dr J. K. St Joseph by permission of the Ministry of Defence (Air), Crown Copyright Reserved.

PLATE 2. Cross at Kilnasaggart, Co. Armagh. It is on or near the Slighe Mhidhluachra, one of the main roads of ancient Ireland, not far from Slieve Gullion. It belongs to the early type of simple incised cross slab. An inscription on one side, saying that the place was given by Ternoc son of Ciarán Bec under the guardianship of S. Peter, seems to date the stone to about 700. See Henry, *L'art irlandais*, i, 157. Photograph by permission of The Archaeological Survey, Government of Northern Ireland. Photograph inset by Dr Henry.

PLATE 3. View of monastic buildings on Skellig Michael, a rocky island off the Kerry coast. The site (in sharp contrast to a city such as Clonmacnois, see Plate XII) is on a shelf on the eastern side of the island about 550–600 feet above the sea. The cemetery lies in the foreground and centre of the photograph, on the left is a boat-shaped oratory, to the right three beehive huts. The flagstones over the entrance may be seen in the farthest of these cells with the well near by. See L. de Paor, 'A survey of Sceilg Mhichíl', *J.R.S.A.I.*, lxxxv (1955), 174–87. Photograph by Mrs Elinor Wiltshire, The Green Studio, Ltd., Dublin.

PLATE 4. (*a*) Initial and script from the Cathach of S. Columba (f. 36ʳ), a Psalter transcribed *c*. 600. Reproduced by permission of the Royal Irish Academy. (*b*) Initial and script from the Book of Durrow (f. 82ᵛ), a seventh-century illuminated Gospel-book. Reproduced by permission of the Board of Trinity College, Dublin. (*c*) Initial and script from the Book of Armagh (f. 157ʳ), opening of the Second Epistle of John. The codex contains a New Testament and a Life of S. Martin, as well as the Armagh 'Patrician' material discussed above. Transcribed early ninth century. Reproduced by permission of the Board of Trinity College, Dublin.

PLATE 5. The Book of Dimma (pp. 104–5), showing the eagle symbol and the beginning of S. John's Gospel. The MS. is one of the Irish 'pocket-gospel' group, and dates from the eighth or early ninth century. It was formerly enclosed in a *cumdach*. The first three gospels are written for the most part in a rapid cursive script, the Gospel of S. John is by a different scribe in neat minuscule bookhand. In the *subscriptiones* the scribe's name, Dimma, is a substitution. The MS. is probably to be associated with Roscrea. See R. I. Best, 'The *subscriptiones* in the Book of Dimma', *Hermathena*, xx (1930), 84–100; P. McGurk, 'The Irish pocket gospel book', *Sacris Erudiri*, viii (1956), 249–70. Reproduced by permission of the Board of Trinity College, Dublin.

PLATE 6. View of Inishmurray, off the coast of Sligo. The dry-stone cashel rises in places to a height of about 13 feet, with flights of steps on the inner face of the wall. One of the entrances may be seen in the photograph. Inside the cashel (right foreground) is the principal church, with *antae* visible at the east end. See Leask, *Irish Churches*, i, 13–14; W. F. Wakeman, *A Survey of the Antiquarian Remains on the Island of Inismurray*, Lond., Edin., 1893. Photograph by Dr Harold Taylor.

PLATE 7. Athlone Crucifixion. Eighth-century gilt-bronze, possibly part of a book cover. Approximate height 8 in. See M. and L. de Paor, *Early Christian Ireland*, pp. 119–20. Reproduced by permission of the National Museum of Ireland.

PLATE 8. Book of Kells, f. 114^r. The Arrest. Early ninth century. See F. Henry, *L'art irlandais*, ii, 83 ff., especially pp. 100 f. Reproduced by permission of the Board of Trinity College, Dublin.

PLATE 9. B. M. Cotton Vit. F. xi. Psalter, early tenth century. David and Goliath. See F. Henry, 'Remarks on the decoration of three Irish Psalters', *P.R.I.A.*, lxi (1960), C 23–40. Reproduced by permission of the Trustees of the British Museum; the photograph was given to me by the kindness of Dr Henry.

PLATE 10. South cross, Ahenny: east face. Approximate heigh 11 ft. A free-standing, wheel-headed cross of the eighth century, carved in relief. The bosses may suggest a metal-work type. The ornament on the cross is of interlace and spirals, whereas on the socket there are figured scenes. See H. M. Roe, *The High Crosses of Western Ossory*, 1958. Photograph by Dr Henry.

PLATE 11. Cross of the Scriptures, Clonmacnois: west face. Approximate height 13 ft. One of the 'scripture' crosses of the tenth century. See p. 235 above. Photograph by Mr James Bambury, by permission of the Office of Public Works, Dublin.

PLATE 12. Nineteenth-century print of Clonmacnois, showing the accessible situation of the monastic city between the esker or ridgeway which runs across the centre of Ireland and the River Shannon. The path enters near Temple Dowling, one of the earliest buildings surviving here and probably belonging to the Viking Age. Adjacent to it is a seventeenth-century structure. Behind lie the cathedral (a single-chamber building with *antae* and a romanesque doorway inserted into the west gable) and, to the right, Temple Rí, dating from the twelfth century. The round tower (now 62 ft. high) is seen on the left, with the twelfth-century S. Fínghin's church (with tower) beyond. The romanesque Nuns' Church lies beyond the picture to the right, connected with the city by a causeway. The romantic ruin outside the city on the left is that of a medieval castle. The original drawing is by W. H. Bartlett, and is reproduced in his *Scenery and Antiquities of Ireland* (London, 1842), i, 101.

PLATE 13. Cormac's Chapel, Cashel. A somewhat unusual example of Irish romanesque architecture. See above, pp. 271–2, for references. Photograph by Mr James Bambury, by permission of the Office of Public Works, Dublin.

PLATE 14. *Breac Maodhóg*, general view and detail of shrine, formerly contained in a leather satchel. See p. 247 above and references there cited. On the sword held by one figure, see E. Rynne, *J.R.S.A.I.*, xcii (1962), 208–10. Reproduced by permission of the National Museum of Ireland.

PLATE 15. 'Doorty' cross, Kilfenora, east face, showing bishop in the crossing clad in a chasuble and a conical tiara, holding a crozier in his left hand and with his right hand extended in blessing. Beneath are two clerics carrying, the one a tau-headed crozier, the other a crozier of Irish type. At the bottom of the shaft is a scene difficult to interpret, showing what may be birds of prey perched on the heads of two men. Approximate height: 9¼ ft. See L. de Paor, 'The limestone crosses of Clare and Aran', *J. Galway Arch. and Hist. Soc.*, xxvi (1955–6), 53–71; F. Henry, *L'art irlandais*, iii, 193–4. Photograph by Dr. Henry.

PLATE 16. MS. T.C.D. 1441 f. 8ʳ, one of the two eleventh-century codices known as the *Liber Hymnorum*. This folio shows the end of S. Hilary's hymn and the beginning of S. Colman's, written in semi-uncial script with a fine initial, the Irish preface (placed between the two hymns) in a small angular hand, and interlinear and marginal glosses. See Kenney, *Sources*, pp. 716–18; Bernard and Atkinson, *H.B.S.*, xiii, 41–2 (Notes), 43 (preface), 44 (hymn of S. Colman). Reproduced by permission of the Board of Trinity College, Dublin.

WRAPPER. View of Inishmurray. Photograph by Mrs Elinor Wiltshire, The Green Studio, Ltd.

1. Aerial view of Nendrum

2. Incised cross slab from Kilnasaggart

3. Monastic buildings at Skellig Michael

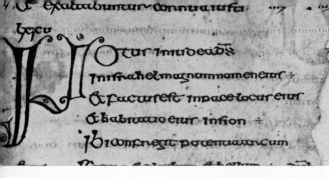

4a. from the Cathach of S. Columba

4b. from the Book of Durrow

4c. from the Book of Armagh

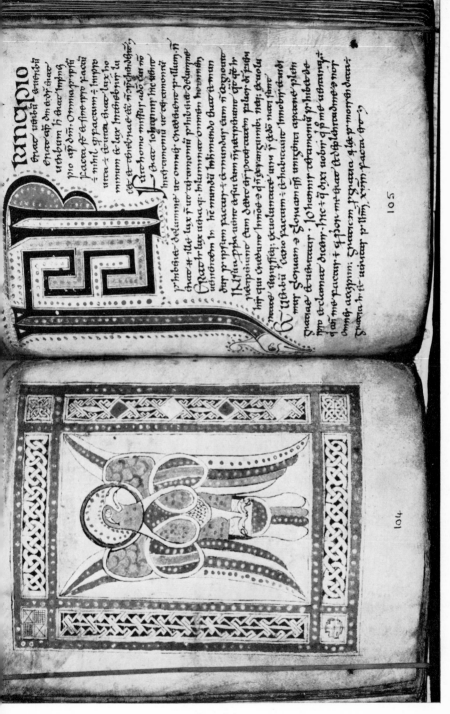

5. The Book of Dimma: commencement of S. John's Gospel and symbol

6. General view of
Inishmurray

7. Athlone Crucifixion plaque

8. The Book of Kells: the arrest of Christ

9. MS B. M. Cotton Vit. F. xi: David and Goliath

10. South cross, Ahenny

11. Cross of the Scriptures, Clonmacnois

13. Cormac's Chapel, Cashel

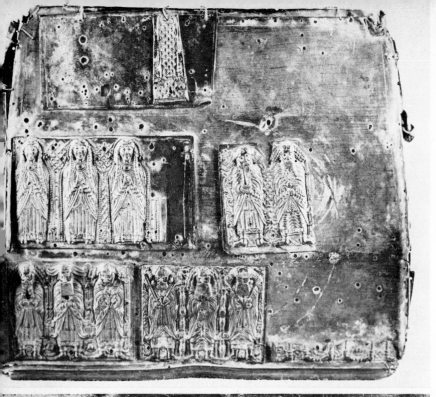

(a)

(b)

14. The *Breac Maodhóg*

15. 'Doorty' cross, Kilfenora

INDEX